Nan Sloane is a writer and activist with e~~xtensi~~ feminism and the Labour Party. As the Dir~~ector~~ and Democracy she campaigned to incre~~ase~~ both civil society and politics, working wit~~h~~ ~~the political~~ spectrum. She has worked with women political activists in the Middle East, the Balkans and Africa and has trained hundreds of Labour women and public representatives in the UK. She is a long-standing member of Labour Women's Network's Management Committee and has a lifetime's experience of politics, including as a local councillor and a member of Labour Party staff. She is the editor of *In Our Own Words: A Dictionary of Women's Political Quotations* and *A Great Act of Justice: The Flapper Election and After.*

'All too often the achievements of working-class women have been excluded from the history books. Yet it was these women who often fought the hardest and had the most to lose. It is up to us to bring to life the hidden history of working-class women and their great achievements. In this book, Nan Sloane takes up that challenge. She unearths the stories of women who, long before the campaign for women's suffrage, fought for workers' rights and played a key role in the birth of the Labour Party. In doing so Nan rightfully honours those women who helped to lay the foundations for other working-class women to succeed.'

Dawn Butler MP, Shadow Secretary of State for Women & Equalities

'An absorbing insight into the role of women in British political history. Remarkable women across the Labour movement were busy influencing policy long before they could vote – fighting for pay, working conditions, childcare, healthcare and social justice – yet there is little trace of their existence. This highly readable, compelling book finally tells the story of these important hidden figures.'

Ayesha Hazarika, political commentator and comedian

'Nan Sloane's engaging book rebalances Labour Party history, putting women front and centre – coincidentally where they've always been, but often overlooked or erased. It is a refreshing and necessary change from the male-dominated history we tend to learn and is essential reading for everyone who values a full and equal perspective of the history of the Labour Party.'

Amy Lamé, writer, broadcaster and activist

'Finally we can see some of the hidden history of our women. Working-class women and their role in politics has been and still is ignored. This book is the start of redressing this balance, and everyone should read it. We have got to stop forgetting the women from the past in the future!'

Jess Phillips MP

'In the immediate pre-war years the suffrage movement and the early Labour movement were intertwined. Yet this is little-known. Great, influential women who shaped twentieth-century politics and drove forward the campaign for the vote, rights at work, the early welfare state and much more have to date been largely airbrushed out of history. *The Women in the Room* sets the record straight.'

Sam Smethers, Chief Executive, The Fawcett Society

THE WOMEN IN THE ROOM

Labour's Forgotten History

NAN SLOANE

Foreword by
Rt Hon Harriet Harman MP

I.B. TAURIS
LONDON · NEW YORK · OXFORD · NEW DELHI · SYDNEY

I.B. TAURIS
Bloomsbury Publishing Plc
50 Bedford Square, London, WC1B 3DP, UK
1385 Broadway, New York, NY 10018, USA
29 Earlsfort Terrace, Dublin 2, Ireland

BLOOMSBURY, I.B. TAURIS and the I.B. Tauris logo are trademarks
of Bloomsbury Publishing Plc

First published in Great Britain 2018
This paperback edition first published 2020
Reprinted 2021

Cover design and illustration by Alice Marwick

A catalogue record for this book is available from the British Library.

A catalogue record for this book is available from the Library of Congress.

ISBN: HB: 978-1-7883-1223-3
PB: 978-0-7556-0056-4
ePub: 978-1-7867-2478-6
ePDF: 978-1-7867-3478-5

Text design, typesetting and eBook by BBR Design, Sheffield
Printed and bound in Great Britain

To find out more about our authors and books visit www.bloomsbury.com
and sign up for our newsletters.

Everywhere women have greater cause to cry for vengeance than men have, and that is why, even for a peaceful revolution such as trade unionism or socialism, the presence and influence of women is absolutely essential.

Isabella Ford

Contents

Illustrations

1. Emma Paterson (TUC Library Collections, London)

2. The inaugural Independent Labour Party National Administrative Council, Bradford, 1893 (By permission of the People's History Museum)

3. Clementina Black (© Mary Evans Picture Library)

4. Margaret MacDonald (By permission of the People's History Museum)

5. Margaret Bondfield (© Alamy)

6. Women's Labour League Conference, Hull, 1907 (By permission of the People's History Museum)

7. Isabella Ford (© Mary Evans Picture Library)

8. Mary Macarthur addressing a strike meeting in Trafalgar Square, 1908 (TUC Library Collections, London)

9. Women chain-makers at work in the Black Country, 1910 (TUC Library Collections, London)

10. Mary Middleton, Mary Macarthur and Margaret Bondfield on the platform at the Women's Labour League Conference, Newport, 1910 (By permission of the People's History Museum)

11. Katharine Bruce Glasier speaking at a Women's Labour League meeting, c.1910 (By permission of the People's History Museum)

12. Marion Phillips at work in the Women's Labour League office, c.1913

Foreword

RT HON HARRIET HARMAN MP

The story of the foundation of the Labour Party is dominated by men such as Keir Hardie and Ramsay MacDonald. And behind them the hundreds of thousands of men trade unionists, the socialist organisations and Marxist parties. But throughout that time and woven through that struggle for progress, was the work of women and their organisations. This book makes visible the role of thousands of women, and their leaders, who otherwise remain hidden from history.

When you read this book you can only be incredulous about how partial and, for that reason, downright inaccurate our history is. Historians now who write about the men while completely ignoring the women who fought against poverty, for a minimum wage, for safety at work and to tackle infant mortality are perpetuating the sexism and discrimination those women suffered. We need positive action to redress this misrepresentation of our past. And this book is a major contribution to that as it reveals the work of a multitude of hitherto invisible women; women who were dedicated trade unionists and ardent members of the Labour Party.

It's quite simply a matter of historical accuracy which makes this book so necessary. I hope that what we will see is a major new genre of women's historical writing – such as Rachel Reeves' biography of Leeds MP Alice Bacon. As we can't leave it to men historians it's something we women can and should do. And what we certainly shouldn't do is throw away our notes and records. My heart sank when I read in this book that the Women's Labour League destroyed many of its own records when it merged into the Labour Party. We must value what we do, keep our records and write about our own struggles to prevent ourselves being invisible to future generations. Most women get on with what they do, day to day. But at a time of struggle and change we need to know what previous generations of women did. And future generations will need to know what we are doing.

Most Labour members are familiar with the founding connection and the ongoing relationship between the trade unions and the Labour Party. But few will know that, just as working men were organising into trade unions to struggle for better terms and conditions, so too working women – who were excluded from men's unions – were setting up women's unions and forming the Women's Industrial Council. These women's unions not only defended women at work but they changed public policy. The National Federation of Women Workers, set up in 1906 by Mary Macarthur, led the strike of women chain-makers in 1910 which forced the implementation of the Trade Boards Act, the precursor of the National Minimum Wage. The women's unions fought on behalf of the women who were recruited into industry to replace men who'd gone off to World War I, so that they would be safe and properly paid. It was only at the end of the war, by which time there were a million women in women's trade unions, that the men's trade union movement had to accept women into membership. They were allowed in but not welcomed with open arms.

The leading lights in the women's unions were also key in the quest for political progress, particularly through the Women's Labour League. Women couldn't participate in the meeting that founded the Labour Party and were only able to watch from the gallery. When the Women's Labour League was absorbed into the Labour Party the women were torn between conflicting loyalties – between their commitment to the cause of women and their commitment to the Labour Party. The Party was a crucial force for social progress but was overwhelmingly masculine. Women could join at a reduced membership rate and that cemented their status as second-class members. But they were pivotal in striving for a whole raft of policies for which Labour women still campaign today. Their demand for free school meals was part of tackling poverty and improving public health and their campaigns for child health services contributed to the establishment of the National Health Service.

This book describes the dogged and important struggles of women fighting for other women. It shows how the trade unions and Labour excluded them and sidelined them. It shows how, even once they were allowed to join, the end of formal exclusion by no means meant inclusion on equal terms. In the trade unions and the Labour Party we are proud of our history. This book is necessary to understand a missing part of that history, the hidden but extraordinary struggle of Labour and trade union women which deserves an equal place in the spotlight.

Acknowledgements

This book could not have been written without the help and (sometimes unwitting) support of many people.

First of all, I am grateful to the staff of the brilliant People's History Museum in Manchester, whose assistance has been invaluable, particularly when it came to allowing me to find and use photographs. I am also indebted to the TUC Library at London Metropolitan University and the Women's Library and Archive at the LSE, in both of which I found new and interesting insights.

This is not an academic book, but it could not have been written without the sterling work of the small band of academic women who have kept alive the memory of early left-wing and feminist women over the years. Many of their works are listed in the Bibliography, and have been invaluable in helping me to understand the environment in which the women I was writing about were working.

Many people over the years have allowed me to lecture them at length about women they've barely heard of, and their interest, positivity and enthusiasm have helped to keep me going. Credit is also due to everyone who has read chapters, commented, asked tricky questions, criticised bad grammar or suggested new angles, as well as to a large number of Labour women for their good-humoured and sisterly tolerance of my occasional eccentricities. I am grateful to all of you.

I am also indebted to my editor, Jo Godfrey, and the team at I.B.Tauris who saw the book through the publication process, and who turned out to be right about the title.

My husband, Christopher, and my children and grandchildren have, as always, put up nobly with my obsessions, vagaries and intermittent neglect. I am (I hope) more appreciative than I might sometimes appear.

Last, but by no means least, I would like to thank all those people who have been mystified, amazed or simply confused by the idea that it might be possible that there were politically active women in the early part of the last century who were not either suffragettes or members of the Pankhurst circle or both. Your polite bemusement kept reminding me of the reason I decided to write about those women in the first place, so thank you! This book is for you.

Nan Sloane
June 2018

Preface

Some years ago, I ran a training course for women candidates for public office which included a section on the history of Labour women. This involved showing pictures of various female characters from Labour's early history and asking people to identify them. Most recognized was Emmeline Pankhurst, but almost all others were greeted with bemused shakes of the head. After a time this pattern began to irritate. Why were Labour and trade union women so unknown? Why was nobody interested in them? And why had we allowed the suffrage movement, and one face of it in particular, to define all women's political activism before the First World War?

Eventually I dropped the history module, but I continued to ask the questions. I looked for books, but there were very few and those that there were tended to be out of print. There were short entries about individual women in biographical dictionaries, and Wikipedia provided its usual mixed bag of information, but there seemed to be huge gaps. The more I complained about this, the more people began to point out to me that if I thought there should be a book I couldn't find about a subject I was interested in, perhaps I should write it myself. In the end, I thought I might try.

As soon as I began to research, I started to find women whose stories do not feature in most histories of women's activism, and certainly not in accounts of either the suffrage movement or the Labour Party. Trade unionists, socialists, feminists, pacifists and social campaigners emerged in crowds from dusty archives. There were women who believed in universal rather than just female suffrage, women who organized the poorest and most exploited workers and women who campaigned against the wars of rampantly imperialist governments. Women I thought I knew something about turned out to have had much more interesting and relevant lives than I had realized. Others were no more than names and characters fleetingly glimpsed through the minutes of meetings, or reports of a strike or campaign. To give the book a shape I decided to frame it as a history of the Labour Party, but it had to be a history with the women added back in.

The approach of the 2018 centenary of some women getting the vote had focused minds on the history of the suffrage campaign, and with that had come the realization that relatively few working-class women had been involved in it. As a result there was a search on to find working-class suffragettes. Yet I had found working-class women fighting for so much else, including money and dignity and the right to work. Together with middle-class allies working-class women had set up unions and benefit clubs and campaigned for better factory inspection regimes and shorter hours. They did this in parallel with the suffrage movement, but very rarely as part of it. Some middle-class suffrage campaigners – most notably Sylvia Pankhurst – bridged the divide, but by and large working-class women were not suffragettes, and did not necessarily regard the vote as the sole key to improving women's daily lives. Why were these women not celebrated in the same way? *The Women in the Room* is an attempt in part to find some answers to this question.

As soon as the book came out in September 2018, it became apparent that for many people the explanations I proposed were both novel and confusing. Everybody knows the suffrage story, and to find it relegated to a relatively subordinate role in the narrative seemed to strike people as both interesting and odd. I had expected the book to be reasonably well received by a small group of people, probably mainly women, with an interest in Labour and trade union history. However, it soon became clear that there was a much wider appetite for it than I had imagined. I found myself invited to speak to all kinds of meetings and groups around the country. People seemed amazed to hear that not all women before the First World War had been suffragettes and delighted to find that they had been and done so many other things as well, or even instead. People I had never met bought the book and contacted me to say how much they liked it. It even got good reviews in serious publications.

Inevitably, some people wanted to talk about the position of women in politics now, and the focus on suffrage meant that this almost always took the form of questions about women in Parliament. When the book was published, Theresa May was still in office leading a Conservative government with support provided by the Democratic Unionist Party, also led by a woman. Scotland had a female First Minister, and both the Scottish Conservatives and Scottish Labour were led by women. Labour had more women MPs than any other party, and there was a lot of concern about, and discussion of, the barriers women in politics faced, particularly in terms of the deteriorating political culture and the possible reasons for Labour's failure ever to have elected a female leader.

Then in the 2019 general election, the Labour Party achieved a historic milestone. For the first time in their 101-year electoral history women constituted more than 50 per cent of the Parliamentary Labour Party, and, at the time of writing (December 2019), might yet elect a woman to lead the party. It has taken Labour a little over a century to reach gender equality in its representation at Westminster, and it happened because Labour women – the political descendants of the women in this book – worked for it over several decades. Every inch of ground, at every level of decision making and representation, had to be fought for. At one point progress was so glacial that even Barbara Castle, who never described herself as a feminist, had to concede that something should be done to make sure that more women got into Parliament. For every male ally there were dozens prepared to resist. For every woman who thought it mattered there were half a dozen more who thought it did not.

For many of the women featured in this book this would have seemed an extraordinary battle to choose. They believed that once the campaigns to get rights and votes were won, they would be absorbed into the system and accorded an equal place within it. They could not have been more wrong. In particular, the expectation in 1918 that, now that at least some women had the vote, many would soon find their way into Parliament rapidly turned out to be an illusion. None of the political parties was particularly keen to stand women candidates in seats they could win. Only one – Sinn Féin's Constance Markiewicz – of the handful of women candidates who stood in 1918 was elected. The first two MPs to take their seats – the Conservative Nancy Astor and the Liberal Margaret Wintringham – got in through by-elections and succeeded their husbands. Labour did not get any women elected until December 1923, when Margaret Bondfield, Dorothy Jewson and Susan Lawrence all scraped in with slim majorities which they lost again at the next election in October 1924.

When George Bernard Shaw, playwright, socialist and activist, wrote to the trade unionist and future cabinet minister Margaret Bondfield to commiserate with her on the loss of her Northampton seat, the problem was all too clear. 'You are' he wrote:

> 'the best man of the lot, and they shove you off on a place where the water is too cold for their dainty feet just as they shoved Mary [Macarthur] off on Stourbridge and keep the safe seats for their now quite numerous imbeciles'.[1]

Unfortunately, when the Labour Party was reorganized in 1918, women had accepted a near-fatal flaw in the new rules as applied to them. For the first time the party introduced individual membership for both men and women, but the subscription for women was pitched at half that for men. In addition, women were organized into separate Women's Sections at local level, and although four places were reserved for them on the party's ruling National Executive Committee, they were not given a universal welcome, and in many quarters were seen as second-class members. There was much discussion of whether or not newly enfranchised women were 'ready' for politics, and most people accepted that they would need to be educated in the mysteries of political life. In the meantime, they would have to wait for equal rights and equal treatment until a future point of 'readiness' was achieved. Needless to say, this never quite seemed to arrive. The disastrous consequences of this approach meant that as late as the 1960s there were Constituency Labour Parties at whose meetings women were required to sit silently at the back, providing refreshments and, outside the meetings, running jumble sales and committee rooms. The later slogan 'Labour women make policy, not tea' arose all too often out of bitter experience.

One way and another, women thus found it extremely difficult to get a firm foothold on the political ladder in the decades after 1918. They often found themselves in marginal seats, their tenure tended to be short-lived, and few of them achieved real prominence. Margaret Bondfield's parliamentary career was fleeting and ended in the disaster of the 1931 general election, when all nine Labour women MPs lost their seats. Ellen Wilkinson, who returned to Parliament in 1935 as the sole Labour woman, was better known for her work outside Parliament than in it. After 1945, when twenty-one Labour women were elected, there was no progress at all until 1992. At times the numbers even went into reverse. In both 1970 and 1983 the level of female Labour MPs fell to ten. All too often Labour women were not just unheard but also almost invisible.

When, in the 1980s, a degree of impatience began to build, two distinct but connected streams of activity began to develop. First, women decided to take on the 'readiness' issue by providing themselves with tough, effective training and support which would mirror aspects of what men tended to get through trade unions and other bodies. This led to the founding of Labour Women's Network, the first independent Labour women's organization since the absorption of the Women's Labour League into the party in 1918. Second, women began to campaign for the party to take positive action to make sure that women were selected as candidates in seats they could have a reasonable prospect of winning. This resulted in 1994 in the introduction of controversial all-women shortlists for half of all 'winnable' seats which did not, for one reason or another, have a sitting Labour MP. The use of this mechanism has successfully driven progress in Labour women's parliamentary representation ever since.

Margaret Bondfield herself would have been horrified at the notion of all-women shortlists. She would have seen them for what they are – an admission of her party's dismal failure to give women a fair and equal chance over many years and an acceptance of the institutional nature of that failure. However, she might also have regarded it as an example of the party's occasional ability to face internal problems fairly and squarely and act decisively and effectively to rectify them. And she would surely have been gratified by what Labour women have achieved over the decades, and greatly interested to see how they progress.

The success of Labour women in achieving equal parliamentary representation is mirrored in huge increases in women's political participation at other levels. But there are still many challenges for them to face, including the culture of politics and the future of the Labour Party itself. The women who managed to get into the rooms of Labour's beginnings would be very proud of their political descendants, and also greatly intrigued to see what happens next. But that only time will tell.

Nan Sloane
December 2019

Organisations and Acronyms

This list includes all the principal organisations involved in the story of the early Labour Party, together with their acronyms, if they had them. Trade unions are not listed unless they had a specific role; neither are other political parties.

ASRS   Amalgamated Society of Railway Servants, moved the resolution at the TUC in 1899 to found the Labour Representation Committee, involved in the Taff Vale case in 1900–1.

BSP   British Socialist Party, formed out of the Social Democratic Federation in 1911.

CIU   Working Men's Club and Institute Union, founded in 1862.

CMA   Chain Manufacturers' Association, set up in 1907 to represent chain-making employers in the Black Country.

EFF   Election Fighting Fund, set up in 1912 by the NUWSS to support Labour candidates in favour of women's suffrage.

Fabian Society   Research and campaign group set up in 1884, one of the founding organisations of the Labour Representation Committee.

FWG   Fabian Women's Group, founded in 1908 by Charlotte Wilson.

ILP   Independent Labour Party, set up in 1893, one of the founding organisations of the Labour Representation Committee.

LRC   Labour Representation Committee, founded in 1900, became the Labour Party in 1906.

LRL   Labour Representation League, set up in 1869 by the TUC to promote working-class candidates.

NAC   National Administrative Council, the elected executive committee of the Independent Labour Party.

NASL   National Anti-Sweating League, founded in 1906.

NEC   National Executive Committee, the elected executive of the Labour Representation Committee and then the Labour Party.

NESWS   North of England Society for Women's Suffrage, affiliated to the National Union of Women's Suffrage Societies.

NFWW   National Federation of Women Workers, established in 1906 by Mary Macarthur and others, absorbed in 1918 into the National Union of General Workers (NUGW), now the GMB.

NSWS   National Society for Women's Suffrage, the first national suffrage organisation, founded in 1867 by Lydia Becker and others.

NUWSS   National Union of Women's Suffrage Societies, formed in 1897, umbrella body for suffragist groups.

NUWW   National Union of Working Women, founded 1875 in Bristol.

PLP   Parliamentary Labour Party, established following the 1906 General Election.

PSF   People's Suffrage Federation, founded in 1909.

SDF   Social Democratic Federation, founded in 1881. Marxist, led by Henry Hyndman, and the first socialist party in Britain.

SJC   Standing Joint Committee of Industrial Women's Organisations, established in 1916.

SLP   Scottish Labour Party, founded in 1888.

TUC   Trades Union Congress, founded in 1868.

UDC   Union of Democratic Control, anti-war group set up in 1914 by Ramsay MacDonald and others.

WFL   Women's Freedom League, which broke away from the
             WSPU in 1907.

WIC   Women's Industrial Council, founded in 1894 by Clementina
             Black and others from the Women's Trade Union
             Association, research and social reform group working mainly
             on women's employment issues.

WIL   Women's International League for Peace and Freedom,
             founded in 1915 following the International Congress of
             Women at The Hague.

WLL   Women's Labour League, founded in 1906, absorbed into the
             Labour Party in 1918.

WNC   War Emergency: Workers' National Committee, established
             by Arthur Henderson to bring disparate parts of the
             movement together during World War I.

WPPL   Women's Protective and Provident League, umbrella and
             support group for women's trade unions, founded in 1874 by
             Emma Paterson, changed name in 1891 to Women's Trade
             Union League.

WSPU   Women's Social and Political Union, founded in 1903 by
             Emmeline and Christabel Pankhurst, militant wing of the
             suffrage movement.

WTUA   Women's Trade Union Association, founded by Clementina
             Black in 1889, became the Women's Industrial Council in
             1894.

WTUL   Women's Trade Union League, known before 1891 as the
             Women's Protective and Provident League.

Timeline

1867   Lydia Becker and others founded the National Society for Women's Suffrage.

       Representation of the People Act, also known as the Second Reform Act, which extended the vote from 1 to 2 million men.

1868   Foundation of the TUC.

1869   Twenty-two-year-old Millicent Fawcett first spoke on a public platform in support of women's suffrage.

1870   First Women's Suffrage Bill.

1874   Emma Paterson founded the Women's Protective and Provident League.

1875   Emma Paterson and Edith Simcox became the first women delegates to the TUC.

1881   Social Democratic Federation founded.

1883   Women's Co-operative Guild founded.

1884   Representation of the People Act, also known as the Third Reform Act, which enfranchised about 60 per cent of men.

       Fabian Society founded.

1888   TUC passed first equal pay resolution, moved by Clementina Black.

       Matchgirls' strike.

1889   Dockers' strike and the start of the 'new unionism'.

1892   Keir Hardie first elected to Parliament.

1893   Independent Labour Party founded.

1897   Establishment of the National Union of Women's Suffrage Societies.

1899   Start of South African (Boer) War.

1900   Labour Representation Committee founded.

1903   Women's Social and Political Union founded.

1904   Adult Suffrage Society founded.

1905   Start of Women's Social and Political Union militant suffrage campaign.

1906   Parliamentary Labour Party founded; the Labour Representation Committee became the Labour Party.

        Women's Labour League founded.

        National Federation of Women Workers founded by Mary Macarthur.

1907   Women's Freedom League founded.

1908   Fabian Women's Group founded.

1909   Lloyd George introduced the 'People's Budget'.

        People's Suffrage Federation founded.

1910   Chain-makers' strike.

        Start of the Great Unrest period of social and industrial action.

        Conciliation Bill and 'Black Friday'.

1911   Death of Mary Middleton and Margaret MacDonald.

1912   Conciliation Bill failed.

        National Union of Women's Suffrage Societies joined with the Labour Party to set up the Election Fighting Fund.

1913   Death of Emily Davison at Epsom.

        Prisoners (Temporary Discharge for Ill-Health) Act (also known as the 'Cat and Mouse Act') passed.

1914   Outbreak of World War I.

1917   Speaker's Conference on Electoral Reform.

1918   Representation of the People Act enfranchised 60 per cent of women and virtually all men.

      End of World War I.

      Parliament (Qualification of Women) Act allowed women over the age of 21 to stand for election.

      First women candidates stood in a general election.

      First woman MP elected but did not take her seat (Constance Markievicz).

      Margaret Bondfield became the first woman member of the TUC Parliamentary Committee (General Council).

1919   First woman MP took her seat (Nancy Astor).

1921   Death of Mary Macarthur.

1923   First Labour women MPs elected (Margaret Bondfield, Susan Lawrence, Dorothy Jewson).

      Margaret Bondfield became the first woman to chair the TUC.

1924   First Labour government; Margaret Bondfield became the first woman government minister.

1928   Representation of the People (Equal Franchise) Act introduced universal suffrage.

1929   Margaret Bondfield became the first woman cabinet minister and Privy Counsellor.

Note on Text

Pre-decimal currency is denoted in pounds, shillings and pence (£ s d), in which one pound sterling (£1) = twenty shillings (20s or 20/–) and one shilling = twelve pence (12d).

Introduction

On a drizzly Tuesday in February 1900 a group of men representing trade unionists, socialists, Fabians and Marxists gathered in a meeting-room in London to make yet another attempt to establish an organisation capable of getting working-class men elected to Parliament. Previous efforts had had very little success, and attacks on trade union rights, in particular, were beginning to alarm them. The body they set up was called the Labour Representation Committee; six years later when 29 of its candidates were elected to the House of Commons it changed its name to the Labour Party.

No women took part in that first conference, but several watched from the public gallery. Among them was Isabella Ford, an active socialist and trade unionist who would have been familiar to most of the men assembled below. She had been asked by her friend, Millicent Fawcett, to attend and report back on what happened. Millicent was the president of the National Union of Women's Suffrage Societies (NUWSS), and Isabella had been involved with the suffrage movement for a long time. A few years later Isabella would become the first woman to speak at a Labour Party conference, moving a resolution on votes for women, but at the Party's inception she and every other woman in the hall was silent.

Throughout Labour's history, even in its earliest years, women were present in the room, but they were not always recorded or remembered. They came from many different backgrounds and they worked for the causes they believed in as organisers, campaigners, negotiators, polemicists, public speakers and leaders. They took on the vested interests of their time; sometimes they won. Yet the vast majority of them have been forgotten by the labour movement that they helped to found. Even Margaret Bondfield, who became Britain's first woman cabinet minister, often barely merits a footnote. Yet women made real and substantial contributions to Labour's earliest years and had a significant impact on the Party's ability to attract and maintain women's votes after World War I.

Beside Margaret and Isabella, in many of the rooms in which the Labour Party found its early feet, remarkable women wait to be rediscovered. This book tells their story.

◆ ◆ ◆ ◆ ◆

Almost all of the Labour founders, thinkers and leaders whose words and deeds are chronicled are men; the very term 'Labour giant' conjures up the male rather than the female. Towering figures such as Keir Hardie, Ramsay MacDonald and Arthur Henderson are, for different reasons, remembered and revered or reviled. Early photographs of Labour and trade union committees and conferences show rank upon rank of carefully posed men in period clothes, hats and facial hair. Occasionally a woman appears, seated somewhere near the front, perhaps, or standing self-effacingly towards the back. From time to time women's names appear in attendance lists, or as speakers in debates or at meetings. Sometimes, as in the case of Emmeline Pankhurst, these names are memorable from other contexts, and it is surprising to find them in Labour settings. Others are vaguely familiar but without association; others still are completely unknown. Yet all are part of the story which saw the Labour Party grow from a marginalised pressure group in 1900 to a party of government in 1924.

Decades of work on the part of hundreds of women enabled Labour to position itself credibly as the natural home for women once they were enfranchised, and this in turn influenced the course of British politics in the 1920s and beyond. Women were very effective at influencing both policy and strategy long before they could vote, not only through extensive networks of contacts and relationships but also through research and public speaking tours. They developed considerable experience as election campaign managers, particularly through the various suffrage organisations. By taking on what were considered difficult and unpopular issues such as infant mortality, public health and free school meals, they laid some of the foundations of the welfare state. A few were national figures in their own right and could attract tabloid-style press coverage. When the trade unionist Mary Macarthur got married, for instance, the media wrote articles about her dress and her hat speculating that, as a modern woman, she might choose to carry a briefcase rather than a bouquet.[1] Leaving these women out of the political history of the early twentieth century, or seeing them only through the prism of female suffrage, is to lose part of our political story.

Just as most Labour and trade union history is written about men, so much of women's political history from this time is written about suffrage. The fight for female suffrage was, of course, very important, but it was by no means the only activity in which women were engaged, and nor did all women agree about it. There were many other campaigns for women's rights going on at the time, including the early stages of the long battle for equal pay (today still not entirely won), for an equal right to work and to have equal access to the better-paid jobs (still not entirely won either), for adequate childcare and health care, for reproductive and social rights (again, all still the subject of contention in some quarters) and for minimum and living wages. Many women believed that until women had economic power the vote would be of little use. Suffrage was indeed one of the major causes of the day, but not for all women, and not always in the way we now believe.

For many working-class women, the great struggle was for enough to live on rather than the vote. The history of this period is littered with industrial activity among women as well as men, with some strikes, such as those involving the Bryant & May matchgirls and the Black Country chain-makers, achieving national prominence. A tiny group of trade union women toiled ceaselessly to organise the most exploited workers in the economy, often without the support of male colleagues and sometimes in the face of their active opposition. Some of these women were also active members of the Labour Party, some, such as Mary Macarthur, were among its first female parliamentary candidates, and some, such as Susan Lawrence, Marion Phillips and Margaret Bondfield, went on to become MPs and ministers. This book, therefore, gives weight to both industrial organisation and suffrage, and as a consequence looks at each from a slightly different angle. Not all trade union women supported a limited female suffrage based on property, and by no means all female suffrage campaigners supported working women's economic liberation.

The fact that so many Labour and trade union women opposed the limited property-based franchise demand made by much of the suffrage movement meant that they could be characterised as being opposed to women's interests altogether. In her memoirs, published in 1931, Sylvia Pankhurst wrote:

It is ... a curious fact that the women who secured political office when the citizenship of women was achieved had none of them taken a prominent part in the struggle for the vote; the first woman Cabinet

Minister having remained during the greater part of her public life uninterested in the question.[2]

This was hardly fair; the early history of the Labour Party was littered with women who had worked all their lives to advance women's interests, even if they had not always construed them as being entirely bound up with the vote. But the prevalence of one version of the suffrage campaign, together with the use of that campaign as shorthand for women's rights campaigns generally, has led to the effective erasure of Labour women from most versions of women's history.

Many trade unionists and socialists had a class-based analysis of women's predicament and as a result did not believe that enfranchising middle-class women would help working-class communities. In 1910, 40 per cent of men still could not vote and for many women of the left, particularly those involved in trade unions, universal adult suffrage was at least as important as votes for women. Indeed, until suffrage campaigners were prepared to support abolishing the property qualification it was hard to see how trade unionists could support an objective which would have enfranchised the wives of their employers but not themselves or their neighbours. The movement for universal adult suffrage, which was vilified by many female limited suffrage campaigners, was in fact large and active, and it included almost all of the early Labour leaders. Universal adult suffrage was Trades Union Congress (TUC) policy for decades, and both the Labour Party and the Women's Labour League supported it through conference resolutions for many years. There was also little sympathy for the militant suffrage campaign. Few working-class women could take the risk of fines or prison; they could not pay fines, and prison would have lost them their livelihoods and put them into the workhouse.

Our view of women's political activity during this period is even more constricted by seeing it mainly through the history of one of the smaller suffrage organisations – the Women's Social and Political Union (WSPU) – which, although originally set up by socialist women, soon moved very far from its roots and became actively hostile to Labour and to the women Labour represented. As a result, not only do we lose a sense of the breadth and depth of the suffrage campaign itself, but we also lose sight of the sheer scale and vibrancy of women's fight for their economic and social rights. Women fought for equal pay and the minimum wage as well as the vote, and the battles for clean air, decent housing and maternity benefits affected the lives of millions.

In fact, women had been campaigning for their rights for decades. The late nineteenth century was an age of campaigns and campaigners, and women participated in most of them. The success of the anti-slavery campaign in the early part of the century had made people understand that it was possible to achieve social progress by both changing public opinion and pressurising government, and there was almost no aspect of life to which this approach could not be applied. Caroline Norton's long fight for women to have access rights to their children had been the first of an extensive list of women's campaigns covering everything from education to prostitution, and property rights to employment. Women had initially not been allowed to speak on anti-slavery platforms, but before long they were addressing public meetings up and down the country. In 1869, at the age of 22, Millicent Fawcett became the first woman to speak on a public platform in support of women's suffrage, and she was followed by hundreds of others. By the end of the century socialist women, in particular, were busy and popular public speakers.

Many of these campaigning women were from middle-class backgrounds and a small number of them chose to immerse themselves in Labour and trade union work. While it is not the case that all early female trade unionists and socialists were bourgeois, it is undeniably true that a great many of them were, and that this was both a weakness and a strength. It was a weakness when, as was sometimes the case, the women concerned did not care overmuch for the class on whose behalf they were organising or campaigning, but saw it as part of a greater moral or social crusade. Working-class men, in particular, often resented the interference in their affairs of 'middle-class ladies' and there were a number of attempts to keep them off the floor of the TUC. Middle-class women did not always help themselves, either, and sometimes adopted a hectoring, rather school-marmish tone that was calculated to irritate the men (and many of the women) with whom they were dealing.

On the other hand, being middle class was a great strength in terms of the time, energy and money women could commit to their chosen causes. Working-class women faced a daily struggle to earn enough to feed their children and themselves and to hang onto the few jobs open to them. The best of the middle-class women understood this, and actively worked for a day when all women would have access to decent jobs, equal pay, childcare and political agency. Some (though by no means all) middle-class women had money, too; Emilia Dilke's donations kept the Women's Trade Union League going for many years, while Margaret MacDonald's income both supported the Women's Labour League and enabled the infant Labour Party to set up its electoral machine. Some working-class women did also achieve leadership roles. Margaret Bondfield had been apprenticed as a shop assistant at the age of 14 and Mary Middleton, who went on to become secretary of the Women's Labour League, had started work as a servant when she was 12. Years later, Mary observed that in her opinion it was the ability of women from different backgrounds and with different skills to work together so well that made women's organisations so successful.[3]

Another reason given for dismissing women's contribution to the early Labour Party is that many of the leading women were married to leading men. That this is true is unavoidable, but it does not automatically follow, as some commentators seem to feel that it does, that these women were subservient, or only acting in their husbands' interests. Margaret MacDonald was an experienced and gifted statistician with a formidable body of work in her own right behind her long before she married Ramsay, and Katharine Bruce Glasier was one of the Independent Labour Party's most high-profile public speakers, capable of drawing larger crowds than most of the men, for years before she married John. Because socialism at this time was regarded almost as a religion, socialists were likely to choose to marry one another and to live lives jointly dedicated to the cause. To undermine or dismiss women's contribution because of their marital status is effectively to accept the contemporary view of their involvement and worth.

Victorian and Edwardian society believed that men and women inhabited separate social, political and economic spheres, and that to move out of them was to 'unsex' oneself. Needless to say, women were much more constricted by this than men, and for middle- and upper-class women especially the price for breaking out of the female sphere could be high. For many working-class women, particularly if they had no option but to rely on themselves rather than their men, separate spheres was an almost unattainable ideal, but for upper- and middle-class women they were a reality. Largely educated at home, girls remained in their fathers' care until they married. They then devoted their time to their husbands and children and were expected to remain supportively and silently in the background. Despite the fact that single women could keep some control over their lives, remaining single was regarded as failure. Married women had virtually no civic, social or economic rights; the young Millicent Fawcett was propelled into the campaign for married women's property rights when, having been mugged, she attended court and heard the charge read out as 'stealing from the person of Millicent Fawcett a purse containing £1–18–6d, the property of Henry Fawcett'. Divorce had been available to women since 1857, but only in extreme circumstances, while access and custody rights when it came to children were heavily restricted.

The first Married Women's Property Act was passed in 1870, but not until 1884 did women cease to be, in legal terms, their husbands' 'chattels'. Women took the whole of their husband's name on marriage; thus the author and social reformer Beatrice Webb was routinely referred to as 'Mrs Sidney Webb', to the point at which some works by her are still occasionally attributed to him. Women could neither vote nor stand for political office, and to speak or be known in public was seen as not quite 'nice'. Many a well-known female author hid her modesty behind a male name, and as late as 1887 Beatrice Webb could take exception to the journalist Annie Besant's practice of speaking on public platforms, remarking that 'it is not womanly to thrust yourself before the world'.[4]

The penalties for women who challenged or flouted the conventions were severe. They could easily find themselves in precarious circumstances, unable to get employment in any 'respectable' house or business and shunned by 'respectable' people, and they could also lose both their children and their support networks. The middle classes were obsessed with the morals of the workers, and much social reform directed at women was as much about changing personal or sexual behaviour as about preventing the poverty which was believed to produce it. Working-class people aspired to respectability because the price of anything else was so high. The careful balancing acts between conventional and unconventional lives achieved by many of the women in this book look all the more remarkable when seen in the context of their times.

Many progressive women thought that both marriage and divorce laws needed urgent reform, and that the nature of Victorian marriage accounted for the tendency of some women to reject it. In 1890 the social reformer, trade unionist and novelist Clementina Black, for instance, published an article in the *Fortnightly Review* in which she observed that:

> At present the strict letter of the law denies to a married woman the freedom of action which more and more women are coming to regard not only as their just but also as their dearest treasure; and this naturally causes a certain unwillingness on the part of the thoughtful women to marry.[5]

For some women, remaining single was a conscious choice for other reasons. Although homosexuality was illegal at this time, lesbianism was not, and there were undoubtedly a number of such relationships which endured for years and brought much happiness. Margaret Bondfield's declaration in her autobiography that she 'had no vocation for wifehood or motherhood, but an urge to serve the Union – an urge which developed into "a sense of oneness with our kind"'[6] is frequently taken at face value, but in point of fact it is entirely capable of more than one interpretation. Margaret also said of her long-term companion Maud Ward:

> our partnership lasted many years. ... I certainly had the best of the arrangement by which she ... was housekeeper for both when in lodgings, and later when she bought a house at Hampstead which she was good enough to share with me.[7]

Similarly, the suffragists and trade unionists Eva Gore-Booth and Esther Roper lived their whole lives together and are buried in the same grave, and any reading of their relationship leads almost inescapably to the conclusion that their love for one another was profound. But posterity has tended to be rather squeamish in its willingness to recognise their relationship for what it almost certainly was, and their biographer concluded that it was not sexual.[8] Another (male) historian says that 'Their lives were filled with a huge circle of friends and acquaintances of both sexes and the satisfaction of pursuing a series of worthwhile causes.'[9] Clearly, not all women who lived together were lesbians; friends often shared accommodation because it was cheaper, maximised limited resources and ensured a degree of companionship. Not all single women were gay, any more than all married women were straight. But to deny the possibility of lesbian relationships, however discreet they may have been, constitutes a denial of an essential element of women's political and personal history. It is impossible at this distance to be certain about anybody's sexuality or sexual life, but that does not mean that we should not accept that those lives existed, or, for instance, that the love between Esther and Eva should not be as much recognised and celebrated as that between Margaret and Ramsay MacDonald or Katharine and John Bruce Glasier.

Throughout the period covered by this book there was a lively debate about whether or not married women should work, and what kinds of work any woman should be allowed to do. Some people thought that women should be excluded from paid work altogether, others that they should give work up when they married. Some people thought there were moral issues, others thought children suffered if their mothers worked, some thought working-class women had no option but to work when men's wages were so poor, while a very few thought that women had as much right to work in whatever trade they chose as men had. Again, some of these debates are still with us, as the briefest of glances at some media outlets demonstrates. Objection was often made to the hard and heavy nature of much industry, with the suggestion that it would be better for women's health and welfare if they were restricted to domestic duties. But this was often a point put by either men or middle-class women, the latter of whom were likely to have servants; most working-class women knew only too well that domestic toil, with several children, no labour-saving devices and no help to carry food, children or coal up what might be several flights of stairs was as hard as any work in a factory, and, in one's own home, was unpaid into the bargain. Working-class women fought the Factory Acts, designed to improve working conditions, as hard as any employer; every restriction of hours meant a concomitant restriction of wages and some people even objected to the introduction of compulsory education in 1870 on the grounds that family incomes would fall (as they did) and that children would have less to eat (which some did, leading to a national campaign for free school meals).

The doctrine of separate spheres had its influence within the labour and trade union movements as well as society as a whole, and many men in the movement, however progressive in other ways, reverted to the stereotypes in their own lives. Even Keir Hardie took a traditional line when it came to his own family. His wife, Lillie, remained at home in Scotland bringing up their children virtually single-handed while he toured the country and made occasional foreign visits. She travelled with him more once the children were grown up, and he was very keen to see her properly recognised, but she had little or no independence and was generally reckoned to have had a difficult life. Their two sons were apprenticed as engineers, but there were no such plans for their daughter, Agnes (usually called Nan), who was expected to stay at home helping her parents until she married.

In some marriages women were able to take a more public role, but even then it seemed important to emphasise the degree to which they conformed in other ways. When Ramsay MacDonald, whose wife Margaret was one of the leading Labour women of her day, came to write his biography of her he found it necessary to spend many pages explaining the degree to which she fulfilled norms that neither she nor he had accepted while she was alive. As a result the book only really becomes interesting when he gets to the chapter titled 'Preparation', where it becomes clear that the life for which she is preparing is political rather than domestic. Many other women, including Mary Macarthur and Margaret Bondfield, neither of whom was in any way saintly, are written about by contemporaries in terms almost worthy of Dickensian heroines. Consequently the real women often become hard to see, and have to be gleaned from their own writings or chance accounts from people they met. Male politicians have had substantial biographies written about them which are (usually) able to produce rounded views of their subject because it was possible to see men as both flawed and interesting because of those flaws; women, however, were allowed no flaws, and so become less interesting to biographers, especially if they left no memoirs of their own.

Margaret Bondfield was actually one of a small number of prominent Labour women to write an autobiography, but disappointingly it seems to contain very little of the woman other people described. Much of it is very worthy, and some parts – such as a lengthy account of a visit to the United States – are downright dull. Written many years after the events it describes it seems like an attempt to forestall any further inquiry, and in this it was entirely successful until 1978 when the journalist Ross Davies began to research Margaret's life for a proposed biography. He found that very few of her papers seemed to have survived, many having been destroyed by her before her death in 1953. The archives of her male contemporaries had been deposited in various libraries and universities, but he could not find anything of Margaret's and gave the project up. Later it transpired that what had survived of Margaret's papers had been taken to the United States by the academic Helen Lockwood, who had died before being able to deal with them. Helen's papers, including whatever there were of Margaret's, were deposited at Vassar College in New York State, and there they have remained ever since. Meanwhile there is still no modern biography of the most prominent female trade unionist and politician of her day, the first woman to chair the TUC or become a cabinet minister or Privy Counsellor. She remains largely unknown, not just to the women who have followed her, but to history generally.

The women in this book were, as a rule, largely unrepresentative of women in the society in which they lived. Whatever fame (or notoriety) some of them attracted came in part from their novelty value rather than their ordinariness. Very few people were socialists, hardly any women were or would have described themselves as feminists, and pacifists of any kind were a tiny minority. Yet many of the women in this story would proudly have called themselves all three. It is sometimes difficult when reading about them now to remember how tiny a minority they were, and how much they must sometimes have felt it. The Huddersfield suffragist Florence Lockwood, for instance, was part of a delegation to the International Woman Suffrage Alliance conference in Budapest in 1913, and recorded in her diary that she 'felt a sense of ease to be a dwarf among these women, instead of standing out as something exceptional and eccentric, as I appear at home'.[10] Even suffrage campaigners, who now loom so large in our consciousness, were a tiny minority of women, though many thousands more might take part in the processions and marches they organised.

The same question of perspective applies to the Labour Party. Seeing it as it was seen by contemporaries requires us to forget what we now know about its subsequent rise. In 1906, when Labour had its first significant election successes, hardly anybody seriously thought that it was anything other than a minor fringe party. Very few people, including most of its members and leaders, imagined that it would ever be capable of forming a government. The Labour Party belonged to the political margins, and struggled to get support even from trade unionists. However, despite this it attracted remarkable women and men, and punched far above its weight in terms of influence and access. Like all small left-wing organisations (and some large ones) it was prone to navel-gazing and infighting, but the particular mix of people it contrived to bring together meant that it always had at least a glimpse of the bigger picture. Its trade union members made sure that the economy was always to the fore, and its internationalist ideals meant that it understood how serious the threat of war was long before many parliamentarians.

World War I is also one of the major filters through which the early twentieth century is viewed. Its effect was so cataclysmic that those who survived it often looked back to the pre-war period as one of halcyon happiness in which the summers were perfect, life was gracious and everyone knew their place. This impression was, of course, created by the middle rather than the working classes and has been assiduously fostered by the producers of fiction and film ever since. In fact, for working people, pre-war conditions were appalling, and the years leading up to 1914 were fractious and full of the fear of revolution. The war brought an end to industrial unrest as well as militant suffrage activity, and neither the Labour Party nor the suffrage movement emerged unchanged in 1918.

As hostilities ceased the Party was reorganised, its constitution rewritten and its internal clock reset. In 1914 it had been in existence for less than 15 years, and had had significant parliamentary representation for only eight. It had been a small, if influential, party grouping in a traditional three-party political landscape dominated by the Conservatives and Liberals, in which Labour came a poor fourth behind the Irish Parliamentary Party. By the time hostilities ceased it had effectively become the third party and its leaders had gained valuable experience of government. The old, infant, pre-war party seemed distant, especially since its hero, Keir Hardie, had died in 1915. Labour in the 1920s was larger, stronger and more successful than it had ever been, but the women's organisations that had helped to build it had been left behind in the far-off pre-war years.

This book begins with the establishment of the TUC in 1868 and takes the story up to the 1918 general election at which the first women voted. As a result, some elements of women's history have of necessity had to be omitted. The Women's Co-operative Guild, for instance, was a fascinating and influential organisation which achieved a great deal and of which many socialists and trade unionists were members. But the co-operative movement never affiliated to the Labour Party, and there has not therefore been space for a detailed examination of the Guild's activity and influence. Similarly there has been very little space to look at women in local government in any kind of depth, despite the fact that many prominent Labour women were involved in it; even Margaret Bondfield, notable mainly for her trade union work during this period, was for a time a councillor in Woolwich. Indeed, the process of deciding what to include and what to leave out has demonstrated all too clearly how many other books about these women there are waiting to be written, and how many more interesting and significant women are still waiting to be rescued from the dustbin of history.

The late nineteenth and early twentieth centuries were a ferment of progressive movements and campaigns, and women were involved in almost all of them. Leaving them out of the narrative, or disregarding them if they were not part of the militant suffrage campaign, diminishes our understanding of the present as well as the past. This book restores women to the rooms of Labour's early history and in doing so expands and enriches our insight into women's remarkable achievements before they had the vote.

∽ 1 ∾

Trade Unionists

In the autumn of 1875 the Trades Union Congress (TUC) gathered in Glasgow for its annual meeting. Its rise since its inception had been meteoric; from a gathering of 34 delegates in Manchester in 1868 it had become an organisation representing over a hundred unions and local trades councils. It represented working people and their interests to government, and through its offshoot, the Labour Representation League (LRL), it had helped get two working men elected to Parliament. However, until the 150 delegates foregathered on a rather cold and damp morning in October 1875 the TUC had never been attended by a female delegate or addressed by a woman's voice. History was about to be made.

When Emma Paterson and Edith Simcox arrived in Glasgow in 1875 they had no role models to inspire or guide them. In a world dedicated to the idea of separate spheres for women and men they were about to enter one of the most assertively male bastions possible, and not only to enter it, but to speak in it, challenge it and fight for the interests of the women they represented. Although Emma Paterson is usually credited with being the first woman to speak at the TUC it was in fact Edith Simcox who had that honour. The men gave the new delegates a very civil welcome, but there was no question of allowing them any real influence. Apart from anything else many of the men simply found the idea of women organising either themselves or anyone else faintly alarming. In a world in which working-class men were struggling to be taken seriously many thought that 'lady trade unionists' might make them seem ridiculous. On the other hand, some were interested and even intrigued; Mr Rolley, chairman of the Sheffield Trades Council and president of the TUC, met Emma Paterson in Glasgow and was sufficiently impressed to invite her to Sheffield to try to organise women in the silver and electroplating industry.

As both Emma and her audience at that visit would have known, Sheffield had played a particular and at times controversial part in the

founding of the TUC less than a decade previously, and had long been at
the forefront of the fight for the right to organise.

The Combination Act of 1825 had made it illegal for workers to
combine for the purposes of trying to improve pay and conditions and
severely restricted the right to strike or picket. Many other Acts of
Parliament restricted the rights of workers to control their pay and
conditions, and of unions to control their own funds. Since industrial
action was thus a perilous undertaking, unions usually presented
themselves as mutual benefit or friendly societies, taking subscriptions from members to provide assistance when they were out of work,
ill or died. This left little legal recourse open to people to challenge the
appalling conditions suffered in a great many industries. Over the next
few decades, however, the developing middle class became increasingly
interested in the condition of the working classes, and researchers and
thinkers began to investigate what could be done to reduce poverty, ill
health and destitution. Inevitably, this included consideration of the issue
of trade unions.

In 1865 the secretary of the Sheffield Typographical Society, William
Dronfield, read a paper on trade unionism at the annual Congress of the
National Association for the Promotion of Social Science (commonly
called the Social Science Association). The Social Science Association
had been established in 1857 to bring together organisations interested
in questions such as public health and education. These groups included
the Society for Promoting the Employment of Women, which had been
set up by women involved in the Langham Place group, one of the earliest
feminist organisations in Britain. The Social Science Association was,
generally speaking, on what would now be described as the centre left
of the political spectrum, but it was also unquestionably middle class
and suffered from many of the prejudices of its time. In 1860 it had
published a 'Report on Trade Societies and Strikes' which was favourable
to the case for trade unions, and which was so thorough that Beatrice
and Sidney Webb later pronounced it to be 'the best collection of Trade
Union material and the most impartial account of Trade Union action
that has ever been issued'.[1] This was all very encouraging, except that
when the members of the Association came up against an actual working-
class person reading a paper to them they found Dronfield's voice hard to
hear, and both his presentation and the discussion which followed it were
entirely omitted from the report of the Congress's proceedings. When
Dronfield complained to Samuel Nicholson, president of the Manchester

and Salford Trades Council, Nicholson is reported to have said, 'Why not have a congress of our own?'[2]

The following year, 1866, a series of events occurred which collectively became known as the Sheffield Outrages. The secretary of the Saw Grinders' Union, one William Broadhead, instigated what was more or less a reign of terror in the town in order to punish employers and strike-breakers and 'persuade' people to join the union. A canister of gunpowder was thrown into a house, threatening letters were sent, and Broadhead himself paid a man £20 to murder an employer who was reducing his wage bill by taking on large numbers of apprentices rather than adult men. Since he admitted to all this under an amnesty while giving evidence to the subsequent Royal Commission on trade unions, Broadhead was not prosecuted. His justification was that, had unions been allowed to operate openly, and had employers not used underhand and even illegal practices, the measures he had taken would not have been necessary.

The Royal Commission (set up at least in part at the request of the Sheffield Trades Council) failed to recommend the decriminalisation of either collective bargaining or strike action. However, three members of it issued a minority report which called for the legalisation of trade union activity and, crucially, the protection of their funds. Trade union leaders were encouraged, since they knew that there was a good chance of the minority report being enacted if there was a new government. The political situation was unstable, a general election loomed and the opposition Liberal leader, William Gladstone, was broadly open to reformist ideas. The unions were also buoyed by the widening of the franchise in 1867 to a whole section of working men who were likely to vote Liberal. In 1868 the anticipated election duly took place. The Liberals secured a 100-seat majority and Gladstone was able to form his first administration. Union leaders now lobbied to persuade his government to repeal the 1825 Combination Act, but they knew that to be seen as having the authority to speak for the movement they would have to have one voice. Thus in 1868 the first meeting of the TUC took place in Manchester, and the new organisation campaigned successfully for the implementation of the minority report. The Trade Union Act of 1871 cast most of its recommendations into law, and remained one of the principal foundations of all subsequent trade union legislation until the end of the twentieth century.

Even before the TUC was formed, trade unionists had been discussing how to get working-class men elected to Parliament, and this was one of the first issues discussed at the inaugural meeting. Very few trade unionists at this point were also socialists, and although a number had been Chartists a couple of decades previously,[3] their focus was on breaking into the system as it existed rather than changing the system altogether. The Liberal Party had absorbed many Chartist campaigners, and although the right wing of the Party was still effectively the old eighteenth-century Whig alliance, the left was a loose combination of Chartists, radical religious Nonconformists such as Unitarians and Quakers, and socially and economically progressive middle-class men. These groups tended to be broadly sympathetic in theory to improving the lot of the labouring classes, and even to legalising trade unions, but there was a difficulty. Mill owners, particularly in the north of England, were often Liberals and sometimes even radical – except when it came to providing adequate pay and conditions for their own employees. Thus relations between the TUC and the Liberal Party were not always easy, and became increasingly tense as labour and socialist political organisations began to proliferate and flex their muscles.

In 1869 the TUC set up the LRL. This aimed to get working men elected to Parliament, ensure that men who could vote were on the electoral register, and keep an eye on proposed industrial legislation. It allowed individual membership and had a rudimentary system of branches around the country. But it had no political programme and, since it had a large executive council composed of 32 members, there was an inherent scope for conflict. In particular, there was disagreement about whether their candidates should be independent of all parties or run as Liberals; this dilemma within the labour movement continued for decades, not being fully resolved until after World War I.

The 1871 Trade Union Act represented a degree of success for the TUC, but the Criminal Law Amendment Act passed in the same year outlawed picketing, thus making even legal strike action very difficult to undertake successfully. What Gladstone's reforming Liberal government had given with one hand it had taken away almost immediately with the other and trade unionists across the board were furious. The need to have working men represented in Parliament was seen to be pressing. There was talk of setting up a separate political party and local men were urged by the LRL to 'organise … not as mere consenting parties to the doings of local wirepullers, but as a great Labour party – a party which knows its own strength and is prepared to fight and win'.[4] However, nothing came of this, at least in part because nobody was prepared to do anything to make it a reality, and the LRL soon fell back on generalised support for Liberal candidates.

At this stage a man called Henry Broadhurst became secretary of the LRL and brought to it a new level of drive and efficiency. Broadhurst was the foremost trade unionist of his generation, going on to become one of the first working-class MPs and the first working-class government minister. A stonemason by trade, he had been apprenticed at the age of 12 and in his mid-20s moved to London to work on the clock tower of the new Houses of Parliament. This brought him into contact with radical groups, and his successful leadership of industrial disputes led him to become a full-time officer of the Stonemasons' Union. By 1873, when he became secretary of the LRL, he was 33 years old and a powerful and influential figure.

Broadhurst proposed to the TUC that they should raise an electoral fund for Labour candidates, but, like Keir Hardie 20 years later, he could not persuade them to contribute financially to make their political aspirations a reality. Instead delegates passed a motion supporting local action and effectively leaving everyone with pretty much a free hand. Most working men who stood for Parliament did so as Liberals with the support of trade unionists as well as local Liberal members. But for the 1874 general election the LRL did produce a list of Labour candidates, the first in any election, and two were successful; Alexander Macdonald and Thomas Burt for Stafford and Morpeth respectively. Broadhurst stood in High Wycombe but lost. In 1875 he became secretary of the TUC's Parliamentary Committee (which became the General Council in 1918) and began his long dominance of the TUC and its work.

◆ ◆ ◆ ◆ ◆

Most trade unions excluded women from membership on the grounds that they should also be excluded from the workforce. For most men (and many women), the presence of women in the workforce not only violated the doctrine of separate spheres but also directly caused unemployment and low pay. Women were prepared to accept much lower rates than men for doing the same jobs, and as a result they were widely used by employers as cheap labour and even to break strikes. Because they were excluded from apprenticeships they were also excluded from many of the industries in which trade unions were most likely to develop, and where they were employed as semi-skilled or unskilled labour there was a continuous campaign to get them out. There were also heavy concentrations of women workers in industries such as domestic service, confectionery and laundries, but there were no unions affiliated to the TUC for any of these trades, at least in part because at this stage trade unionism was still largely dominated by the older craft unions.

As well as having principled objections to women in industry, many male trade unionists were irritated by the practical problems. Women were difficult to recruit and even harder to retain in membership, and it was years before the men came to see equal pay rather than exclusion as the answer to undercutting. Almost the only exceptions to this attitude were some of the unions which developed in the Lancashire cotton industry. They had admitted women on equal terms (though on a reduced subscription) for many years and were large and influential. In 1875 the East Lancashire Amalgamated Power Loom Weavers' Association had been successful in achieving some measure of equal pay for its male and female members and affiliated 20,000 members to the TUC. It was one of the few unions to understand that women could not be excluded from industry altogether and that improvements in working conditions and pay for both women and men were part of the same struggle.

The cotton weavers of Lancashire were unusual, however, and most of the jobs which women could get in factories or mills were pretty grim. They were often repetitive or dangerous, with high levels of injuries, very long hours, and no compensation for the diseases caused by chemicals or industrial processes. Such working conditions were often thought to have a coarsening effect on the moral character of the women themselves and much middle-class effort was expended on trying to 'reform' female workers. The principal alternative to industry was domestic service, where conditions were poor and pay even worse. At least a woman working in a factory or mill had some small measure of independence, but those in service or working in the burgeoning retail industry had virtually none. Many women had no option but to work at whatever they could get, and lower-middle-class as well as working-class women lived in constant fear of destitution. A great many married women would much rather not have worked but had no option but to seek employment either outside the home or inside it as a homeworker. Homeworkers tended to earn the worst pay of all, and to be exploited to such an extent that they and their children lived permanently on the verge of starvation. Virtually all single working-class women needed employment to survive. Women generally were often subject to harassment and assault and could be hired and fired at will. They were classed with immigrant Irish, Jewish and Chinese labour as threats to working men's wages and had little or no protection from anyone. For many the choices were stark, with the dreaded prospect of the workhouse always looming as the alternative to starvation.

The difficulties of organising women were increased by their places of work. They were more likely to be employed in small, scattered workshops, in domestic service, or in their own homes where they were difficult to reach. They were usually so poorly paid that the penny a week that men in skilled industries could afford for union membership was beyond their reach, and even if they could pay it, the ephemeral nature of their employment, the tendency for it to be short-lived, and the likelihood of their being sacked by their employers at no notice made them hard to keep track of, and their subscriptions hard to collect. This applied to millions of unskilled men too, of course, and partially accounts for their also remaining largely unorganised prior to the 1880s, but it was particularly true of women and continued to be so for decades. Moreover, any increase in women's pay that the unions secured was often viewed with disfavour by men, since they thought that better pay would attract more women to work, and that more women would further undermine their own position.

There were also social factors. Young women entering the workforce frequently did so as children, and believed that they would leave it once they married. Working-class women married earlier than those of the middle classes, so that teenage girls were inclined to view their working lives as transitory. If they came back to work later, as widows, deserted wives, single mothers or wives with sick or disabled husbands or husbands who simply could not or did not earn enough, they still wanted to hope that employment was temporary. The trade unionist Edith Simcox said:

> The fact that women only work for wages for a short part of their life, while many more hope and believe that they will not need to do so always, makes the state of her trade seem a matter of less importance to each young woman as she enters it than it would be if she intended from the first to work at it for life.[5]

Joining a trade union was not worth women's while, or, if it was, it wasn't worth it for very long.

It also required a degree of courage. Many men were not at all keen on their wives and daughters joining trade unions, and many were actively hostile. As the Leeds trade union organiser Isabella Ford noted: 'It is a common excuse amongst the girls … that they do not join a union because their fathers do not urge them or care for them to do so.'[6] After years devoted to the organising of women she and others knew that unless men changed their opinions there was unlikely to be much progress. To make matters more difficult, men often felt perfectly comfortable shrouding their hostility to working women in a cloak of moral concern or simple superiority. Henry Broadhurst spoke for the majority of people when he said that:

> [men] had the future of their country and children to consider, and it was their duty as men and husbands to use their utmost efforts to bring about a condition of things where their wives should be in their proper sphere at home, seeing after their house and family, instead of being dragged into competition for livelihood against the great and strong men of the world.[7]

Every year, almost without exception, the TUC discussed what to do about women in the workforce. Although there were always a few individuals willing to speak up for them, the majority took the accepted view that industry was no place for the female sex, and especially not for married women. They supported legal restrictions on women's working hours as well as their exclusion from certain trades, but did not at the same time look for an increase in women's rates of pay to make up for the reductions in hours which the Factory Acts they supported entailed. This acted as even more of a disincentive to women to join them. Thus, until the arrival of the general unions in the late 1880s, the few women who were organised were found almost exclusively in women-only trade unions.

Clearly, if women were to be part of the trade union movement there would have to be a new approach to the problem, and in 1874 one appeared in the shape of the Women's Protective and Provident League (WPPL). The driving force behind it was Emma Paterson, a young woman of considerable skill and flair and a great believer in the power of women acting together.

Emma was born in London in the spring of 1848 when the wave of revolutions which eventually deposited Karl Marx on English shores was sweeping Europe. Her father ran a parish school in Hanover Square in the West End of London. This gave Emma experience of both the poor families whose children her father educated and the rich ones who lived in what had always been a fashionable area. The school was also situated close to a workhouse, which must have provided the young Emma with a very clear idea of what happened to people – especially women – who failed to survive in the cut-throat economy of the mid-nineteenth century.

Educated at home, Emma's first job was to help her father to teach the younger children. This did not last long and she was soon – if briefly – apprenticed to a bookbinder. She then worked again as a teacher and, for a short unhappy period, a governess. At 18 she took a job assisting a female clerk at the Working Men's Club and Institute Union (CIU). This had been set up in 1862 to bring working men's clubs together and help them to found new ones. In this it had been highly successful, and clubs had sprung up all over the country. However, these were not working men's clubs as thought of now: their primary function was to provide education as well as entertainment, and they were (at least at first) strictly teetotal. The CIU was a middle-class body designed to teach the working classes self-reliance and organisational skills, and, crucially, keep them out of the public houses and away from the demon drink. In July 1867, at the age of 19, Emma was promoted to the post of assistant secretary. She never looked back.

For the next five years she worked in this post, drawing from it many lessons in both organisation and networking. By its very nature, the CIU had developed a wide array of funders and patrons, many of whom were wealthy society figures with charitable or radical inclinations. In her position as secretary she came into contact with a huge range of people, from Lord Brougham (who was also the president of the Social Science Association and had presided over the meeting at Sheffield at which William Dronfield read his ill-fated paper) to the working men who ran clubs up and down the country. She also met the leading trade unionists of the day, and learned about the struggles of organised labour. She gained a thorough understanding of the model of wealthy philanthropists funding working people to organise themselves as well as an extensive list of contacts. These she would later put to good use.

In early 1872 Emma left the CIU (which presented her with a gold watch and an illuminated address which referred to her 'practical ability and good judgement')[8] and took up a post as secretary to the National Society for Women's Suffrage (NSWS). This was one of the earliest of the suffrage groups and through it Emma again extended her network of contacts to include people such as the young Millicent Fawcett. For some reason, however, this job did not last long, and the causes of its termination are shrouded in a degree of mystery. According to one version of the story Emma left when she married, but Emilia Dilke, who later worked with her for many years at the WPPL, said that Emma had told her that she was sacked because 'my bodily presence is weak and my speech contemptible'.[9] Either way, she married Thomas Paterson, with whom she had worked at the CIU, in 1873 and departed with him for a 'working honeymoon' in the United States.

Emma Paterson's introduction to the idea of women's trade unions is usually attributed to this visit, and while it may well be true that this was when she first thought of applying her organisational expertise to them, it is inevitable that her experience beforehand must have informed her thinking. Women-only unions in Britain were rare but not unknown, but her visits to groups such as the Female Umbrella Makers' Union in New York, which was run by women for women, must have made her consider what might be possible, and, more importantly, how she could facilitate it.

When the Patersons returned from America Emma set about making her ideas a reality. At 26 she was at the height of her power and energy, and she used both them and her previous experience to the full. She wrote a series of articles for *Labour News*[10] about the plight of women workers and the need for them to be organised. She followed this up in July 1874 with a conference for which she raided the address book she had built up during her time at the CIU and the NSWS. The result was the formation of the WPPL, with Emma Paterson as secretary and a committee of supporters, philanthropists and male trade unionist sympathisers lending names, help and credibility as well as, in some cases, donating funds.

The purpose of the League was not to be a trade union itself, but to foster the development of women's unions. It encouraged women in as many trades as possible to organise themselves, supporting them with a starter fund, advice, help with recruitment and access to a network of women in other trades. It assisted with negotiations, and helped the new unions to set up benefits funds to cover sickness or unemployment, although at this stage neither strike nor lock-out pay were covered. The WPPL was financed by subscriptions and fundraising as well as donations from wealthy benefactors, some of whom also sat on the committee. Each new union was expected to become self-supporting within the WPPL's orbit. It had its own newsletter – the *Women's Union Journal* – and took a strong line on women's rights to self-determination when it came to their employment. As a concept it owed very little to the Female Umbrella Makers' Union of New York and a great deal to Emma's experience at the CIU, and it was by far the most successful attempt to resolve some of the organisational problems of women's unions until the advent of the National Federation of Women Workers in 1906.

One of the problems that Emma Paterson and the women working with her saw was the lack of any female voice at the TUC, despite the fact that this body frequently discussed women's employment, made policy on it, and represented that policy to government. In particular, the WPPL believed that legislation to restrict women's hours and the industries in which they could work was designed not to improve women's lives, but to control them in ways which would improve men's. They maintained that, while legislation might be necessary to protect children, it was insulting for women to be treated in the same way. They wanted women to be able to make choices for themselves and to resolve issues of hours and pay through organisation and action in the same way that men did.

One of the main drivers of the growing women's movement in the second half of the nineteenth century was the fight to open up education and employment for middle-class women. Emma's interaction with both the Social Science Association and the NSWS had brought her into contact with women from the Langham Place group, members of which had been instrumental in the recent establishment at Cambridge of women's colleges, and which in 1859 had also set up the Society for Promoting the Employment of Women. Obviously, middle-class women getting into universities and the professions was a very different matter from working-class women 'choosing' to work 12–15 hours a day in a dark, airless factory or foundry, and this point was frequently made by the male proponents of restriction. From the women's point of view, however, all occupations should be open to all women, and to force working-class women out of manual trades just as middle-class women were forcing their way into the professions was counter-productive. A woman excluded from nail-making was unlikely to be able to find work as a teacher or clerk, and the WPPL and others foresaw significant increases in women's unemployment and poverty if they were not permitted to work at the same trades as men. They thought that, properly organised and represented, women would be able to arrive at their own agreements with employers, and that this would more effectively shorten hours and increase pay than the various Factory Acts.

Working women had grounds for particular concern when it came to the arbitrary shortening of working hours. In 1875 there was a Royal Commission on the Factory and Workshop Acts, and Emma Paterson brought 130 working women together to give evidence directly to its chair, subsequently writing that evidence up and presenting it to the Commission. She reported that the women 'agreed that any further reduction of hours, if accompanied by a reduction in wages, as it probably would be if brought about by legislation, would be objectionable'.[11]

In 1874, as part of a lengthy all-male debate on the Factory Bill then before Parliament, the TUC had agreed unanimously that measures to restrict the labour of women and children should 'ultimately be extended to all branches of industry as far as practicable'.[12] Stonemason Alfred Walton said that, in spite of 'a new school of political economy which preached the doctrine that they ought not to interfere with the labour of women and children', trade unionists had 'a duty as men to require protection for those who could not protect themselves'.[13] In Emma Paterson's opinion Mr Walton's view of the men's 'duty' seemed not to include organising women at all, and she noted that they had failed either to recruit women into the male unions or help them form their own. In one of her *Labour News* articles she had written:

> At three successive annual congresses of leaders and delegates of trades unions, the need of women's unions has been brought before them, and each time someone present has asserted that women *cannot* form unions. The only ground for this assertion appears to be that women *have not yet* formed unions. Probably they have not done so because they have not quite seen how to set about it.[14]

The WPPL set out to rectify this, beginning with the Society of Women Bookbinders, the Society of Shirt and Collar Makers and the Society of Women Upholsterers. The National Union of Working Women was also established in Bristol. The first three of these were allowed to affiliate to the TUC for 275, 39 and 92 members respectively, and in September 1875 Emma Paterson (for the Bookbinders and the Upholsterers) and Edith Simcox (for the Shirt and Collar Makers) travelled to Glasgow to put the women's viewpoint to the TUC on equal terms.

As the first woman to speak at the TUC, Edith Simcox attracted a certain amount of press attention. A nameless 'Special Correspondent', writing for the *Sheffield Daily Telegraph*, observed that the speeches were 'with rare exception … heavy, oppressive, and very misty', but that the 'sensation of to-day was the speech of Miss Simcox' who was 'enthusiastically received, and did not seem at all disconcerted in rising to address the gentlemen present'. With possibly more than a touch of sarcasm, he observed that it was 'marvel that so much shrewdness should still be ticketed "Miss Edith Simcox"'.[15] Had he known Edith rather better he might have known that very little disconcerted her, and that by the time she addressed Congress she was an accomplished and energetic organiser of women workers.

Although she was only a little older than Emma Paterson, Edith Simcox's background demonstrated the gulf between the lower and upper middle classes. Whereas Emma had received a decent education which included music and some German and Italian, Edith could speak three languages fluently and a little of three more, as well as having taught herself a grasp of Latin and Greek. She came from a family which valued learning, and had access to good educational opportunities. However, although her two brothers were able to go to university (both becoming academics at Oxford), that door was closed to her as to all women: Emily Davies and Barbara Bodichon did not establish Girton College at Cambridge until 1869, which was too late for Edith. Like other serious-minded young women of the age, she saw social reform as both a duty and a release, and plunged into it with a will. But unlike many other women of her class, she realised very quickly that trade unionism was essential if women were to have control over their own lives. While many women saw charitable work as the best way of 'saving' working women, Edith thought that women must be able to create change for themselves, and that they could do this through trade unions. She never married, but was for many years in love with the novelist George Eliot (Mary Ann Evans). In 1875 Edith and her friend Mary Hamilton set up a shirt-making co-operative, and this provided her with both employment and the opportunity to be a delegate to the TUC. She had helped Emma Paterson to found the WPPL, and spent a great deal of time travelling the country organising, speaking and providing advice and support to women's unions at every stage of their development.

Both Edith and Emma's first speeches at the Glasgow TUC were about factory inspection. This was an issue of considerable importance, since although there was some legislation covering industrial safety, sanitation and working hours, enforcement was largely inadequate, especially where women were concerned. Already there were tensions between the 'middle-class ladies' and men like Henry Broadhurst over this and other issues; over the years these would broaden into a running battle.

The 1875 TUC also held a lengthy debate about the representation of the labouring classes in Parliament. There was still no serious idea of creating a new political party; the concept of party (or caucus) itself was only just beginning to take shape in its modern form and was generally regarded with suspicion. The Second Reform Act of 1867 had extended the franchise so that it included a significant number of the urban working class, doubling the electorate from 1 to 2 million men. This presented obvious opportunities, but there was little clarity about how they should best be seized, and a real concern that working-class men who were eligible to vote were not getting their names onto the electoral register. In this debate Edith Simcox made a short, careful speech agreeing that there needed to be more working men in Parliament and noting that power was slowly being transferred from the middle to the working classes. Neither she nor Emma Paterson mentioned women's suffrage, and it was not in fact until 1880 that the issue was raised by the working-class suffragist Jessie Craigen. But Edith's intervention made it clear that the politics of the problems of working people were of as much interest to women as to men, regardless of whether or not they had the vote.

In 1879 Emma Paterson wrote that 'The admission of women as delegates at the Trades Union Congress ... does not appear to excite opposition or jealousy on the part of the Men's Unions, as was once feared would be the case.'[16] This may indeed have been true for most delegates, but the atmosphere very quickly soured when it came to the Parliamentary Committee and, in particular, its secretary, Henry Broadhurst. Among other things, the 1878 Factory and Workshop Act restricted the employment of women and children, but also expanded the factory inspection system which had existed since 1833. The WPPL had opposed the restriction of women's hours but, being of a practical turn of mind once the legislation was through, they turned their attention to ways in which the lot of working women could be improved despite it. The factory inspection system did offer some opportunities: inspectors were expected to look into conditions and safety as well as working hours, and the service was seriously underfunded and understaffed. At the 1878 Congress the East Lancashire Power Loom Weavers moved a motion instructing the TUC's Parliamentary Committee to 'take immediate action to secure the appointment of a number of respectable and practical working men as assistant inspectors'. Emma Paterson was immediately on her feet moving an amendment to add the words 'and women' after 'men'. This was seconded by the male delegate from the Manchester and Salford Trades Council and Miss Merrick, from the Bristol-based National Union of Working Women. There were six female delegates that year, four of whom spoke in the ensuing debate. However, Henry Broadhurst was scathing in his response. He thought it seemed 'extraordinary' that, having opposed the Factory Act, the 'lady delegates' should now behave in this way. He urged Congress not to 'place itself in the ridiculous position of asking Parliament to appoint as inspectors those who had been the most determined opponents of the Act'. But in this view he turned out not to be in a majority: when Emma Paterson pressed the amendment to a vote it was passed by 46 votes to 33.[17]

The next 11 years saw a dismal series of events unfold. Each year the Parliamentary Committee failed to do anything at all to secure the appointment of women factory inspectors, and each year the women's organisations and their supporters got an instruction through Congress requiring them to do so. In 1880 Henry Broadhurst gave a masterly demonstration of what women were then (and are sometimes still) up against. He observed that:

> His friend Mr Cooke had said that women should be the inspectors of women. He [Mr Broadhurst] ventured to say that if the women themselves were canvassed it would be found that they would much rather be inspected by men. (*Great laughter and applause.*) He only spoke from his own experience. (*Continued laughter.*) The lady delegates at that Congress were women of great persuasive powers and fascinations and were most active in canvassing others for the promotion of their own views and special ends ... Why could not the ladies be reasonable for once in their lives? ... But they knew how unreasonable ladies were. In whatever they went in for their idea was 'all or nothing'. Half-measures never satisfied them.[18]

Over the years the debates became repetitive, and irritation was evident all round. They even began to undermine women trade unionists' faith in the TUC as an avenue for addressing their grievances. In 1889 Eleanor Whyte, who led the charge after Emma Paterson's early death from diabetes at the age of 38, said:

> Year after year this question had been brought before the Congress, and the vote had been carried in favour of women ... [it was said that] women were not suitable because there were some silly women. Were there not silly men? They would not give the post of inspector to a man who was not qualified, neither to a woman. If women are not to have

any benefits, why let them waste their time in coming to Congress? ...
Let it be decided this time, so that they might have no more tricks.[19]

By 1891 there was a new secretary of the Parliamentary Committee
and in that year the resolution to appoint women factory inspectors
finally met with no opposition from the platform. To applause, Eleanor
Whyte announced that she was not going to move an amendment. But
by now the seeds of distrust had deep roots. She added that she hoped
that 'when the time came to appoint them they would not mention
women under their breath, but that they would speak out distinctly and
say women should be appointed'.[20] The first two women factory inspectors
(Lucy Deane and Adelaide Anderson) were appointed in 1893. In 1895
more were appointed and a separate women's section of the Factory
Inspectorate established. This was the first time that women had been
appointed to senior, responsible and relatively well-paid government
posts, and success was due in large measure to the courage and tenacity
of Emma Paterson, Edith Simcox, Eleanor Whyte and other women trade
unionists during this period.

In 1884 the Third Reform Act broadened the male franchise again,
taking about 60 per cent of men into the electorate. A bid to include an
element of female suffrage was dropped by Gladstone in order to get the
support of the Irish MPs for the main Bill, but nevertheless it did bring
several million more working men into the orbit of electoral politics for
the first time. At the same time a new, more militant trade unionism was
beginning to develop among people who were not part of the traditional
aristocracy of the craft unions. This process was first brought to public
attention, not by the dockers, who staged a famous strike in 1889, but by
the equally famous matchgirls' strike of 1888.

Thanks to the journalism of the socialist and Fabian Annie Besant
and others this strike achieved national notoriety, and awakened people
to the horrendous conditions in which many women and girls were
working. The WPPL raised £400 (about £36,500 in current values) for
the strike fund, and helped the women organise themselves into a union.
The strike lasted for two weeks and the workers won almost all of their
demands. The Matchmakers' Union survived the strike for a few years,
sending delegates to the International Trades Union Congress in London
in 1888 and affiliating to the TUC for the last time in 1898, but, like
most women's unions, it struggled to keep going. However, the strike itself
heralded a fundamental change in trade unionism which brought manual

and unskilled workers into the movement and challenged the dominance of the older craft unions.

The new general unions accepted more trades into membership and grew quickly to become giants. In 1891, a mere two years after they were founded, Will Thorne's Gas Workers and General Labourers' Union affiliated over 27,000 members, while Ben Tillett's Dock, Wharf, Riverside and General Workers' Union affiliated 40,000. Unlike the women's unions, these new unions prospered and grew, forming the basis of what are today, respectively, the GMB and Unite. Together with the huge delegations of miners they dominated the TUC for many years. But, unlike the miners, many of the new men were socialists, and took a very different view of the Liberal Party from the craft unions and their MPs. They also felt less threatened by competition from women workers, and were prepared to recruit them. Thorne, in particular, understood the value of organising women, and in 1894 the Gas Workers became one of the few mixed-sex unions to send a female delegate to Congress.[21]

This 'new unionism' had its effect on the WPPL, too. The untimely death of Emma Paterson in 1886 could have meant the end of it, but her colleague Emilia Dilke was made of sterner stuff and announced in the *Women's Union Journal* in January 1887 that 'the work of the League must go on'.[22] The appointment of Clementina Black as secretary, combined with Emilia's flair and determination and the commitment of a number of others, ensured that it did.

Clementina Black was an author and socialist in her early 30s. She was a friend of Karl Marx's daughter Eleanor and a member of the Fabian Society, and she possessed both organisational ability and political intelligence. She understood how different aspects of issues might be connected, and was one of the founders of the Consumers' League, organising boycotts of companies such as the matchmakers Bryant & May and encouraging people to understand that the power of their purchasing decisions could be used to improve the lives of women workers. Clementina left the WPPL in 1889 to found the more radical Women's Trade Union Association (WTUA) in the wake of the matchworkers' strike, and although her tenure was brief she left her mark.

Emilia, Lady Dilke, was a rather different character. Born Emily Francis Strong in 1840 into an artistic family, she had attended art school in Kensington as a student before marrying Mark Pattison, an Oxford don much older than herself. The marriage was very unhappy, allegedly providing the material for George Eliot's portrayal of Dorothea and Edward Casaubon in the novel *Middlemarch*. After Pattison's death in 1884 she married Sir Charles Dilke, who was a Liberal politician and MP and notorious for his involvement in a scandalous divorce case. This marriage was much happier; Emily changed her name to Emilia and continued her work on the two passions of her life – art, in which field she developed a substantial and lasting reputation as a critic and historian, and the liberation of women, in particular working-class women.

Emma Paterson probably came across Emilia during her time at the CIU, so that when she went to work on setting up the WPPL Lady Dilke (or Mrs Mark Pattison as she was then still called) was an obvious person to draw in to work on it with her. After Emma's death Emilia and Clementina Black set about reorganising and restructuring the League so that it reflected the changing times. They abolished the original funding model, which had relied on wealthy benefactors, and replaced it with a system of affiliation open to trade unions which had women members. In return for a fee of a halfpenny per female member the WPPL provided speakers and organisational and administrative support for both single-sex and mixed unions who wanted to recruit women. Emilia and others travelled the country speaking to meetings small and large, both encouraging women and, not infrequently, taking male trade unionists to task for not supporting women enough. Another breach with the past came when Emilia instituted a strike fund; Emma Paterson had never thought one necessary, but in the heightened climate which existed during and after the industrial unrest of the late 1880s strikes were increasingly seen as the only way in which to improve the lot of working people. In 1891 the League appointed Annie Marland (subsequently Marland-Brodie) as possibly the first full-time female national trade union organiser.[23]

Before her death, Emma had observed that, while the middle classes felt very comfortable with the concept of a 'provident' league which paid benefits to deserving members, they were much less so with the more proactive 'protection' element, which sought to improve women's wages and conditions. 'Rich people,' she said, 'were always ready to urge women to be provident on seven shillings a week.'[24] She personally favoured the dropping of both words, and by 1891 the WPPL had become the Women's Trade Union League (WTUL).

The late 1880s was also the point at which Henry Broadhurst's resentment of 'middle-class ladies' reached boiling point. He was not by any means alone in this feeling, but his position as secretary of the Parliamentary Committee gave him a unique opportunity to vent it.

For almost a decade the women had been defying him over the issue of factory inspectors, and now the whole question of women and their pay, on which he also held strong views, looked as though it might suddenly go the women's way. At the 1887 TUC, Richard Juggins of the Black Country Nut and Bolt Makers had managed to persuade Congress to pass a resolution to 'prevent the employment of females in the making of chains, nuts, rivets, bolts, or any such articles that are made from iron or steel, such work not being adapted to their physical constitution'. In his speech he said that the conditions under which the women worked were degrading and demoralising, and their pay very low. Clementina Black retorted that conditions were worse in matchmaking and tailoring, that Congress did not pay proper attention to women workers, and that the real issue was the pay the women were receiving, not the presence of the women themselves. Clementina and Eleanor Whyte, the only other woman present, voted against Mr Juggins' motion, but it was passed by a huge majority.[25] The matter seemed to be closed.

Clementina Black, however, was not prepared to let it go. During the ensuing year negotiations were held and a common position arrived at. Juggins was converted to the idea that equal pay rather than exclusion might be the answer. In 1888, Clementina sent in her credentials for the Congress to be held in Bradford, and also submitted the motion she and Juggins had agreed. It read: 'That in the opinion of this Congress it is desirable, in the interests of both men and women, that in trades where women do the same work as men, they shall receive the same payment.'[26] Henry Broadhurst's response to this seems to have been to try to exclude Clementina as a delegate on the grounds that delegates had to be active in a trade, and she was not. Undeterred, she went to Bradford anyway and challenged the ruling. The Standing Orders Committee upheld her challenge, and she duly moved the first equal pay resolution to be debated at the TUC. In seconding it, Richard Juggins said that he 'had come to the conclusion that nothing but better pay for women could cure the evil, and they had therefore resolved to organise women as soon as possible'.[27] He also said, however, that an employer in the Black Country had told him that once the women were paid the same as the men he would cease to employ them,[28] so his motives may not have been quite as high-minded as Clementina would have liked. Clearly quite a lot of groundwork had been done before the meeting, and the motion was passed unanimously. But as with factory inspectors, nobody in any position to do so had much intention of doing anything with it, and in the event it was more than 80 years before a Labour government passed equal pay legislation.

In 1889 Broadhurst tried to exclude women delegates again. In particular, he took exception to Edith Simcox, who had attended several times over the preceding years. Speaking from the platform, Broadhurst said that 'Miss Simcox was not clearly the class of person who was entitled to sit in the Congress as a labour representative. The committee were determined that they shall not pass credentials of this kind any more.'[29] But by this point he had made one too many enemies across the board, and when the young firebrand Keir Hardie moved a motion of no confidence in him it was passed by 177 votes to 11. In 1890 he was finally forced from office by a combination of Hardie and the 'new unionists' who had no patience with him. He had become irredeemably Liberal in his politics, and there was even a whiff of financial misdoing around him. Change was in the air.

Inevitably, this discontent also crept into the issue of labour parliamentary representation, and in 1891, in the run-up to the 1892 general election, there was a lengthy debate as to how real labour representation was to be achieved. Hardie wanted there to be a parliamentary fund into which every union would pay a penny per member, but this was roundly defeated. The resolution that was eventually passed effectively continued the call from previous years for independent labour representation and, while urging 'the United Trades of this country to seize every opportunity to select, nominate and return Labour Representatives to the House of Commons', reiterated that such representatives should be 'independent of party politics'.[30] At the 1892 election three Independent Labour MPs were elected, and the following year Hardie and others formed the Independent Labour Party (ILP) with no formal involvement from the TUC.

Since women trade unionists were excluded from both the TUC's Parliamentary Committee and Parliament itself, they found political influence of any kind very hard to get. The Parliamentary Committee of the TUC was entirely male, and remained so until 1918. Congress was not receptive to the WPPL's arguments about women's organisation and work, and it did not (and indeed could not) function as a channel between its few women members and Parliament.

By the mid-1890s, the attendance of women delegates at the TUC had begun to fall. There were several reasons for this, including the fact that, with the advent of the new unionists, TUC meetings had become more aggressive, more prone to shouting matches and more of a power struggle between old and new union elites. But there were other reasons, too. As Eleanor Whyte had suggested, women's trust in trade union men to represent their interests was low. In all the years during which the issue of women factory inspectors had been debated and agreed by Congress, women had not been included in a single TUC delegation to government or consulted about how Congress's decision should be implemented. Moreover, while the new unions had recruited women to their ranks, they had made little move to put them into official positions; Emma Paterson's observation two decades earlier that the mixed cotton weavers' unions were not all they seemed since 'the women paid only half-contributions and were excluded from management [of the union]'[31] still held true. In addition, there was a slow decline in the women-only unions, which generally fell by the wayside once their driving forces died or moved on, and which in any case found the funds for delegates difficult to find as their numbers dwindled. In 1895 the adoption of the block vote for decision making, the exclusion of delegates from trades councils and the requirement that all delegates be employed in a trade combined to exclude women still further. In 1890 there were ten women delegates to the TUC; by 1898 this was down to two.

Partly to compensate for this, Emilia Dilke and the WTUL developed a different strategy for influencing male trade unionists. They had in the past run very successful fringe meetings about the organisation of women; this they now converted into a full-blown reception which proved very popular. But by now some of the more fundamental differences of opinion between male and female trade unionists had begun to fade, too. The women's resistance to protective legislation weakened and then vanished altogether as it became clear that in reality it would be impossible to drive women out of the workforce. Indeed, there were whole areas of employment in which there were virtually no men, and where women were entirely at the mercy of unscrupulous employers. Women in these industries were often omitted from the limited protection of the Factory Acts and frequently had no one to speak for them: the campaign to get laundresses included in the legislation was a case in point. The battle on their behalf was waged almost entirely by the WTUL, who surveyed over 60,000 women working in the industry, presented evidence to Parliament directly, and was successful in forcing improvements for some of the most vulnerable women of all. Emilia Dilke had faith in working-class women, and knew how to deal with the most senior levels of the establishment, so that, to a considerable degree, the annual battles on the floor of Congress had become an irrelevance.

◆　◆　◆　◆　◆

When the TUC gathered in Plymouth in 1899 there was, for the first time since 1875, just one female delegate. Margaret Bondfield was the 24-year-old assistant secretary of the National Amalgamated Union of Shop Assistants, Warehousemen and Clerks, one of the very few women holding a senior position in a mixed union. She had started her working life at the age of 12, but at 14 she had been sent from her West Country home to Brighton to take up an apprenticeship in a shop. A move when she was 19 from Brighton to London had brought her into contact with a wider range of people, but it was complete chance that brought her into the trade union movement. She bought some fish and chips in Fitzroy Street, and wandered around Fitzroy Square reading the newspaper in which they were wrapped. She thus saw a letter from James Macpherson, the secretary of the Shop Assistants' Union:

> urging shop assistants to join together to fight against the wretched conditions of employment. I was working about 65 hours a week for between £15 and £25 per annum, living in. Here I felt was the right thing to do, and at once I joined up.[32]

The union knew a good thing when they saw it, and immediately gave her plenty of work to do. When she became a member of its executive committee, which met on a Sunday, she was told by her church that she would have to choose between it and the union. Without hesitation she chose the union. In 1898 she was appointed as assistant secretary, noting later that 'I was given equality of status by Macpherson'.[33] The Shop Assistants' Union was very small, but already Margaret was regarded as a rising star.

When she arrived at Congress, however, expectations of her seem to have been fairly low, since she was asked to do the kind of 'nice' little job often given to women. This was to move the vote of thanks to the international speakers. The representative from the United States had expressed surprise that there were not more women delegates in the hall. The delegate from Denmark explained that in his country there was only one union covering all trades. Margaret knew open goals when she saw them and did not miss. In her speech she said that she was:

> extremely obliged to Mr O'Connell for his remarks concerning the absence of women delegates from the Congress. She was amazed to find herself the only female delegate in attendance when there were so

many toilers of her own sex. She hoped that such a thing would not happen at any future Congress.

She went on to suggest that delegates were indulging in a good deal of talk and not enough action, and concluded by suggesting that Congress might 'show that they were not above learning from even a little nation like Denmark by dropping pettifogging differences and grasping the real principles of trade unionism'.

She sat down to 'loud applause' and the verbatim record of Congress remarks that 'Miss Bondfield ... surprised and delighted Congress with her stirring speech'.[34] During the rest of the week she spoke on a number of other issues, but in particular was asked to support the resolution from the Doncaster branch of the Amalgamated Society of Railway Servants (ASRS) on labour representation. This she did, observing that what they needed was a 'labour representative body capable of taking its own stand on any particular question' and that they were not likely to get 'any redress in the House of Commons until the Labour members formed an appreciable party in that assembly'.[35] Again, she sat down to applause.

In her autobiography, Margaret Bondfield plays down her part in this Congress, merely saying that she was invited to speak on the 'historic resolution calling for the setting up of the Labour Representation Council' as a result of her 'precocious utterance' in her first speech.[36] But it is clear from the amount of interest surrounding her at the time that the impression she made was considerable, and it turned out to be lasting. The rest of her life was to be spent in the labour and trade union movements, and she led the way for women in both.

∞ 2 ∞

Socialists

When Margaret Bondfield spoke at the Trades Union Congress (TUC) in 1899 she was already a member of a political party. The Social Democratic Federation (SDF) was Britain's first and oldest socialist party, and Margaret had been recruited to it by the general secretary of the Shop Assistants' Union. He convinced her that it was the place for young, committed socialists to be. In her autobiography Margaret skated rather quickly over her SDF membership, simply saying that she 'did not like the emphasis on the need for a bloody class war ... I discovered that there was another socialist group, the ILP [Independent Labour Party]. I soon transferred my membership to this evolutionary body, and studied the Fabian tracts.'[1]

In fact, she remained a member of the SDF for several years, probably at least until 1907. At the beginning of her political life the Marxism of the SDF seemed new and exciting, dominated by towering men of principle such as its leader, Henry Hyndman, and a beacon of hope for the future. People spoke of being 'converted' to socialism of all kinds and were evangelical in their campaigning. Socialist speakers filled with missionary zeal toured the country seeking souls to save, and although Margaret Bondfield's efforts were largely reserved for trade union work, she shared the sense of possibility socialism seemed to offer. For young people, especially, the newness of it was inspirational; for a generation wanting to slough off the restrictions and conventions of the Victorian age it seemed a harbinger of what the twentieth century might bring.

Socialism in England actually had roots which went back to the Diggers and Levellers in the seventeenth century. In the early nineteenth century the industrialist and philanthropist Robert Owen came to the conclusion that the industrialised society which had made him rich needed reform, and he began to see capital and its ownership as part of the problem. His mill at New Lanark was run on what were then revolutionary lines with decent working conditions, education for children, and the removal of very young

36

children from the workplace. He was interested in both the infant fledgling co-operative movement and ideas of a utopian society, and in 1825 he tried to set up a new kind of community at New Harmony in the American state of Indiana. The first known use of the word 'socialism' in England also dates from this time: Edward Cowper, writing to Owen in 1822 about an unnamed woman, said that '[She] seems well adapted to become what my friend Jo. Applegath calls a Socialist.'[2] By 1827 Owen himself was using the term in his *Cooperative Magazine* to suggest that the principal difference between Malthusian political economists and socialists was whether 'capital should be owned individually or commonly'.[3]

Neither the early trade unions nor the Chartist movement of the 1830s and 1840s were themselves socialist in either origin or aspiration, although both had people in them who would now be described as such. It was not until German refugees from the 1848 revolutions in Europe began to arrive in London that socialism as an economic and political ideology began to filter into the British consciousness. However, the scope of its early influence should not be exaggerated. Karl Marx's *Das Kapital* was not translated into English until after his death, and the few British people who read it did so in a French version. For many people socialism was a foreign import to be regarded with suspicion. The German Social Democratic Party, founded in 1869, scored an early success by gaining 12 seats in the federal Reichstag in 1877, but there was little sign of this being replicated in Britain, and, indeed, there were no socialist candidates of any kind in the 1880 general election. When, in 1881, the anarchist leader Prince Peter Kropotkin visited England in the wake of the assassination of Tsar Alexander II of Russia he complained about the 'ridiculously small audiences'[4] he found himself addressing, and even the death of Karl Marx in 1883 failed to trouble the front pages of the nation's newspapers.

The SDF which the young Margaret Bondfield joined was founded in 1881 by Henry Hyndman, a wealthy businessman with an interest in social and economic questions. In the 1880 general election he stood in Marylebone as an independent radical Tory, but withdrew when it became clear he had no support. He then spent some months researching and thinking about reform, before discovering Karl Marx's *Das Kapital* and becoming, if not actually a socialist, at least a fellow traveller of sorts. In 1881 he brought together representatives from radical groups in London to form the Democratic Federation, the first meeting of which was held in the office of the German Social Democrats in Soho. It was not initially a socialist organisation, but by 1884 Hyndman had moved from interested support to full-scale conversion, and the group became the SDF. It had a new socialist programme and an executive committee which included three women: Eleanor Marx, Amie Hicks and Matilda Hyndman. Eleanor Marx subsequently chaired the executive, making her not only one of the first women to be elected to a senior role in a British political party, but also the first woman to occupy a leadership post in such a body.

Of these three women, only Amie (also known as Annie) Hicks could be described as being in any way working class. A ropemaker by trade, she and her husband had six children and lived for many years in New Zealand, returning to London in 1880. She soon became involved with the SDF, and remained a member for most of the rest of her life. In the late 1880s she joined the Women's Trade Union League (WTUL) and worked with Clementina Black and others on a variety of campaigns. She sat on the SDF executive for only two years, but was an important influence on both it and, later, many younger women in the labour and the suffrage movements. Two of her daughters followed her: Frances (also known as Amy) attended the TUC as a delegate on more than one occasion in the 1890s, and Margaretta became a full-time organiser for the SDF's successor body, the British Socialist Party.

Amie Hicks and her daughters are easy to trace, but Matilda Hyndman is a very different matter and illustrates how quickly women become invisible if they do not write their own memoirs, publish diaries or contribute to periodicals. She was born in Sussex in about 1850 and married Hyndman in 1876. In his autobiography he recorded that 'We had been lovers for many years before, and it was fitting we should be wedded on Valentine's Day.' In an unusually self-aware moment for a man of famously considerable ego he went on to recognise that 'Had I followed her advice in business and politics we should certainly have held a much more secure and satisfactory position than that which we occupy to-day.'[5] For some years she helped to run a scheme providing free school meals and seaside holidays to poor school children; her husband reports that she distributed 'fully 30,000 meals'.[6] In 1889 she was a witness at the trial of a destitute woman who had drowned her child.[7] When she died in 1913 the *Daily Herald* described her as 'alive with earnestness and zeal' and said that her bereaved husband could rejoice in 'the proud consciousness that the ardent and genial helpmeet who is gone made the noblest use of her years, and that her memory is bright and kindly in the minds of many thousands of rebels'.[8] But in fact the rebels forgot her very quickly; even her grieving husband remarried within 12 months.

Eleanor Marx was born in 1855 after her parents' arrival in England and became, after her father, both the best known and the most politically active of the family. She had early thoughts of the stage, but the Paris Commune of 1871 and its bloody aftermath plunged her into political activism on her own account. She quickly became a leading light in socialist circles, though since she also had to stay at home and look after her ageing parents she did not achieve full independence until after Karl Marx's death in 1883. A year later she began living with Edward Aveling, a married man who was unable to get a divorce from his wife. Eleanor used his name and was thereafter known as Eleanor Marx Aveling. Edward Aveling was a convinced socialist, but he was also untrustworthy and unfaithful, and his relationship with Eleanor came to show all the hallmarks of what would now be called coercive control. Together, however, they were major figures on the British socialist scene for a number of years, and Eleanor developed new ideas on the links between socialism and feminism. But in the 1890s a series of blows, culminating in Aveling's secret marriage to a student half his age, left her depressed and despairing, and in 1898 she committed suicide by drinking prussic acid.

In the SDF's early years Eleanor Marx was an important figure, though by the end of the first year of its life both personal and political tensions between the members had become apparent. Henry Hyndman was not always an easy man to work with, and he had a long-running feud with Friedrich Engels in which he considered Eleanor Marx an enemy. He had earlier fallen out with her father after plagiarising Karl's work for his own book *England for All*. Hyndman's socialism was not particularly well thought through, and was blended with a nationalist streak which, given their internationalism, Eleanor and her supporters found unpalatable. Hyndman also had a dictatorial style of leadership and, since most members of the SDF executive were strong characters with pronounced opinions of their own, this made for friction. By the end of 1884 things were coming to a head. Eleanor, the socialist designer William Morris and their supporters set up the Socialist League in opposition to the SDF. Eleanor was in no doubt as to who was to blame for the split. Hyndman, she told her sister Laura, 'forced things to such a condition that it was impossible to go on working with him'.[9]

Within a few years the Socialist League itself had split, and Eleanor, Edward Aveling and others formed the Bloomsbury Socialist Society. The League's troubles had manifested themselves at an early stage in the form of infiltration by anarchists who had no commitment to the parliamentary road to socialism. A few favoured terrorism and the so-called 'propaganda of the deed', although Peter Kropotkin himself soon came to the conclusion that 'a structure based on centuries of history cannot be destroyed with a few kilos of dynamite'.[10] People who had found Hyndman impossible now found anarchists to be even worse, and there was a steady drift back to the SDF. Without its founders, the Socialist League continued as an anarchist body until 1901, when it finally collapsed.

Meanwhile the SDF found itself in the eye of a storm created by the 'Tory gold' scandal of 1885. This involved Conservative Central Office,[11] election expenses, and the SDF leadership in the shape of Hyndman and H. H. Champion who both turned out to be more than a little naïve when it came to electoral strategy. Indeed, for men who thrived on conspiracy theories and stories of government spies and plots, they were astonishingly gullible, mainly because their hatred of Liberals far outstripped their distrust of Tories. If Conservatives were bad, Liberals, especially radical Liberals, were worse, because they promised so much but when it came to it delivered so little. Moreover, the little they did deliver was likely to persuade people that reform might be possible on a gradual basis and without a revolution, making socialism not only unnecessary, but even downright dangerous. For many in the SDF an honest Conservative was better than a weasely Liberal, and in 1885 this resulted in one of the most damaging episodes of labour history.

That year's election was one which Gladstone's Liberals were expected to win, and the Conservatives were desperate to stop them. The election marked a turning point in electoral history for a number of reasons: it was the first at which most adult men could vote, and the first in which most constituencies were voting for one, rather than two, MPs. It was also fought on new constituency boundaries which had been drawn up in an attempt to recognise differences between communities and the need for them to be represented appropriately. Faced with what they thought was an uphill battle, Conservative Central Office hit upon a novel plan to minimise the Liberal Party's chances. It bribed the SDF to the tune of £340 (about £30,500 in current values) to stand in two marginal seats and split the Liberal vote. Hyndman and Champion agreed to the plan without telling anyone else. Unfortunately, the seats they chose were Kennington and Hampstead, neither of which was either marginal or likely to vote for working-class men standing as socialists. The results were disastrous. John Fielding in Kennington got just 32 votes, while Jack Williams in Hampstead got 27. The only other SDF candidate, the future MP and cabinet minister John Burns, stood in Nottingham with no secret Conservative funding and got a much more respectable 598 votes. Predictably, the deal soon leaked out, and the 'Tory gold' storm broke over the whole socialist movement.

The Treasurer of the SDF objected, as treasurers are wont to do, to money being paid into his accounts from a dubious source without his knowledge. The SDF splintered again, with the Socialist Union splitting off to pursue a more honourable course. Every other socialist organisation tried to distance itself from the scandal but the aura of corruption hung over all the socialist parties for many years. Even Keir Hardie later found himself taunted with questions about his campaign funding and whether or not he was a spy or a closet Tory.

But the episode flagged up other problems, too. The decision about which seats to stand in had been taken by men who had very little electoral experience and who seem to have believed that middle-class Liberal voters would flock to the socialist standard once it was raised. Jack Williams had been imprisoned the month before on a charge of obstruction as part of a campaign for the right to speak at open-air meetings without police harassment. Laudable though this campaign was, his conviction made Williams easy to present to the electors of Hampstead as a dangerous revolutionary. Moreover, there had been no attempt to build any kind of base in either of the London constituencies, whereas, although he knew he was unlikely to win, Burns had been nursing Nottingham for some time. Hyndman and Champion had failed to understand the political differences between voters in the north, where the scale of industrial organisation could, in theory, create fertile ground for socialism, and those in London, where trade unions were weaker and socialism was more likely to be perceived as the province of a few cranks. This inability at the top of the party to appreciate political realities would dog the SDF throughout its existence, and was one reason why it failed, at either local or national level, to provide the breakthrough vehicle for the parliamentary representation of working people.

◆　◆　◆　◆　◆

The break-away Socialist League was not the only organisation to find itself with an anarchist problem: the Fabian Society, founded in 1884, was also targeted. In the light of the Society's twenty-first-century incarnation as a pillar of respectability on the centre left this may seem surprising, but in fact it was completely in tune with its origins.

The Fabians began as a faction in an organisation called the Fellowship of the New Life, which was not, as might be suggested by the name, a religious organisation, but one which advocated simplicity of life, communal living and a constant search for perfection. Adherents tended to be pacifist and vegetarian and women and men could join on equal terms, although in practice members were mostly youngish men.

The Fabian Society is sometimes described as an 'offshoot' of the Fellowship, but in fact its creation was the result of a classic disagreement over aims and objectives before either organisation had actually been formed. One group of idealists wanted the spiritual to be paramount, while another was at least as much interested in material issues. In November 1883 the materialists appeared to have the upper hand, persuading a meeting to pass a resolution which condemned the competitive (or capitalist) system which 'assures the happiness and comfort of the few at the expense of the suffering of the many' and called for the reconstitution of society 'in such a manner as to secure the general welfare and happiness'.[12] The spiritualists objected that this conflicted with their aims, and a working group was sent away to try to resolve the differences. A month later it returned with a plan which concentrated entirely on the spiritual, including a paragraph on 'Principle' which required the 'subordination of material things to spiritual'. This was irritating to the materialists, but what probably annoyed them more than anything else was that the meeting was informed that 'a Fellowship would be formed on this basis, whether it was accepted or rejected by the majority'.[13]

When the Fabian Society's first secretary, Edward Pease, came to write its history he was discreet about whatever manoeuvrings and discussions occurred over the Christmas period, but in January 1884 a small group of about 20 people came together to set up a new society. They took their name from the Roman general, Fabius Cunctator, on the grounds that 'For the right moment you must wait, as Fabius did most patiently … but when the time comes you must strike hard, as Fabius did, or your waiting will be in vain, and fruitless.'[14] They based their aims and rules on the materialist resolution passed at the Fellowship meeting in November, and determined to run a programme of meetings, research and other activities.

From the beginning, the new Society attracted women. Four were present at its founding meeting, including the philosophical writer Caroline Haddon, who had advanced views on social issues and advocated polygamy. In March 1884 a paper written by her on the subject of 'The Two Socialisms' was read and discussed at a Fabian meeting; this seems to have been the first occasion on which socialism itself was mentioned rather than vague phrases such as the 'reconstruction of society'. Caroline ran a girls' school in Dover and was also financing the future sexologist Havelock Ellis to do his medical training. The following year she published a hugely controversial piece of polemic called *The Future of Marriage* which outraged respectable Victorians. She does not seem to have been an active Fabian for very long, but did remain a member of the Fellowship of the New Life for a number of years.

Perhaps the best remembered (and still best loved) of the first Fabian women is Edith Nesbit. At this stage she had not achieved her lasting fame as the author of children's books such as *The Railway Children*. She and her husband, the writer and journalist Hubert Bland, had a notoriously open marriage into which she had entered at the age of 18 when already heavily pregnant. By 1884 she had been married for four years, borne two children, and discovered that Hubert had children by at least one other woman besides her. Against all the Victorian conventions, Edith smoked, refused to wear corsets and wore her hair short. But an open marriage had pains as well as pleasures. When Edith had a stillborn child her friend Alice Hoatson moved in to help look after her; nine months later Alice gave birth to Hubert's child, which Edith agreed to treat as her own. Despite Edith's protests Alice remained with them and nearly 30 years later Hubert died in her arms. Both Edith and Hubert believed in free sexual relationships, although it is noticeable that it was usually Edith who had to deal with the practical consequences of his affairs as well as her own. Nor did Bland necessarily take the view that this freedom should apply to his children; when in 1908 the writer H. G. Wells tried to elope with one of his daughters Bland was outraged and threatened to horsewhip him.[15] George Bernard Shaw, himself an early Fabian, described 'Bland's very attractive wife Edith Nesbit, who wrote verses ... and upset all the meetings by making a scene and pretending to faint'.[16] Given that her third child – named Fabian after the Society – was born in 1885, the fainting may not have been quite so much of a pretence.

Edith had gravitated towards socialism early in life, and like many young people had briefly been a member of the SDF. In the Fabians, however, she found a style of socialism that suited her, and devoted much of her time to it, lecturing, speaking and writing on a variety of issues and co-editing the Society's magazine with Hubert. After her children's books started to be successful at the turn of the century she became less active, though Hubert remained an influential Fabian almost until his death in 1914.

The Society began on a very small scale, meeting in the sitting rooms of its executive members and holding gatherings at which members and invited guests read and discussed papers on current topics. They also intended to write and publish tracts and reports and both Edith Nesbit and Robert Owen's granddaughter Rosamond Dale Owen were members of the seven-strong Pamphlets Committee. The first tract, called *Why Are the Many Poor?*, appeared in April 1884 and was very popular, being reprinted several times. George Bernard Shaw, who had been hesitating between the Fabians and the SDF, read it and decided that he would find more likeable and like-minded people in the Fabian Society. Later, when he became secretary, he added a note to the minutes of the first meeting he attended to record that 'This meeting was made memorable by the first appearance of Bernard Shaw.' Whether it was memorable to the other members or just to him he did not say.

A few months after its foundation the Society accepted Charlotte Wilson as a member, a decision which Shaw described as bringing 'a sort of influenza of Anarchism' in its wake.[17] Charlotte was a Cambridge-educated anarchist with a stockbroker husband and a house in Hampstead, and she spearheaded the anarchist attempt to infiltrate the Fabians. In November 1884 she read a paper on 'Anarchism' at a Society meeting. In January 1885 she was elected to the executive. This was a small body, comprising only five members including Shaw, Hubert Bland and the secretary Edward Pease, and since the remaining two were anarchists the clashes which followed were intense. In June a proposed pamphlet on housing had to be voted on clause by clause by the Society's general meeting; perhaps unsurprisingly only 17 members were present for this.[18] The anarchists got alterations to the Society's rules agreed and fought a running battle over membership. But the two biggest struggles were over a proposed publication known as Tract 4, and the vexed question of whether or not to work for reform through parliamentary means.

Tract 4 was intended to explain collectivism and anarchy. It was called *What Socialism Is*, but since nobody could actually agree on a definition there was ideological wrangling from the outset. Believing that she had the members' support, Charlotte persuaded them that the full text should be referred back to a general meeting for a final decision rather than being left to the Pamphlets Committee. The anti-anarchist faction managed to remove responsibility for Tract 4 from the Pamphlets Committee and give it to the executive, who would decide on the text to be put to members. At the same time they beefed up the executive's anti-anarchist faction by agreeing to add four more members, including Edith Nesbit and the journalist Annie Besant. When the draft finally went to a full Fabian meeting it was extensively discussed and partially amended. In its published form it contained separate sections on both collectivism and anarchy, but there was no attempt to bring them together. In a masterly piece of fence-sitting the introduction explained that there were basically two kinds of socialism:

> a Collectivist Party supporting a strong central administration, and a counterbalancing Anarchist Party defending individual initiative against that administration ... In view of this ... the theories and ideals of both parties, as at present formulated, are set forth below; though it must be carefully borne in mind that the majority of English socialists are not committed to either, but only tend more or less unconsciously in one or other direction.[19]

The tract itself is attributed to 'certain members of the Fabian Society', but the section on 'Anarchism' is headed 'Drawn up by C. M. Wilson on behalf of the London Anarchists'. In the dozen pages of this pamphlet as a whole lie a succinct and oddly elegant statement of the fundamental tension that has afflicted the labour movement to one degree and in one form or another ever since. *What Socialism Is* was published in 1886, but was not well received and was never reprinted.

The question of whether or not to participate in the electoral system was one on which there was substantial disagreement among early socialist groups. It came to a head later the same year when, after a three-day conference, the Fabians decided to put the matter to a public meeting open to anyone who described him or herself as a socialist. On Friday, 17 September 1886, therefore, about 70 people gathered at Anderton's Hotel in Fleet Street, a venue often used by radical and left-wing groups. Fabian Society executive member Annie Besant proposed:

> That it is advisable that Socialists should organise themselves as a political party for the purpose of transferring into the hands of the whole working community full control over the soil and the means of production, as well as over the production and distribution of wealth.[20]

William Morris, then still a member of the Socialist League, moved an amendment to add:

> and whereas no Parliamentary party can exist without compromise and concession, which would hinder that education [of the people] and obscure those [Socialist] principles, it would be a false step for Socialists to attempt to take part in the Parliamentary contest.[21]

The chair, Sidney Webb, then had to manage a debate which grew so heated that Anderton's Hotel subsequently banned the Fabian Society from holding any more meetings on its premises.[22] The amendment was defeated and Annie Besant's resolution was passed by 47 votes to 19. The subject would come back again, and be argued with passion on both sides, but effectively the game was over so far as the Fabians were concerned. Unlike the Marxists of the Socialist League, the Fabian Society had been able to repel the anarchist takeover and Charlotte Wilson, conceding defeat, resigned the following year to spend more time working on anarchist organisation and publications with Prince Kropotkin. The Fabians, on the other hand, continued to recruit new members, attracting women as disparate as Edith Simcox, Clementina Black, South African writer Olive Schreiner, designer May Morris (daughter of William) and the (then) Liberal Emmeline Pankhurst. Political differences were no bar to being a Fabian, and active socialism was not a prerequisite. For some years to come the official Fabian view continued to be that the best plan was to work with the Liberals and that a separate labour or socialist party would, without significant trade union support, be doomed to fail.

There was one other area in which the Society took some early decisions which would have significance for the future. Initially it had a very definite London bias, but early in 1886 Annie Besant persuaded the executive to allow local Fabian Societies to be formed around the country. Growth thereafter was steady, helped on considerably by the publication in 1889 of *Fabian Essays in Socialism*. These were written by seven members of the executive, including Annie Besant, whose contribution was called 'Industry under Socialism'. George Bernard Shaw wrote two of the essays and edited the volume as a whole. It was immediately successful, presenting as it did a version of socialism untainted by dynamite or revolution, and it brought new members and donations as well as a wider audience for Fabian ideas. In 1890 the Society was able to organise an extensive speaking tour of Lancashire and Yorkshire which resulted in more new groups being formed. This in turn began to open up a gulf between the London-based members, who were largely middle class, and the new local societies, most of whose members were working class, and some of whom were refugees from the nearly defunct Socialist League.

By the start of the 1890s the Society was maintaining a team of travelling speakers who toured the country giving lectures and appearing on platforms at meetings and demonstrations. One of the brightest and most sought-after stars of this group was the young Katharine Conway, who was a member of the Bristol Fabians. The daughter of a Nonconformist clergyman, she had been educated at Cambridge before moving to Bristol to teach in a school. Here she became a convinced socialist and an able public speaker. The mixture of brains, looks and a compelling stage presence made an irresistible combination, and soon her name alone was enough to fill a hall. The Society's lectures secretary, W. S. de Mattos, who was responsible for organising 500–600 speaking events a year, noted that 'She has a peculiar magnetic influence over her audiences, and larger audiences could be drawn for her than for almost any other lecturers.'[23] She spoke at all kinds of meetings, from endorsing candidates in the 1892 general election to supporting strikers and preaching at the Manchester Labour Church on 'Socialism: the Light of the World'. She was in the Ladies' Gallery of the House of Commons to see Keir Hardie take his seat in 1892 and in September of that year went to the TUC in Glasgow where she shared platforms with the great names of the movement and danced at social events until the early hours of the morning. But despite her youth (she was then 25) and her slightly raffish reputation she was the only woman included in the steering group set up at that TUC meeting to make arrangements for the founding of the ILP in the New Year, and when the Party was formed she was the only woman to be elected to its national executive.

The ILP was founded at a conference held at the Bradford Institute in January 1893. The steering group took responsibility for the detailed arrangements, even arriving early on the day to prepare the hall. Katharine Conway's contribution was to scrub the floor. She was very excited at the prospect of the ILP, writing later that 'The Labour party is in league with life, and works for liberty that man may live.'[24] Though her style seems florid and overblown now, she embodied and was able to communicate the welling up of hope that socialism then seemed to represent. Young women were not supposed to hold strong opinions, much less express them, but Katharine was fearless in doing both as well as in challenging the opinions of men much older and more experienced in the movement than she was. Later she declined simply to retire into domesticity once she had married; she and her husband, John Bruce Glasier, were among the first of Labour's 'power couples', and had a lasting influence on the Party's development.

The ILP which Katharine helped to establish is sometimes described as being wholly the project of Keir Hardie, but in fact it was the result of a collective effort which included socialist journalists, trade unionists and new, localised grass-roots parties, particularly in the north of England and in Scotland. These last wanted to be independent of both the Liberal and the Conservative parties, but lacked co-ordination, resources and, most critically, money. Some local labour parties had grown from existing Trades Councils, while others had sprung up as socialist groups. The Scottish Labour Party (SLP) had been established by Hardie in Glasgow in 1888 but had made no electoral headway. In much of Lancashire and Cheshire the working-class vote remained stubbornly and unyieldingly Tory; in Yorkshire it clung to the Liberals. Events, however, had begun to prise these adherences loose, and none more effectively than the Manningham Mills strike of 1890–1.

Manningham Mills in Bradford was a vast, physically dominant textile factory which at one point was among the largest in Europe. It employed thousands of people making high-quality woollen cloth, silk, velvet and other products, and had made its owner, Samuel Cunliffe Lister, an extremely rich man. The same could not be said, however, for his employees. They suffered considerably from the down-turn in trade in the late 1880s, and in December 1890 5,000 workers, including many women, went on strike rather than accept a reduction in their (already low) wages. The West Riding of Yorkshire woollen trade had not become industrialised as early as the cotton spinners in Lancashire, and trade union growth had lagged behind accordingly. West Yorkshire also had a long and deep-rooted history of religious Nonconformity and Chartism, and both of these traditions had found an accommodating home in the broad church that was the Liberal Party of the mid-to-late nineteenth century. Many of the major mill owners were Liberals, with some counting themselves as radical. At the 1885 general election Liberals were elected in almost all of the wool and mining seats of the West Riding where working-class voters were often in the majority. Some Liberal MPs were large employers in the industries in which they had made or inherited their money. In the febrile industrial atmosphere which had grown up in the wake of a weak economy and the new unionism, some kind of clash was inevitable.

The Manningham Mills dispute became a national cause célèbre, with widespread sympathy for the strikers, and speakers such as the London dockers' leader Ben Tillett and the socialist and trade unionist Isabella Ford arriving to address large meetings and marches. Isabella, who lived in Leeds and had seen grim poverty at close quarters before, said later of the young women she supported through that winter:

> We found some of them desperate with hunger, and supplied a breakfast of tea and bread and butter every morning. One poor girl with a drunken father and an invalid sister collected 10s and ran away with it. To her it represented wealth, and I am only sorry there was not more in the box. She had awakened to the right to possess something.[25]

The strike lasted 19 weeks but was ultimately lost. During it the Liberal-dominated Bradford Council used police and troops to break up demonstrations and marches,[26] and many (though not all) Liberals sided decisively and without question with Lister. After the strike a group of workers set up the Bradford Labour Union mainly to fight local council elections; its rules required that 'operations shall be carried on irrespective of the convenience of any political party'. The following year brought a general election, and the Bradford Labour Union saw its chance. Wanting a high-profile candidate, it originally persuaded Robert Blatchford, the hugely popular editor of the *Clarion*, to stand in Bradford East. But Blatchford withdrew as the election approached and attention then switched to Bradford West where Ben Tillett was prepared to stand. The Liberal candidate was Alfred Illingworth, a major mill-owner who had been a Bradford MP since 1880. Tillett used the election to drive home the differences between Gladstonian Liberal industrial policy and the needs and demands of working men. Illingworth himself was portrayed as 'having got rich on the pence of the work people'.[27] The Liberals locally were condemned for failing to support working men to get elected and for sending the troops in to attack the Manningham Mills strikers. There were repeated attempts to persuade local groups to abandon Illingworth for Tillett and electioneering became heated and occasionally rowdy. In the event Tillett came in third and Illingworth narrowly won; Bradford West would have to wait until 1906 to get its first Labour MP.

Since the 1870 Education Act there had been an exponential increase in working-class literacy, and journalists such as Joseph Burgess and Robert Blatchford supplied socialist news and comment through the *Workman's Times* and the *Clarion*. Keeping papers such as these going was hard work, as Keir Hardie constantly found with his *Labour Leader*, but Burgess and Blatchford combined political and industrial news with items which would appeal to wider audiences and thus contrived to keep their heads above water. This meant that far more people became aware of what had happened in Bradford than would have been the case even a decade earlier, and more labour unions and electoral groups were set up. Together with the socialist and feminist lawyer Richard Pankhurst, Blatchford helped to found the Manchester and Salford Independent Labour Party, the constitution of which required 'That all members of this party pledge themselves to abstain from voting for any candidate for election to any representative body who is in any way a nominee of the Liberal, Liberal-Unionist or Conservative parties.'[28]

This was an even clearer declaration of independence than that laid down by the Bradford Labour Union, and pointed the way to what might be possible next. The spread of labour unions and electoral associations in the north of England rather than in London, and among working men rather than middle-class intellectuals, also suggested where the main push for electoral success should be. However, as the Fabian Society argued,[29] independent candidates or small organisations acting alone without adequate finance were bound to fail and, as Hardie found when he tried to get the TUC to agree to a levy in order to support candidates in 1891, the unions were still reluctant to put their money into a new party when so many of their members and leaders were Liberals.

The SLP failed to get any MPs elected in Scotland in 1892 and fell victim to the usual combination of personal disputes and Liberal influence. The unions did not entirely trust Hardie, and there was some resentment of his pre-eminence. Unlike the Manchester and Bradford labour organisations the SLP had no clear statement of separation from the other parties and there were several attempts to reach electoral pacts with the Liberals. The Party was unable to impose discipline at the grass-roots level, and could not even prevent its own officers from supporting or actually standing as Liberal candidates; all five of the SLP's own candidates in the 1892 election were soundly beaten by Liberals. In England, labour candidates had marginally more success, and Keir Hardie was elected in West Ham South after a long and difficult campaign in the face of strong opposition.[30]

The election was also significant for the Liberal Party's concerted appeal to working men in the areas in which they thought their support was greatest. In 1891 the Liberal Associations had adopted the radical 'Newcastle Programme' (named after the place where the conference was held that year). This had a heavy focus on Irish Home Rule, which was a touchstone issue for both Liberals and socialists, but it was also a direct attempt to shore up the Liberal vote in Scotland, Wales, the north-west of England and rural areas. When the election came it did indeed have this effect; although the result was a hung parliament the Liberals did well in their target areas and Gladstone was able to form a minority government with the support of the 81 MPs of the Irish Parliamentary Party (IPP). The socialist and labour inability to agree a common programme, let alone field successful candidates standing on it, was brought into sharp relief by both the Liberal success and the ability of the IPP to maintain some semblance of discipline despite a recent and traumatic split. Indeed, the IPP (also known as the Home Rule Party) offered reflective socialists a possible model for what a successful labour party might be. For several decades it was the third-largest party in Parliament, sitting as a permanent, independent and cohesive bloc. It was the first party able to enforce parliamentary discipline, the first to have a recognisably modern election machine and the first to understand how to use the power its electoral strength gave it. Even after the spectacular fall from grace of its charismatic leader Charles Stewart Parnell in 1890[31] and the subsequent rupture in the IPP ranks, the Irish MPs were still able to influence successive governments. This looked attractive to socialists who, even once committed to parliamentary action, still did not believe that they would be able to replace either of the existing major parties.

What was required was someone prepared to take the bull by the horns and make something new happen, and that person turned out to be Joseph Burgess. Born in a Lancashire cotton town and sent to work from the age of six, he had worked his way into journalism, and by the early 1890s he was based in London editing the *Workman's Times*. This paper was widely read and therefore used by many progressive campaigners to reach their audiences. Burgess himself had both a practical outlook and organisational ability, and he had been advocating the need for independent labour representation for some years. In April 1892 he published an editorial calling for action rather than aspiration. He invited readers to send him their names, and undertook to connect them to like-minded people in their own localities so that they could set up independent labour parties.

Names forwarded to him were listed in the paper, and in all well over 2,000 appeared. The paper followed what happened in specific areas and ran stories about new groups being set up. All this created an atmosphere of interest and activity, as well as a sense of momentum.

In June the National Independent Labour Party (London District) was set up with the journalist Shaw Maxwell as secretary and Burgess a member of the Executive Council. There were discussions, in which Keir Hardie participated, about creating some kind of network of labour clubs and parties, but two problems rapidly became evident. The first was that the SDF did not wish to join, opting instead for a position of 'benevolent neutrality'. The second was that the new northern groups, particularly those in Bradford, were not going to allow Londoners to call the tune. Thus, when the steering group for the Bradford conference was formed in Glasgow it was already evident that the initial strength of the new party was going to be outside London, and that it would almost certainly not be able to command support across the socialist movement.

As a result of all this preliminary work the conference which gathered on the newly scrubbed floor at the Bradford Institute in January 1893 turned out to be one that had grown from the roots up rather than the top down. The shape of the conference had been determined by the small steering group set up under Keir Hardie at the TUC in Glasgow, but its flavour and make-up were substantially the consequence of Burgess's creation of so many local parties. For the first time the majority of delegates at the founding of a political party were working class, with many coming from Yorkshire and Lancashire and very few from the south of England or even London. The SDF was represented, but not by its metropolitan leaders, and while the Fabians had sent several delegates they were greatly outnumbered by the northern working men gathered in the hall. This signalled in a very visible way the change that had occurred over the preceding ten years; no longer was socialism the preserve of a few intellectual and middle-class people. Carried by the new unionism, the economic down-turn of the late 1880s and the indefatigable journalism of men like Burgess and Blatchford, it had gathered much greater strength among labouring communities in the north. The balance of power in the movement had shifted.

Unfortunately, the balance when it came to women had not shifted at all, and the 120 delegates present included only three. Of these, Katharine Conway had by far the highest profile, and she and Margaret Reynolds, from Jarrow, were both Fabians. The only other female delegate was a

Mrs Bullock, who was included in the Bradford Independent Labour Party delegation but was also listed as representing the Women's Labour Union. There were women (including Eleanor Marx) in the gallery as observers, but overall the new party was thoroughly male.

Like many labour conferences before and since, proceedings began with an argument about delegates' credentials. George Bernard Shaw, who was one of those involved, retired to the gallery from which he shouted at delegates until the conference resolved to accept him. The meeting then moved on to discuss a name for the new party. The Glasgow delegation wanted to call it the 'Socialist Labour Party' on the grounds that 'in Scotland the Labour Party had come to the conclusion that it was best to call a spade a spade'.[32] A delegate from London moved to amend this to the Independent Labour Party. Katharine Conway spoke in support, observing that the new party had to appeal to an electorate which as yet had no clear idea of what socialism was, and that even people speaking on its behalf might be 'put to confusion at the first debate ... because they did not understand socialism'.[33] Once the title had been settled there was a discussion about the Party's objective; in the end this was agreed as being 'to secure the collective ownership of the means of production, distribution and exchange'.[34]

If Burgess was responsible for the grass-roots organisation, it was Keir Hardie who drove decisions about the structure. He wanted to be as clear as possible about where authority in the ILP lay, and thought that there was already a tried and tested model available in the form of the TUC, with a national executive, a decision-making conference and a degree of autonomy for local bodies. The executive would assist with local organisation and, crucially, with candidates and election campaigns. This is effectively the structure adopted by the Bradford conference, the only significant difference being that in order to emphasise its subservience to Conference they called the executive the National Administrative Council (NAC), and made contributions from local parties compulsory rather than voluntary, as Hardie had initially envisaged.

At the end of the first day the conference set up a small (all-male) committee to draw up a policy statement and report back the next morning. This it duly did, returning with a set of proposals which were moved as a whole. There was then a debate on the different sections. At the end the new ILP emerged with a clearly socialist economic and social policy, including an eight-hour day, provision of support for the elderly, sick and disabled, the abolition of the employment of children under the age of 14, and free 'unsectarian' education up to and including university level. There was an attempt to replace the word 'unsectarian' with 'secular' which fell for lack of support; controversy over the role of religion in the provision and content of education was already widespread, and would years later become one of the first problems for the new Parliamentary Labour Party (PLP) in 1906. There was a requirement to provide 'properly remunerated work for the unemployed' without stating how this should be done. The section concluded with a restatement of the commitment to collective ownership.

The 'Industrial' section included the abolition of overtime and piecework, a proposal to which some of the trade unionists present objected. A Mr Hoskins from Slaithwaite in Yorkshire wanted to add a requirement to eliminate the employment of married women, which he considered 'one of the greatest curses of the country'.[35] This was defeated, but only by 45 votes to 32. In the 'Political' section the first item was a commitment to enfranchising the 40 per cent of men who could not vote, as well as all women. An amendment was moved to delete this whole section and replace it with 'The ILP is in favour of every proposal for extending electoral rights and democratising of the system of government.' This was unanimously carried. The deleted section included the payment of members on all elected bodies (a matter of considerable moment to working-class people who could not afford the time off necessary for public office), shorter parliaments, the abolition of the House of Lords and the monarchy, the introduction of referendums and the payment of election expenses from the rates. The more general wording blurred the new party's commitment to electoral reform and the extension of the franchise while allowing it to claim that it supported both. The suffrage issue would return in increasingly contentious form over the succeeding years.

There remained the question of how the new Party should conduct itself at elections. In order to preserve its independence delegates set up a Central Election Fund which would be run by the NAC, which was specifically prohibited from accepting donations which came with conditions. A compulsory affiliation fee was agreed in order to give the Party a regular and independent source of income, although in practice this proved difficult to collect. The unfortunate experience of the SLP, combined with fears about any repetition of the 'Tory gold' scandal, meant that considerable attention was paid to candidates, each of whom would be required to sign an undertaking that he subscribed to the objects and programme of the ILP, that, if elected to Parliament, he would 'form one of the ILP there, and sit in opposition no matter which party is in power', and that he would observe discipline in Parliament in 'advancing the interests of Labour, irrespective of the convenience of any political party'.[36]

Thus the ILP both emphatically declared its independence from the old parties, but also said equally clearly that it saw no prospect of ever forming a government itself.

The NAC elected to implement the conference's decisions was drawn up on geographic lines to ensure that neither it nor the Party was dominated by Londoners. Those elected included Burgess, Edward Aveling and Katharine Conway. Shaw Maxwell, who had been both secretary of the London Independent Labour Party and chair of the SLP, became secretary. Keir Hardie did not stand. In the official photograph of the new NAC Katharine is seated behind Maxwell and peers hopefully out from a sea of moustaches, waistcoats and rather self-conscious poses (see Plate 2). In June 1893 she married John Bruce Glasier, and although she continued to tour the country speaking at meetings and events she did not stand again for election to the NAC. Her husband, whom she recruited to the ILP before marrying him, edited the ILP's paper, the *Labour Leader*, and Katharine wrote comment pieces for it, including a women's column called 'Iona'. John Bruce Glasier was elected to the NAC in 1897 and remained there for over 20 years.

The creation of the ILP marked a new phase for the labour movement. Northern Fabian Societies, many of which had been struggling, almost immediately converted themselves into ILP branches, leaving only Liverpool with any real Fabian presence. As a result the Fabians became more London-based in fact as well as perception. When, in 1894, they were left a substantial amount of money there was a fundamental difference of opinion between people such as Shaw and the Webbs, who wanted to use it to found the London School of Economics, and a new generation of activists who thought that it should effectively be passed to the ILP to build electoral capacity. The Webbs won the argument, but the tension between London-based groups such as the Fabians and more practically minded campaigners in the country was a theme which would be repeated many times in the years to come.

Despite the energy and enthusiasm of the Bradford conference the ILP nationally was slow to get off the ground. The NAC was large and unwieldy, and its geographic spread meant that meetings were expensive to hold. Apart from lecturing and speaking on platforms, there seemed to be some uncertainty as to what to do next, and in any case there was no money to do anything much with. There were a number of successes in local elections of various kinds, but this trend had actually begun before the ILP was formed. On the other hand, membership and affiliated groups grew and people were attracted by what seemed like socialism without either the Marxist dogmatism, the anarchist attachment to dynamite, or the Fabians' open attachment to the Liberal Party.

Among those who joined the new party was Isabella Ford, the Leeds socialist and feminist who organised working women in Leeds and Bradford. She and her older sisters, Bessie and Emily, came from a wealthy Quaker family with a strong social conscience, and all three were campaigners for women's rights. Emily was a well-known religious artist, and all three sisters had from their youth engaged in social work in industrial Leeds. However, they had struggled to find ways of helping working women that were not simply charity. Their mother's friend, Emma Paterson, had suggested that they might like to get involved in trade unionism, and they had never looked back. Isabella, in particular, immersed herself in industrial issues, and had been one of the leaders of the 1889 Leeds tailoresses' strike.[37] She had quickly developed a national reputation as a skilled public speaker and organiser and a useful person to have on a committee. She had been a founder member of the Fabian Society, and was an active member of the National Union of Suffrage Societies and a writer and commentator of note.

The Ford sisters lived at Adel Grange in Leeds and people came from all around the world to stay with them. None of the sisters conformed to the Victorian idea of a repressed spinster, and their friends included the socialist and gay rights campaigner Edward Carpenter, the anarchist Prince Kropotkin, the South African feminist novelist Olive Schreiner, the American suffragist Susan B. Anthony, and many trade union, socialist and suffrage leaders. Their vast network of friends and colleagues meant that they were present at one time or another in almost every left-wing or progressive movement of the late nineteenth and early twentieth centuries.

Thus it was hardly surprising that they were among the first members of the ILP. Several years later Isabella ascribed her final decision to join to a visit to a labour club in Colne Valley, where, she said, the men held a tea party for the women, adding:

A party, that included the education of men, which had hitherto been so much neglected, as well as the education of women, that gave the one such skill and dexterity, and the other wider and truer views of life, was the party for me, I felt, and so I joined it.[38]

Not everyone was so enthusiastic. The prominent Fabians Beatrice Webb and her husband, Sidney, were sceptical, and many members of the Society took some convincing that a fourth party, which would never be able to match even the Irish MPs in numbers, could be effective. The SDF became increasingly hostile, although members at the local level often worked well with ILP members. But generally speaking there was satisfaction with what had been achieved.

Divisions within the Liberal Party meant that there was a fair prospect of a general election, when the new party's possibilities could be tried out at the ballot box. Sure enough, the prime minister, William Gladstone, resigned in March 1894 and his Liberal successors seemed to have very little interest in implementing the Newcastle Programme. Disillusion with the Liberal government was setting in fast, and even the Fabians wavered in their allegiance. This did not last, however, and it was not long before they drifted back to their policy of 'permeating' the Liberal Party with socialism. Many of the unions, whose parliamentary representatives were, with the exception of Hardie, all Liberals, saw no reason to change their approach. The ILP had support from the wool and cotton unions of the Pennine belt, but none from the miners of the coalfields of the West Riding (which then included the modern South Yorkshire), South Wales or Durham. Had the Liberals been wise, this imbalance might have continued indefinitely and caused the ILP to wither away as other small parties had done, but their own north–south divide was as much a problem for them as it was for Labour, and ultimately they proved unable to take advantage of their strength.

Foundations

A little over two years after the Bradford conference the ILP suffered an unforeseen and crushing disappointment in the 1895 general election. It was so bad that Beatrice Webb considered that:

> The ILP [Independent Labour Party] has completed its suicide. Its policy of abstention and deliberate wrecking is proved to be futile and absurd; Keir Hardie has probably lost for good any chance of posturing as MP, and will sink into the old place of a discredited Labour leader.[1]

In the long run this analysis turned out to be wrong in almost every respect, but it was a reasonable prediction at the time. The ILP had fielded 28 candidates and every single one, Hardie included, had been defeated. Discontent with the Liberals, rising imperialist feeling, hostility to Irish Home Rule and a longing for competent government had resulted in the election of a Conservative administration with one of the largest Tory majorities in history. It left both the Liberal Party and the ILP in varying states of disarray, and seemed to usher in the prospect of a prolonged period of Conservative office. The Fabian opinion that socialism alone could not win elections, and that the best strategy was to 'permeate' the Liberal Party with socialist opinions, appeared justified. The future for socialism looked bleak.

Yet the party had gone into the election with high expectations. A series of surprisingly respectable performances in by-elections between 1893 and 1895 had made people think that socialism had a chance of breaking through. The media saw a real danger of the new party making gains, and the Liberals were seriously alarmed at the prospect of losing votes to the left as well as the right. How, then, did the Party's earliest venture into major electoral politics end in such disaster?

The ILP was the first political party of the left to be founded with a sitting MP. Keir Hardie was a national figure whose fame went well beyond the very small socialist circles of the late nineteenth century. His great oratorical skills could attract huge crowds, and he was both loved and hated by the popular press in almost equal measure. They loathed and feared his principles, but they liked his ability to make news and sell papers for them, and he had a much higher profile than any of his contemporaries. In the ILP's first couple of years he constantly toured the country whipping up enthusiasm and support. After a few months he was joined by other speakers, many of whom could also command large audiences on their own account. Organisation and support on the ground was patchy, but where it did exist it was strong enough to give the impression of being greater than it actually was. Combined with the excitement of by-elections, this created a sense of purpose and momentum which had the dual effect of distracting attention from the party's inherent structural weaknesses while magnifying its apparent achievements.

By-elections in the late nineteenth and early twentieth centuries were much more frequent than they are now. In 1893 alone there were 29;[2] eight were in Ireland and therefore not of concern to the ILP, but the remainder, at least in theory, were possibilities for ILP candidates. The first real opportunity came within days of the Bradford conference when one of the two Liberal MPs for Halifax died. The ILP's Treasurer, John Lister, was a local landowner, philanthropist and councillor, and was thus the obvious candidate. The by-election was held in February, and Lister stood on a programme which was a mix of Gladstonian Liberalism and socialism. This had the effect of peeling some votes away from the Liberal candidate, and to everyone's astonishment Lister polled over a quarter of the votes.

Unfortunately, the next by-election in which the ILP took an interest brought it up against all the forces which wanted to restrict it. Henry Broadhurst, the erstwhile Trades Union Congress (TUC) general secretary who had been ousted in 1890, had lost his parliamentary seat in 1892. When the Liberal MP for Great Grimsby resigned a by-election was set for early March 1893. The ILP wanted to field a contender, but Broadhurst had already secured Liberal support and was standing as a Lib-Lab candidate. Worse, it soon became apparent that he was being supported by H. H. Champion, who had been involved in the 'Tory gold' scandal of 1885. Having later been expelled from the Social Democratic Federation (SDF), Champion had become a Fabian and editor of the

Labour Elector, advocating the formation of a class-based party with trade union support. He had been present when the ILP was founded, but his habit of acting without consulting anybody, combined with a reputation for untrustworthiness, meant that he was often regarded with suspicion. Even so, Hardie had accepted financial assistance from him in West Ham South in 1892. In Great Grimsby Champion's unilateral decision to back Broadhurst effectively froze the ILP out of a seat where it might reasonably have expected to find support. In the event Broadhurst lost, not returning to Parliament until the middle of 1894 when he won a by-election in Leicester, but the ILP found itself in the position of having been both outflanked and embarrassed. It did its best to repudiate Champion, but the episode raised pointed questions about the party's ability to field candidates in 'winnable' seats if even some of its own supporters preferred a Liberal nominee.

When delegates arrived in Manchester for the ILP's second conference in early 1894, therefore, resentment at both Champion's interference and Broadhurst's hostility was high. There was also some anxiety about the relationship with the trade unions, who had money and influence and no inclination to share either with the ILP. Individual unionists such as dockers' leader Tom Mann were members, but the TUC as a whole was at best ambivalent. Its secretary, miner Charles Fenwick, was himself a Lib-Lab MP and a strong opponent of socialism. At the TUC in 1893 Hardie had tried and failed to get a resolution through disconnecting Congress from the Liberal Party, but even the influential John Burns MP, who described himself as a socialist and whom Keir Hardie had initially wanted as ILP secretary, fully intended to remain in Parliament as a Lib-Lab member. Events during the latter part of the decade would begin to change many trade unionists' minds about the Liberal Party, but this would take time, and in the meantime the ILP found itself without significant support from organised labour.

Although it was only a year old, the party's constitution was already the source of dissatisfaction and debate. The 1894 conference managed to agree some changes, the most important of which in practical terms was to resolve the National Administrative Council (NAC)'s inability to take decisions. Its unwieldy size, combined with its geographic composition, had effectively paralysed it, and during the first year it met only twice. At the Manchester conference its size was reduced from 15 to nine, Tom Mann was persuaded to take over as secretary and the post of president was set up to be occupied by Keir Hardie. The new all-male NAC was heavily dominated by men from Yorkshire and Lancashire, and the ILP could thus almost be described as a northern, rather than a national, party.

Katharine Bruce Glasier (formerly Conway), who had been a member of the first NAC, was not even present at the party's second conference. There were still very few women delegates, but despite this the conference held its first discussion about the role of women in the party. The Fabian and trade unionist Enid Stacy moved a resolution on 'The Place of Women in the Movement'. She proposed the formation of women's associations to run alongside the ILP branches on the grounds that this would 'tend to equip women for the intelligent use of their increasing political power'.[3] The resolution was seconded by a male delegate from Liverpool and carried unanimously.

There then occurred one of those incidents with which women in politics were (and are still) all too familiar. As the vote was being taken Robert Blatchford, a man with a talent for drama and hugely popular as the editor of the *Clarion* newspaper, entered the room. He was 'enthusiastically received' and the Chairman invited him to take a seat on the platform and say a few words. Never one to disappoint an audience, he referred to Enid Stacy's speech and:

> spoke playfully of the danger the movement was in of being captured by the ladies. He was glad, he said, to see one or two delegates present standing up for their sex in a manner which was common to their sex.[4]

His remarks were received with applause; the feelings of Enid Stacy and the two other women present can only be imagined, particularly when a little later the delegates who had voted for her resolution and applauded Blatchford's remarks declined to elect her to the NAC.

Neither Blatchford nor the assembled delegates can have been ignorant of Enid's work and reputation. Together with Katharine Conway she had been one of the moving spirits of the Bristol Fabian Society, and as a result of serious strikes in the city in 1889 she had become a trade union activist as well, organising women working in the confectionery and laundry industries. She was interested in communal living, suffrage and women's ability to control their bodies and their fertility. When the ILP was formed she was already famous as a public speaker, able to fill halls and make herself heard in even the most difficult of circumstances. At 25 years old she was an impressive figure with firm opinions and no hesitation about expressing them. Since there were only three women delegates in the room Blatchford could not seriously have imagined that the movement was in any danger of being 'captured by the ladies', but this kind of humorous 'gallantry' was commonplace. That the ILP went on to employ Enid as one of their most popular travelling speakers indicates the power of her abilities.

The year which followed continued to offer by-elections, including one in Sheffield Attercliffe in July, where the local Liberal Party refused to back a working-class candidate. This brought a number of people to understand that although the Liberals wanted working men's votes they had no intention of handing over any real power, and prompted a rush of new members for the ILP. Among them was the young Ramsay MacDonald, who had been working for a Liberal MP but now thought that the Liberal Party would never either represent people like him, or allow him to represent others. Within days of joining the ILP he was officially adopted as the ILP candidate for Southampton for the general election.

A month later Joseph Burgess made a decent showing against a victorious Broadhurst in the Leicester by-election and the ILP began to convince itself that it might do well in the forthcoming general election. These hopes were underpinned by victories in local municipal contests, where it was possible both to get elected and to influence local policy and events. The original Bradford Labour Union had been founded to get local councillors elected, and now the national party increasingly found encouragement in contests for council seats and places on school boards and boards of guardians. Women were able to stand and to vote in some of these elections, and met with a degree of success. Margaret McMillan, like Enid Stacy a Fabian and touring speaker for the ILP, was elected to the Bradford School Board in 1894, and in the same year Emmeline Pankhurst was elected to the Chorlton Board of Guardians. Boards of guardians were responsible for workhouses and other forms of 'relief' for the destitute. Like many other people who now saw them for the first time, Emmeline was shocked by the conditions in the institutions for which the Board was responsible, and campaigned vigorously to improve them.

In 1894 some women became eligible to vote in rural, parish and urban district council elections and to be elected to them as councillors.[5] Isabella Ford was elected to Adel cum Eccup Parish Council near Leeds in 1895. A couple of years later the ILP had six women on boards of guardians (and 28 men), and three women (plus 45 men) on school boards. Isabella remained the party's only elected female councillor until the early twentieth century.[6] Socialist men also did well on the wider range of councils for which they could stand,[7] and in some places were able to build an electoral base which they presumed would stand them in good stead for parliamentary elections.

Nationally, the ILP remained resolutely independent, but this did not stop there being a fair amount of co-operation with other parties locally. In the north ILP members might work with the SDF on local councils, but in London, where the ILP was small and enjoyed little support, its members joined together with the Liberals on the County Council (LCC) to form the Progressives. This helped the Fabians to continue their policy of 'permeation' of the Liberal Party with socialist ideas. They were able to point to the Progressive party as an example of what their policy might be able to achieve, but in fact the LCC was almost its only success, and despite much hard work by Beatrice and Sidney Webb, in particular, permeation was largely ineffectual when it came to the national Liberal leadership either in or out of Parliament.

By the beginning of 1895 it was evident that the general election was near, and the ILP conference which gathered at Newcastle was full of anticipation. The number of women delegates rose to eight (out of just over a hundred in total). At the 1894 conference the focus had been on organisation; in 1895 delegates returned to some old themes. There was an attempt to change the Party's name to the National Socialist Party which was supported by Amy Morant from Hammersmith but roundly opposed by Emmeline Pankhurst and Enid Stacy. In what was described as 'a vigorous speech', Enid advised the Party to turn its fire on the 'Tory wirepullers and the Liberals' rather than on one another.[8] Keir Hardie made a rousing speech from the platform and the NAC agreed that changing the Party's name in the run-up to a general election would be 'inopportune', so the proposal fell.

On the other hand, Enid Stacy scored a signal success by being elected to the NAC, taking second place in the ballot. There was also a brief debate about whether or not women should be specifically included in the section covering political rights in the party's policy statement. Mrs Pearce from Glasgow argued that they should be, and won her point, so that although the ILP's election manifesto did not directly mention women's suffrage it did say that the party was 'in favour of every proposal for extending electoral rights to both men and women and democratising the system of government'.[9] This brief discussion illuminated the problem both the ILP and, later, the Labour Party faced when it came to suffrage issues: all women lacked the vote, but so too did 40 per cent of men, most of whom were the poorest in society. Socialists were reluctant to support enfranchising middle-class women and not working-class people of either gender, which would have been the effect of retaining the existing property qualifications. It is noticeable that, although he supported female suffrage, the proposal to name both sexes came from Keir Hardie 'in order to avoid opening up a wide question'.[10]

When the anticipated election came in July it showed up all too clearly almost every flaw the party had, and went a considerable way towards bringing people to understand that the ILP alone was not going to be enough to create the kind of breakthrough the socialists were looking for. Although some individual trade unionists stood as ILP candidates they did not enjoy wide support, and the unions as a whole clung to their traditional loyalties. Most voters were not keen on socialism, and many working people were wary of being seen to support it in case they were penalised by their employers. Katharine Bruce Glasier's husband John described Tom Mann's campaign meetings in Colne Valley where:

> It was with difficulty we got the crowd around us. Men and women hung around the houses and the walls and seemed afraid to form part of the meeting … Mann rose and requested the people to come forward as he could not afford to strain his voice. Still they would not move.[11]

Other problems related to leadership, which Keir Hardie, effectively the ILP's leader and certainly its best-known candidate, exercised in an inspirational but essentially individual manner. As usual, he toured the country speaking to enthusiastic crowds, but this meant that he spent very little time in West Ham South, where his majority was by no means secure. General elections at that time took place over several weeks, with each constituency appointing its own election day and results being declared as they came in. Early results could have a very definite effect on the later ones and, unfortunately for the ILP, West Ham South was one of the earliest. Although he lost by less than a thousand votes Hardie was incensed, and he was not slow to turn on the Liberals who detested him. They had not run a candidate against him but were celebrating his defeat by a Tory as a Liberal victory. Given the widespread suspicion of socialism it was perhaps unwise of him to announce that 'The Labour and socialist parties will henceforth vote so as to sweep away the only obstacle in their path – the historic Liberal Party.'[12] This was not taken well by many of the Liberals whose votes the ILP needed, and may have contributed to defeats where polling day had yet to occur. But Hardie's loss was also dispiriting on a wider level and could well have discouraged people from voting for the ILP in other areas. Candidates such as Richard Pankhurst in Manchester and Ramsay MacDonald in Southampton, whose results were declared late, might have won had their polling days been sooner. Other pronouncements did not help either; at one point Hardie seems to have advised voters to write the name of a woman on the ballot paper as a protest.[13] This might have been attractive in principle, but in practice it just made the ILP sound faintly ridiculous.

The 1895 election was, however, notable for bringing together two people who would go on to have a substantial influence on the development of both labour and women's politics. Margaret Ethel Gladstone (who was no relation to the former Liberal leader and prime minister) was from a well-off middle-class family of scientists. Born in 1870, she had lost her mother at birth, but her father, a Professor of Chemistry at the Royal Institute, had brought her up with a broad education and plenty of encouragement for her clever mind. Since he was an active Liberal who had stood unsuccessfully for Parliament and successfully for the London School Board, she also had an early introduction to politics. She had a scientific education at the Women's Department of King's College in London, combining this with the charity work expected of young ladies of her class and the study of political economy at lectures given by Millicent Fawcett. By the time she was 23 she was managing board schools and working for a variety of voluntary groups.

Like other young women engaged in such work, however, Margaret soon came to think that charity alone could not solve the social and economic problems working women faced, and in 1894 she joined the Women's Industrial Council (WIC). This was the successor body to the Women's Trade Union Association (WTUA), which had been set up by Clementina Black in 1889 in the wake of the matchgirls' strike. It had heavy SDF influence, and although it was strongly supported by women such as Amie Hicks, who became a mentor to many young women, including Margaret, it struggled more or less from the start. By 1894 it was clear that there was really only room for one umbrella organisation for women trade unionists, and that the Women's Trade Union League (WTUL), established by Emma Paterson and now run by the formidable Emilia Dilke, had more or less cornered the market. In 1894 the Association was converted into the WIC to investigate women's working conditions. Perhaps influenced by Amie Hicks, Margaret seems to have joined almost immediately. She loved facts and was a gifted statistician; later she would become one of the very few women to be elected to the Royal Statistical Society. She began working in a team of women inquiring into the hours and conditions of wage-earning children, the report of which fed into an Interdepartmental Committee set up by the government to look at the question. She then embarked upon a major report on women's homeworking (published in 1897), as well as taking an interest in alcohol policy and temperance (a significant political issue for a number of decades) and the exploitation of women working in pubs and bars. Some young women embarking upon this kind of life had no intention of marrying, but Margaret was always clear in her own mind that she wanted each woman (in modern terminology) to have it all and to be in control of her own destiny so far as possible.

By early 1895 Margaret had become a socialist and a member of the Fabian Society, and she had already met many leading trade unionists and members of the ILP. At some point before May she came across Ramsay MacDonald, then an attractive young man of 29 with a reputation as a fine public speaker and political journalist. They did not meet at this stage, although it seems likely that Margaret decided almost immediately that they should. MacDonald was the ILP candidate in Southampton, but he had to spend part of the run-up to the campaign in hospital in London. In May 1895 Margaret wrote to him enclosing a cheque for £5 as a donation to his campaign fund. He replied in a formal little note thanking her and saying that his health was improving. Never having met Miss Gladstone, he probably did not expect any further correspondence. However, she promptly responded asking his opinion about an ongoing lockout in the boot and shoe industry. He replied again, and within days she was offering to undertake election work for him. Candidates do not usually turn down offers of help, and soon Margaret was addressing envelopes and writing out canvas cards. 'I am sending you,' MacDonald wrote, 'the whole register for the district of Shirley but please do only what you conveniently can, and mark what you have done.'[14] By this stage they had still barely met in person. Ramsay was spending most of his time either campaigning in Southampton, or in Scotland visiting his mother and recuperating from his illness, but they exchanged frequent letters ranging over a wide selection of subjects. After the election they saw one another more frequently, usually at political events but also occasionally socially.

MacDonald was the illegitimate son of a servant and a farmhand, and he had no money. He earned just about enough to keep himself through journalism and speaking engagements, but he had no private income or steady job. He was socially uncertain and intensely sensitive about the circumstances of his birth, and he was only too well aware of what would be said if he aspired to marry a middle-class woman with a substantial income of her own. Margaret understood that he felt himself to be in a delicate position and in May 1896, a year to the day after she had first written to him, she proposed to him on the steps of the British Museum. After some demur he accepted and, despite reservations on the part of some of her family, their engagement was announced. They were married six months later and set up home at 3 Lincoln's Inn Fields in London. MacDonald was a well-known figure in the labour movement, and Margaret already had a growing reputation of her own. Congratulations flooded in. The members of Long Eaton Trades Council in Derbyshire, for instance, passed a resolution which expressed a widespread and enduring view of Margaret, agreeing that:

> This meeting of the Workingmen of Long Eaton congratulates Mrs J. R. Macdonald on having won the esteem of Comrade J. R. Macdonald which in due time matured into love, and it further resolves that she is one in a thousand.[15]

At the point at which she and Ramsay were married Margaret was not yet known as a public speaker. However, the ILP's list of travelling orators and lecturers included a number of other remarkable women. Enid Stacy, Katharine Bruce Glasier, Margaret McMillan, Caroline Martyn and several others toured the country providing both education and entertainment for audiences large and small. Itinerant speakers could command large audiences, but might also easily find themselves trying to gather stragglers on street corners in the rain. Beatrice Webb, herself no mean public speaker, had initially considered female speakers 'unwomanly', but for women to have any kind of public presence oratory was an essential skill to master. Almost every female activist from the period said that she initially found it very difficult. Margaret Bondfield, for instance, recalling her first experience of public speaking in the mid-1890s, explained:

> I am often asked how I learnt the art of public speaking. I didn't. I discovered it at a great meeting held at the Mile End People's Palace ...

without warning, the chairman called upon me to move the vote of thanks ... Afterwards I was told that I at once responded with a speech which brought down the house, but it was an automatic response, for I was literally stunned with stage fright. I hadn't the faintest recollection afterwards of what I had said.[16]

Isabella Ford, embarking on her speaking career during an industrial dispute in Leeds in 1888, was very nervous, but was told: 'Just get up. Don't much mind what you are going to say, and it will be all right.'[17] She found that this was indeed correct, and that the power of her voice and her conviction could overcome her terror. Famous speakers such as Millicent Fawcett (the first woman to speak on a public platform in support of women's suffrage), Katharine Bruce Glasier and Annie Besant all reported similar trepidation.

Their fears were not without justification. Speaking in public went against everything they had been taught about the female sphere being private and discreet. Worse, the act of public speaking could be terrifying. Victorian and Edwardian audiences regarded oratory as a form of entertainment in which they were fully entitled to participate, and frequent heckling could quickly degenerate into abuse and the throwing of missiles. Alcohol was easily available and crowds often contained a fair share of drunks. Sometimes meetings could be held in halls, where to some extent access could be controlled, but for many political and trade union speakers, women as well as men, the venue could be the street or other open area with an audience composed of whoever was passing by. Speakers were paid their expenses by organisations such as the ILP and sent around the country on public transport in gruelling marathon tours. They usually stayed with members where possible, but otherwise they had to resort to cheap boarding houses. For women there were obvious risks, but it was a very effective way of raising both profile and standing in the movement.

For married couples such as the Bruce Glasiers the life could be a real test of their relationship. Katharine and her husband only rarely found themselves in the same place at the same time, criss-crossing the country in mad dashes from one meeting to another. On one occasion Bruce Glasier recorded that when he was on his way to York and Katharine was going to Darlington they managed to arrange for their paths to cross at Northallerton. They had a lunch of pork pies at a pub after which 'we walk westward from the station and the rain comes gently down. Then we ensconce ourselves in the hedgerow under a tree by a byewayside and have a memorable hour of love.'[18]

Memorable hours of love were rare, however, and the life was generally very tough. Ultimately the price paid for it could be high. Caroline Martyn was one of the ILP's most popular speakers, but her health had never been good and constant travelling and public speaking did not help. She was often exhausted but her schedule was punishing. 'I am just a speaking-machine,' she wrote to a relative, 'I envy you your busy round of life, your constant duties, and your responsibilities.'[19] In 1896 she was elected to the NAC, which spoke volumes for her standing in the ILP but only added to her burden. In July 1896 she was speaking in Dundee, but wrote to her mother that:

> I do not know if it is the weather, which is close and gloomy or what but I have been feeling very queer the last few days … I hope I shall soon be all right. It is very hard to speak in public when you feel faint and ill.[20]

That evening she collapsed with pneumonia which she was unable to fight. She died ten days later at the age of just 29.

The ILP was stunned, but the force of their grief perhaps also concealed a slightly guilty recognition that their demands on her had played a part in the tragedy. Keir Hardie described her as having an unrivalled 'power of intellect and moral-force'.[21] The *Clarion* raised money to buy and equip a propaganda van which bore her name and toured the valleys of the Pennines and South Wales. People were used to sudden deaths, but Caroline's was particularly shocking because of her youth and potential, and because the lifestyle she had chosen had so clearly been a contributory factor in her demise. Scarcely remembered now, she was for her contemporaries a kind of socialist saint who had sacrificed her life for the cause.

As Caroline Martyn's life was ending, the public life of another, much better-known, woman was starting to open. Emmeline Pankhurst had for many years been a supportive wife to her husband Richard, and although she had engaged in a number of campaigns she had not yet emerged as a public personality in her own right. Election to the Manchester Board of Guardians had begun to change that, and had also helped her to gain experience of speaking in public. But it was the conflict of Boggart Hole

Clough in 1896 which brought her to wider attention and launched her on her career as one of the great public speakers.

The campaign for free speech had been going on for over three decades, and centred not on the content of speeches so much as on whether or not they should be made in public at all. The very large crowds some speakers attracted were considered a public order risk, and in London there had been attempts to prevent speakers using public parks. But the police also had a tendency to crack down on opinions they disapproved of. In 1884 the suffragist and SDF member Jessie Craigen was summonsed for speaking at an open-air meeting in Primrose Hill. Socialists suspected that the police were singling them out for special treatment. In 1885 Amie Hicks was arrested for obstruction when speaking at Dod Street in the East End. Other arrests, including that of William Morris, followed. Annie Besant observed that 'Christians, Freethinkers, Salvationists, agitators of all kinds were, for the most part, left alone, but there was a regular crusade against the Socialists.'[22] The arrests led to a huge public campaign to defend free speech, with thousands of pounds being collected for a defence fund and tens of thousands of people turning out in Dod Street to protest. The establishment had no option but to give in; the protests were a greater threat to public order than the original public meetings. But matters did not end there.

In 1887 the SDF and others organised a mass demonstration against unemployment to be held in Trafalgar Square on 13 November. The police tried to ban it, but this just resulted in the crowds being even larger. Marches were organised to come from various parts of London to meet in the Square, each led by a prominent socialist speaker. Annie Besant and the anarchist Charlotte Wilson both led contingents. When they got to Trafalgar Square the marchers were attacked by police and troops, and many were injured. The socialists John Burns and Robert Cunninghame Graham were arrested and both spent six weeks in prison. Annie Besant spoke from the platform and invited the police to arrest her, but, perhaps having learned from their experience with Amie Hicks, they declined to do so. The day became known as 'Bloody Sunday', and public revulsion was increased further by events at a protest against the arrests held on the following Sunday, when a young man called Alfred Linnell was trampled by a police horse and subsequently died.

The free speech debate continued to rumble on over the years, coming to a head again in May 1896 when Manchester City Council decided to stop socialists holding meetings at Boggart Hole Clough. This large open area had traditionally been used by all kinds of people for public meetings, so that when the trade unionist John Harker was arrested for speaking there people were outraged. He was defended in court by Richard Pankhurst and fined ten shillings. The ILP organised more meetings at Boggart Hole Clough, which attracted large crowds. Speakers who were arrested refused to pay their fines and some were imprisoned. Emmeline Pankhurst, easily identifiable by her pink straw bonnet, began to appear on the platform. In June, together with a number of others, she was arrested and charged with breaching public order. In court she was defiant and refused to pay any fine. When her co-defendant Leonard Hall was sent to prison and she was not, she shouted from the dock 'I will not be treated like a child!'[23] When, a little later, Keir Hardie was arrested, he told the court that he intended to call over 400 witnesses; it soon adjourned and never reconvened to finish his case. The government of the day, horrified by the escalation of an essentially local issue, refused to allow the Council to pass a by-law prohibiting public gatherings. The ILP had won, and Emmeline's public career was launched. The lessons she learned from Boggart Hole Clough would serve her in good stead in the future, and her voice would become familiar to many during the early years of the next century.

Richard Pankhurst, however, did not live to hear it. In July 1898 he died from a stomach ulcer at the age of 62. His funeral procession was attended by thousands, but he had died intestate and was heavily in debt, so that his widow was left with serious financial problems. A fund was set up to assist the family, and Emmeline humiliatingly found herself dependent upon charity. All the trustees were men, and there were numerous clashes of opinion over how resources should be allocated. It was more than ironic that a man who had spent so much of his life campaigning for women's economic and political rights should unintentionally have left his wife in such a position, and it had direct consequences in contributing to her increasing impatience with the status quo and the attitudes of the men in both the ILP and in wider society. When, a few years later, she launched the Women's Social and Political Union (WSPU) she was driven at least in part by indignation that, as in the courtroom after Boggart Hole Clough, her sex repeatedly led to her being 'treated like a child'.

◆ ◆ ◆ ◆ ◆

Although the 1895 election result had been disappointing the ILP was not unduly cast down. The loss of Keir Hardie's seat was a blow, but overall the party had received over 44,000 votes which could be considered promising. Certainly the results in Scotland, where no ILP candidate received over 500 votes, were depressing, but then the party in Scotland was in a state of disarray. Elsewhere things looked much more hopeful. The financial position, too, was healthy, with the NAC able to report a surplus in the Parliamentary Fund. However, most of the money raised had come from small subscriptions sent in by readers of the *Labour Leader* and the *Clarion*, and there was very little sign of larger donations, particularly from the unions.

This lack of trade union support did not prevent ideas of socialist unity from persisting, however, and chief of these was the prospect of merger with the SDF. The SDF had polled only a little over 3,000 votes at the election, but still considered itself the true socialist party. Moreover, many of the other very small leftist parties had withered away, and prominent socialists such as Eleanor Marx had returned to the SDF fold. Now in his 50s, Henry Hyndman had started to mellow, and the death of Friedrich Engels in 1895 marked the end of an era. Although there was hostility between the SDF and the ILP nationally, at a local level there was often co-operation, and dual membership was probably by no means unknown. In Yorkshire and Lancashire, in particular, there was considerable overlap, and it was from this quarter that much of the pressure for a merger came.

Unfortunately, this reckoned without either the personalities involved or the ideological differences which persisted. Keir Hardie remained implacably opposed to the SDF; he had never been a member of it and disliked its doctrinaire and sometimes patronising approach to politics and the working class. He and Hyndman were both men of considerable ego, and probably neither would have been comfortable as members of the same organisation. The SDF remained equivocal about peaceful change and vitriolic about many of its former members. Although one or two individual union leaders such as Will Thorne were SDF members, trade unions generally tended to regard it with even more disfavour than they did the ILP. Nevertheless, the 1895 ILP conference had instructed the new secretary, Tom Mann, to explore the possibilities of merger and this he did. Perhaps unsurprisingly, the SDF turned the proposal down out of hand.

From this point on events turned into a full-blown row. The 1896 ILP conference was, understandably after the shock of the election defeat, inclined to fractiousness, and some of this centred on the issues of both the merger and the Party's name. The NAC was instructed to reopen negotiations with the SDF, and there was again a lengthy debate about a proposal to change the ILP's name to include the word 'Socialist'. There was some bad feeling about this, and when Enid Stacy spoke she said that she was 'astonished' to hear that some branches were apparently threatening to leave if the name was not changed, adding that 'Certain sections of the press and public opinion would be only too pleased if they changed their name, but she thought such an action would be detrimental to the party.'[24]

The name change was defeated, but there was then a proposal to add the word 'Socialist' in a subtitle. Emmeline Pankhurst suggested that this strap-line should be 'The British Division of the International Socialist Movement'. This was also voted down.[25]

Throughout the late 1890s debate about the need for unity dragged on. The ILP spent many fruitless hours of each year's conference debating the question of whether to fuse or federate with the SDF. Branches locally might favour a merger, but the national leadership was dead against it and inclined instead towards federation. The ILP also spent a considerable amount of time examining its own structures and rules, eventually resolving in 1899 not to take any further rule changes. In 1900 delegates congratulated themselves that 'For the first time in the history of the Party the Conference left the Constitution without alteration.'[26] But by then the questions of both the party name and its relations with the SDF had become almost irrelevant, and growing threats to the trade unions had begun to focus minds in a new and much more productive way.

The apparent check to socialism in 1895 was matched by developments in industry. The 'new unionism' of the late 1880s and early 1890s had brought new people and sectors into the movement, but it had also galvanised employers into taking steps to defend themselves. In 1893 the National Free Labour Association was set up to supply strike-breakers when they were needed. Employers' federations began to spring up to try to get some unity between firms facing industrial action as well as to lobby Parliament as a counterbalance to the TUC. Worse, there began to be discussions about limiting the powers of the unions and making their legal responsibilities during strikes more onerous, or at least clearer. In 1894 some members of the Royal Commission on Labour had suggested that employers should be able to sue the unions for damages through the courts. Since unions were not legally regarded as corporations this would have required a change in the law, but the mere fact that such a move was being discussed was ominous. Trade unionists became increasingly apprehensive that gains made by collective bargaining and strikes would be lost to legislation or expensive court cases. Events would show this fear to be entirely justified. The more likely legislation looked, the stronger the case for independent working-class representation in Parliament became.

Unfortunately, the unions continued to have little faith in the ILP as a vehicle for this aspiration. For socialists, the ILP was not socialist enough; for everybody else it was too socialist by far. The 1895 defeat did nothing to boost confidence, and the fact that the ILP immediately descended into introspection at the national level only made things worse. Trade unionists began to disappear from the party's NAC, being replaced by journalists and polemicists such as Ramsay MacDonald and John Bruce Glasier. Instead of narrowing, the gap between the ILP and the unions seemed to be growing ever wider.

The ILP was changing in other respects, too. Men and women who were elected to local councils and other municipal bodies began to find that the challenges of office were more complex than socialist ideology would have them believe. Contact with day-to-day decision making made councillors, aldermen and board members more pragmatic. To be outraged by the suffering surrounding them was one thing; to be responsible for doing something about it was quite another. Local government then had much wider powers than it has now, and municipal socialism, which was later to be one of Labour's great achievements, was in its infancy. People elected to local government had to develop a blend of practical and political thinking which had been absent from the Bradford conference, and the growth of local authorities as employers meant that trade unionists were also taking an increasing interest in being elected to them. This brought together several different strands of the movement – sometimes including women – to develop expertise in new areas. These alliances would pay off in forging a base for the Labour Party when it was out of favour nationally, providing day-to-day experience which would prove invaluable in times to come.

◆　◆　◆　◆

In 1899 a new question arose which split the movement and came to define attitudes well into the twentieth century. Rising imperialism had played a part in the 1895 general election, and within a very few years it had reached fever pitch. In 1899 it erupted in the form of widespread and vocal public support for the South African (also called the Boer) War,[27] taking much of the labour movement by surprise and polarising opinion across the board. The SDF, which immediately and comprehensively denounced the war as imperialist and capitalist oppression, acted in line with its long-held view on Britain's colonial expansion. For other parts of the movement, the question seemed more complex. The Fabian Society chose, by a narrow majority, to remain neutral on the issue and make no statement. Margaret and Ramsay MacDonald, Emmeline Pankhurst and a number of others interpreted this as tacit support for the war and promptly resigned in protest. Robert Blatchford took a pro-war stance, while most other ILP leaders, including Hardie and Bruce Glasier, were adamantly against it. The South Africa Conciliation Committee was set up to bring together the disparate anti-war elements to make the case for peace. In the prevailing climate of jingoism this made it highly unpopular, including with many working-class people. Not for the last time, socialists would find this costly when it came to the ballot box.

For most socialist women the issue was clear. They declined to support what they saw as an unjust war and many campaigned publicly against it. Supporters of the conflict were incensed by what they saw as a lack of patriotism, and there was rioting at a number of the Conciliation Committee's public meetings. The Glasgow offices of the *Labour Leader* were ransacked and speakers were physically attacked. In Brighouse near Halifax the ILP's former treasurer, John Lister, was beaten up by a mob, and around the country ILP and other anti-war campaigners had to be protected from the fury of the crowds. Margaret MacDonald, leaving a meeting in a 'fashionable' part of London, was surrounded and threatened by well-to-do women in evening dress. Ramsay MacDonald later described her reaction:

> She deliberately stood and looked them in the face. Those next her seemed taken aback. 'What have you to say?' she asked, and finding no response added: 'Does shame make you women dumb? If a working woman went into the streets as you do, her cheeks would burn with a sense of disgrace,' and she walked unmolested away.[28]

Differences over the Boer War tended to emphasise rather than resolve disagreements between trade unionists and the ILP. Throughout the 1890s attempts to bring the two sides together had continued, but had met with very little success. In 1895 the Parliamentary Committee of the TUC was successful in introducing the card vote system for all major decisions, removing the (often socialist) trades council delegates and banning any delegate who was not either a union official or working at a trade. This removed many ILP members, including Keir Hardie and a number of women, from TUC meetings. For the next few years the TUC was dominated by the Liberal miners on the one hand and the Conservative cotton unions on the other, and although they disagreed on many things they were at one on the need to steer clear of socialism. They were able to enforce this at every level; in a by-election in Barnsley in 1897, for instance, the ILP candidate was allegedly chased away from at least one pit village by miners throwing stones at him.

The other issue upon which trade unionists could agree was the need to resist the employers, but this was easier said than done. Imitating the success of their American counterparts, employers were now beginning to look to the law for redress. A long and punitive lock-out in the engineering industry in 1897 resulted in defeat for the unions, and increasing mechanisation was threatening jobs even as the war was creating more work. A trickle of legal judgments was going against them and affecting their rights both to strike and to picket. In some industries, the unions were not even recognised by the employers; the Amalgamated Society of Railway Servants (ASRS), for instance, though one of the TUC's larger affiliates, could not negotiate on behalf of its members and was therefore unable to protect them from low wages and poor conditions. Lib-Lab mining MPs tended not to consider themselves responsible for or to any industry but their own, and the mining unions took the view that men in other industries should follow their example and get their own MPs. Despite this, however, socialists were beginning to be elected again to the TUC's Parliamentary Committee, and in 1898 the TUC passed a resolution calling on trade unionists to 'give their support, moral and financial, to the working-class Socialist parties'.[29] In *Labour Leader* Keir Hardie wrote about the kind of electoral arrangements he thought would be feasible: 'Trade Unionists, Socialists, and co-operators each select their own candidates, a joint programme having been first agreed upon, and then the expense of the campaign is also borne jointly.'[30]

The process of bringing this coalition together began in Scotland, where the Scottish TUC (STUC), founded in 1897, was more amenable to progress than the TUC as a whole. In late 1898 Keir Hardie persuaded the ILP's Administrative Council to write to both the TUC and the

STUC to secure 'united political action'. The STUC was the first to respond, and the issue was discussed at its Congress in Dundee in April 1899. The secretary of its parliamentary committee, Margaret Irwin, was the first woman to hold such a post in a mixed trade union body, and had spent many years organising women workers in Glasgow. She and Keir Hardie heartily disliked one another, and after the Dundee Congress she complained bitterly to Ramsay MacDonald that:

> [Hardie] was never off the platform all the time ... We find that his presence and the actions of some of his satellites in the Congress have been hotly resented by many of the Delegates and it is openly said that our Congress is being nobbled by Keir Hardie and will be run by him and wasted on the desert air ... it is just a toss up whether the ... Railway Servants and sections of the Miners, who are highly disgusted, will not also formally withdraw.[31]

Nevertheless, Hardie's forceful management of the situation was at least in part born of the sense of urgency that he and others brought to the meeting, and the STUC agreed to support working-class representation. A conference was held in Edinburgh in January 1900 which set up a Scottish Workers Parliamentary Elections Committee, and attention then turned to the question of how to persuade the TUC in the rest of Britain to take a similar course.

The key opportunity was offered by the ASRS, for whom the situation was becoming acute. There was an increasing amount of industrial action in the rail industry, and the threat of legal action was growing, but they had no parliamentary voice. In 1899 its secretary, Richard Bell, had tried to become a candidate in the railway town of Derby, hoping to stand as an Independent on a Liberal ticket, but the union's conference refused to allow him to do so. Doncaster, where the railway industry was significant, was a marginal Conservative seat, while many of the adjacent mining seats were represented by Lib-Lab MPs who did not always regard themselves as accountable to railway workers and whose politics seemed increasingly remote. In early 1899 Thomas Steels, an ILP member and railwayman from the town, wrote in the *Railway Review* that:

> The sending to Parliament of even one direct and independent representative by a powerful trade union, even though that representative never opens his mouth in the House of Commons, will make for more

progress than the sending of 50 Liberals or Tories of the best type, because it will be unmistakeable evidence of Labour's revolt.[32]

It used to be assumed that the resolution which finally prompted the TUC to take action was written by either Hardie or MacDonald or both, but given that Steels himself had strong views on the subject and was a member of his union's executive this seems unlikely. What was certain was that the TUC would require more than just an invitation from the ILP to prompt it to act; there would have to be a resolution submitted by an affiliated trade union which could get through on the floor of Congress. Accordingly, when the Doncaster branch of the ASRS held its regular meeting in the Good Woman Hotel in St Sepulchre Gate[33] it found on the agenda a resolution in Steels' name which read:

> That this congress, having regard to its decisions of former years, and with a view to securing a better representation of the interests of labour in the House of Commons, hereby instructs the Parliamentary Committee to invite the cooperation of all the cooperative, socialistic, trade union and other working class organisations to jointly cooperate on the lines mutually agreed upon, in convening a special congress of representatives from such of the above-named organisations as may be willing to take part to devise ways and means for securing the return of an increased number of labour members in the next parliament.[34]

The resolution was passed and sent to the union's executive for approval. The executive forwarded it to the TUC for debate at its Congress in Plymouth in September 1899. Steels was not a delegate to the TUC that year, so the resolution was moved by James Holmes, an ILP member and railwayman from the west of England. Following a three-hour debate which included Margaret Bondfield as the sole female voice it was passed, and on 27 February 1900 the conference to establish the Labour Representation Committee (LRC), which became the Labour Party, gathered together to hammer out the detail.

‑ 4 ‑

'The Men's Party'

The Memorial Hall in Farringdon Street in London stood on the site of the old Fleet Prison, which had served for centuries as one of London's principal gaols.[1] For many of the delegates who gathered there to found the Labour Representation Committee (LRC) it was a familiar venue used often for both political and religious meetings; the *Clarion* called it a 'Cathedral of Nonconformity'.[2] All of the delegates who gathered there on a damp, drizzly Shrove Tuesday in 1900 were men; even the Independent Labour Party (ILP) failed to interpret its theoretical support for women's suffrage as a requirement to involve women in the new enterprise. Margaret Bondfield, who might otherwise have been present as a trade union delegate, was away on an organising tour of the country. There were a few women in the public gallery, but none took an active part in the proceedings. When, several years later, the trade unionist and socialist Marion Curran referred to Labour as 'the men's party',[3] she was simply reflecting reality.

Despite the fact that the Trades Union Congress (TUC) was in theory hosting the meeting, the majority of the larger unions did not attend. The Amalgamated Society of Railway Servants (ASRS), the Boot and Shoe Operatives, the Amalgamated Society of Engineers and the Gas Workers were the only sizeable unions to send delegates. Almost all of the mining unions declined the invitation; of the textile unions only the Amalgamated Association of Operative Spinners accepted. Quite a few of the smaller unions were present, however, and in all over half a million trade unionists were represented. Although this was less than a third of the total number of trade union members, it was still a significant proportion. The meeting was chaired by W. C. Steadman of the Barge Builders' Union. Steadman was a Fabian, a radical Liberal, the Lib-Lab MP for Stepney, and a member of the TUC's Parliamentary Committee. His union had about 400 members, so that while Steadman himself was a person of some authority his union could be said to be relatively neutral.[4]

The ILP sent virtually all of its most senior members, including Keir Hardie, Joseph Burgess, Fred Jowett (who had been instrumental in the development of the Bradford Labour Union a decade earlier), Ramsay MacDonald and Philip Snowden, an able and intelligent working-class Yorkshireman in his mid-30s. The ILP delegation arrived at the Memorial Hall with a clear idea of what it wanted to achieve and a plan for driving it through. MacDonald and Hardie knew that they could not afford to miss this opportunity and had spent the time between the TUC meeting in Plymouth the previous September and the foundation meeting in February making sure that there would be enough votes in the room to get them what they wanted. Even the Fabians, who had only one delegate (the secretary, Edward Pease), had been squared off before MacDonald's resignation from it over the war. Both Hardie and MacDonald were powerful and compelling speakers, and they came to the meeting having learned some valuable lessons from the experience of running the ILP.

One element of the wider labour movement was entirely missing. The Co-operative Union, which had been invited, was absent. In his report of the conference, Ramsay MacDonald noted that since they had no 'mandate from their last annual conference, [they] were unable to pledge their organisations'.[5] In fact the co-operative movement never affiliated; in 1917 it set up its own political party which, in 1927, came to an electoral pact with the Labour Party.

Prior to the conference there had been a considerable amount of preparation. MacDonald reported that what was effectively a steering committee had met on several occasions to agree the format and agenda. Although the Parliamentary Committee of the TUC had been represented at those meetings it subsequently insisted on its own unilateral revisions. This effectively put down a challenge to the ILP, which was keen to make sure that the new organisation was a partnership rather than just an extension of the TUC's existing structures.

The Social Democratic Federation (SDF), whose relations with the ILP were now fairly poor, wanted the conference to set up an avowedly socialist body committed to class war and the nationalisation of the means of production, distribution and exchange. Their problem was that very few trade unionists agreed with them, and that even some of their own members were not wholeheartedly supportive. Will Thorne of the Gas Workers' Union, for instance, was a long-standing SDF member, but he was also now an alderman with experience of local government decision making, and his political position seemed to be softening. The SDF delegation did not include Hyndman himself, but it did have the secretary of the London Trades Council, James Macdonald (not to be confused with the ILP's Ramsay), and Harry Quelch, who edited the SDF journal *Justice*. Both were coherent and vocal advocates for their party, but neither could make much headway against the prevailing climate and the electoral imperative. Quelch, in particular, was irritated by the debate on class war and socialisation, protesting against the 'humbug of men professing to be in favour of a principle which at the same time they declared they intended to vote against'.[6] The Dockers' Union delegate James Sexton, however, thought that the resolution to include full-blooded socialism 'seemed to be reviving a spirit which had been responsible for more recrimination and bad feeling in the Labour movement than anything else'.[7]

The trade union delegates tended to see the conference as a vehicle for getting some sense into the arrangements for trying to get working men into Parliament, and some were still active Liberals. The hugely popular MP John Burns, for instance, had begun his political life in the SDF, but had been elected to Parliament on a Lib-Lab ticket. Since then he had been steadily moving away from socialism, and would eventually become the first working-class cabinet minister when he joined the minority Liberal government of 1905. He attended the conference in 1900 as a delegate from the Amalgamated Society of Engineers and therefore had to put his union's point of view, but he was by no means alone in his personal antagonism to socialism.

The question of socialism and nationalisation was virtually the only policy issue the conference discussed. It certainly did not make any mention of the franchise, either male or female. Its objective was to get working-class men elected to Parliament, and to begin to develop some kind of collective parliamentary presence. But this did not mean that the suffrage movement did not take an interest in it, and Millicent Fawcett, on behalf of the National Union of Women's Suffrage Societies (NUWSS), had asked her friend, the redoubtable Isabella Ford, to attend as an observer.

When it came to organisation, the TUC Parliamentary Committee and the ILP had a mutual objective in view, which was that each wanted to rein in the influence of the other. But in Keir Hardie and Ramsay MacDonald the Parliamentary Committee found itself up against two of the finest political operators of the day, and the outcome of the conference was a triumph of planning, organisation and oratory for one of the smallest organisations in the hall. The ILP got its way on almost every single issue, including the crucial one of the make-up of the executive committee.

The original proposal on the agenda was for an executive of 28 members, but the ILP knew that this would be difficult to manage. It was also unrealistic in that it included ten members from the Co-operative Societies, provided they decided to affiliate. If the Co-operative members were removed it would leave an executive of 12 trade unionists plus six others (two ILP, two Fabians and two from the SDF). From the ILP point of view this was unbalanced, since the trade unionists would easily dominate. From the TUC's point of view, however, it seemed not unreasonable that if they were being expected to foot the bulk of the bill they should have the loudest say. Joseph Burgess moved an amendment to reduce the size of the executive to 12; seven trade unionists, two from the ILP, two from the SDF, and one from the Fabians. This was seconded by Keir Hardie, who pointed out that smaller committees were both more efficient and less expensive to run. Alexander Wilkie, for the Shipwrights' Union, pointedly observed that 'They were at the starting of a new movement, and he urged them to move carefully if they wished to secure the support of the Trade Unionists.'[8] The SDF suggested that the Fabians should be excluded altogether, but this was not pursued. When the whole matter was put to the vote Burgess's proposal was accepted on a show of hands. But it was narrow, and the unions demanded a card vote, the first in Labour's history. Burgess's proposal won by 331,000 to 161,000.

Unlike the modern Labour Party, the LRC made no provision for individual membership. Only organisations could 'affiliate', a process which required them to declare how many members they had and then pay an affiliation fee which, in 1900, was set at ten shillings per thousand members. All trade unions were eligible to affiliate, as were socialist societies such as the ILP and the Fabians. Later, trades councils were also added to the list. Anyone who was a member of an affiliated organisation could then be involved in the national LRC, and local LRCs could be set up to run election campaigns. There were advantages to this system in that it reduced administration while enabling high numbers of 'members' to be claimed, but there were also disadvantages. For one thing, someone who was actually a member of another, non-affiliated, political party could be a delegate to the LRC conference and influence debates. This applied to men such as Richard Bell, who was a trade union leader but sat in Parliament as a Liberal, as well as to members of the SDF such as Harry Quelch, who attended for some years as a delegate from the

London Trades Council even though the SDF itself left the LRC in 1901. But perhaps the major problem, and one which was to loom large in time, was that virtually all the LRC's income effectively came from trade union funds which, because of the confused state of the relevant legislation, were increasingly subject to judicial rather than parliamentary decisions.

There was a long discussion about how members of the executive should be chosen. The members of the TUC Parliamentary Committee who were present wanted effectively to be appointed without election, but there was no general support for this. Apart from anything else, there was already some resentment at the big unions' domination of the TUC, and the smaller unions had no wish to have it extended to the LRC. In the end it was decided that each group should elect its representatives then and there, and various huddles produced seven trade unionists, including Richard Bell from the Railway Servants, Pete Curran from the Gas Workers and Alexander Wilkie from the Shipwrights. Hardie and James Parker were elected from the ILP delegation, and James Macdonald and Harry Quelch from the SDF. Edward Pease, who was the only Fabian Society delegate, reported later to the Society that he had elected himself.[9]

Finally, the conference chose its officers. Frederick Rogers of the Vellum Binders' Union became the LRC's first chairman, but there was some debate as to who should be secretary. There was a proposal to ask Sam Woods, secretary of the Parliamentary Committee and a Lib-Lab MP to undertake the task, but this did not meet with much enthusiasm. The suggestion that there should be two secretaries was similarly dismissed. The next proposal was Fred Brocklehurst, an ILP delegate from Manchester, but he declined to accept nomination and instead put forward Ramsay MacDonald. The Railway Servants seconded the motion. MacDonald was elected unopposed.

◆ ◆ ◆ ◆ ◆

The secretaryship was an unpaid post, and there was no money for offices, equipment or materials. No organisation had yet formally agreed to affiliate, therefore nobody had paid any affiliation fees, and the TUC Parliamentary Committee, which had come away from the conference feeling more than a little bruised, was not going to pay the costs of an organisation which it did not entirely control. In histories of the Labour Party, MacDonald's unanimous election is usually explained by the fact that he had 'the use of' or 'had access to' his wife's money and therefore did not need a salary. The wife's name is not usually mentioned, nor is it suggested that she had any choice in the matter. In fact, Margaret MacDonald had full control of her own money, and effectively funded the Labour Party wholly or in part for several years. The decision to do this dated back more than eight years to an exchange of letters between Margaret and Ramsay before their marriage.

Middle-class young women were not supposed to have much to do with money in Victorian and Edwardian times. Money belonged in the male sphere, and discussion of it by ladies was held to be vulgar. In any case, the question of allowances and settlements was, at least in theory, usually discussed and agreed between a bride's father and her fiancé before the wedding. But, having proposed to Ramsay, Margaret was not likely to baulk at circumventing other conventions. Their surviving letters show that they had a very thorough discussion, both in writing and in person, about what the basis of their marriage would be. There seems to have been no question of Margaret ceasing to work on her research and reports, nor any of him getting a job with a salary so that he could maintain his family. They decided early on that their life together was going to be political, and the arrangements they made for themselves were worked out accordingly. When it came to money, however, there were some initial problems. MacDonald was acutely aware that he could be accused of marrying Margaret for her £460 a year,[10] which was many times what a working man could earn, and he was also apprehensive about what her family would think when they found out that he was not only a socialist, but also poor, working class and illegitimate. Margaret wrote to him:

Of course if we marry people will chatter ... [they] will, I suppose, say you've married a fine Miss, or that it's convenient for you to have a little more money coming in. I've thought of that ever since I first knew you, a thought that would be much harder for you to bear than anything anyone might say about me. But people who know us and are worth anything won't believe such tales & one must not regard idle chatter.[11]

Her initial thought was that she would give up her income and live 'a simple life right among the working people ... and [give] the rest to Socialist propaganda of various kinds'.[12] MacDonald, who had known real poverty at close quarters and had no romantic notions about it, was understandably horrified. He wrote to her:

> Don't talk of that Quixotic notion of giving it up altogether. Reduce your cost of life to a moral minimum, do service to society, hold the rest as a trustee to the community; but if you knew what it was to have ideal plans for work, a conviction of a strength to carry them out at least to a valuable point and no breakfast, you would see the real immorality of neglecting to use the opportunities you have in life.[13]

Once married they lived comfortably but not extravagantly. Their flat at Lincoln's Inn Fields was on the third floor, they employed no live-in servants, and when they travelled (which they did frequently) it was as much for research purposes as pleasure. By the time the LRC was founded Margaret was in the habit of giving away much of her income, and would not have objected to her money being used to get it off the ground. Until the LRC could afford its own offices in 1904, therefore, it was run from a table in the back room of their flat.

The challenge which faced Ramsay MacDonald the day after the conference finished was considerable. Both he and Keir Hardie knew that the new LRC had the potential to change the political landscape, but they also knew that it would take more than conference resolutions to make such a change happen. Fortunately, in MacDonald, they had a political organiser and operator of real genius.

MacDonald is usually judged by the cataclysm of 1931, when the Labour government he led collapsed and he went into a coalition with the Conservatives. In the ensuing general election the Labour Party was almost wiped out and he himself was expelled from it. By then he was over 60, tired and, like most other people, baffled by the financial storm that had broken on the world in 1929. But the MacDonald of 1900 was a very different matter, and without him there is no doubt that the LRC would have struggled to establish itself. He was a gifted administrator and, despite his occasional prickliness, he had the ability to bring people on opposite sides of an argument together on common ground. This talent he would need to use to the full, given the mutual suspicion of the trade unions and the socialists, the tendency for people to find it perfectly reasonable to be simultaneously a socialist and a Liberal, and a readiness of individuals in all the socialist organisations to turn on their own side rather than the opposition. This was particularly true of the SDF, who loathed most of their former members, including MacDonald. Many trade unionists were also dubious about him, but this was more because they thought him too much of a socialist rather than too little. In her autobiography (written after World War II), Margaret Bondfield reflected that he 'saw the industrial side as so much raw material to be educated into the higher atmosphere of doctrinal Socialism. The rift was in course of creation long before it became visible.'[14] In 1900 the rift lay far in the future, and if the LRC politically owed a good deal to Keir Hardie (also mistrusted by the unions), it owed much of its organisational and electoral success to MacDonald.

His first problem was to create the impression that the LRC was rather more than it actually was. It had no funds, no organisation and no policy platform, and acquiring all of these was going to be challenging. Nevertheless, he had some headed paper printed and started writing to the trade unions inviting them to affiliate. Until fees were paid there would be no money for anything else, so MacDonald spent a considerable amount of time on this. Most – though by no means all – of the unions represented at the foundation conference agreed to join. Slowly the affiliations trickled in, starting with those whose executives could make such a decision without having to ballot their members. The Steel Smelters seem to have been the first, followed by the Railway Servants, whose TUC resolution had led to the conference in February, and Will Thorne's Gas Workers. The two largest dock workers' unions and several smaller unions followed. By May, MacDonald could report real progress to the first National Executive Committee (NEC) meeting in that unions representing 187,000 members had affiliated. By September the figure had risen to 278,000.[15] There had been some setbacks – the Amalgamated Society of Engineers, for instance, had deferred a decision following an inconclusive ballot – but overall there were grounds for optimism.

The other area of concern was what the LRC's relationship with the Liberals should be, and here there was a clear difference of opinion over what the LRC was for. Some of its founders regarded it as a new political party in the making and wanted it to act accordingly, but others saw it as simply a natural development of the TUC's long-standing aim to get working men elected by any means possible, including on a Liberal ticket. The TUC secretary, Sam Woods, wrote to the NEC suggesting that they contact the Liberal chief whip, Herbert Gladstone (the son of the former prime minister) to enlist his support. Possibly unhelpfully, he copied Gladstone into this letter. When the NEC met in May there was a long debate and when the vote was taken it was so narrow that Woods' proposal was only rejected on the casting vote of the Chairman. The issue came back at the September meeting, when it was proposed to contact the Conservative and Nationalist (Irish) parties as well, but this was also narrowly deferred. It was clear that, while the Fabians and their allies considered the LRC a group able to work with other parties and groups, MacDonald and Hardie thought it was a party in its own right, or at least had the makings of one. The justice of this belief was about to be put to an unexpected test.

In October 1900 the government resigned and caused a general election. This is generally known as the 'Khaki Election' because it was dominated by the issue of the South African War. Ironically, given that the war had another two years to run, both the government and the electorate were largely of the opinion that it had been won, and the decision to go to the country was taken at least in part on this basis. Since 1715 Parliaments had served a maximum term of seven years (hence the Chartist demand for annual Parliaments). Given that the Conservative government had a healthy majority there was no need for an election before 1902, but the prime minister, Lord Salisbury, decided that the time was right to renew his mandate. In the event, the Conservatives lost a few seats but were still returned with a majority of 130.

Despite being completely unprepared, the LRC did its best to rise to the challenge. In the Committee's report to the 1901 conference MacDonald rather laconically remarked that 'At the dissolution in September, the membership was incompletely organised.'[16] In fact, in electoral terms it was hardly organised at all. Although there had been some discussion at the foundation conference about candidates, the Committee had been given no steer as to how they should be selected, except to say that their candidatures should be 'promoted by one or other of the organised movements represented by the constitution which this Committee is about to frame'.[17] This was not very helpful when it came to practicalities, so the executive interpreted it to mean that the LRC could support only candidates run by affiliated organisations, and that any candidate so supported must accept the requirement that he be, among other things, 'in favour of the establishing of a distinct Labour Group in Parliament, who shall have their own whips, and agree upon their policy'.[18] This meant that a trade unionist candidate whose union was not affiliated, or any candidate who stood on a Lib-Lab ticket, could not be an LRC candidate, which had the effect of keeping the number of Labour candidates artificially low since so many unions were not yet affiliated. However, it did put down a marker for the future that, as Hardie and MacDonald wanted, the LRC would one day develop into a new and self-contained political party.

Since the foundation conference had not discussed a policy platform the Committee also had to think on its feet when it came to Labour's first manifesto. A single-sided document was produced which listed 16 demands including old age pensions, child maintenance and the nationalisation of land and railways, as well as no compulsory vaccination, public control of the liquor trade and referendums on peace and war. There was no mention of industrial policy, however, and although there was a demand for adult suffrage and equality between the sexes there was no indication of what these might mean, or of how any of the demands were to be achieved. The manifesto went on to say:

> The object of these measures is to enable the people ultimately to obtain the Socialisation of the Means of Production, Distribution, and Exchange, to be controlled by a Democratic State in the interests of the entire Community, and the Complete Emancipation of labour from the Domination of Capitalism and Landlordism, with the Establishment of Social and Economic Equality between the Sexes.[19]

This was a statement of socialist principles so comprehensive that even the SDF felt able to sign up to it. MacDonald observed in the Committee's report that the 'manifesto to the electors in the constituencies where its candidates were running was signed by representatives of all sections of the Labour movement. This is a happy augury for the future.'[20] Some 22,000 copies were supplied free to the candidates, MacDonald accompanying the distribution with a note which advised candidates that 'For the purpose of presenting a proper return to the Returning Officer you may value these leaflets at 3/– per 1000 and set them down as a contribution from this Committee.'[21]

In all, the LRC centrally spent just £33 (equivalent to about £2,800 now) on election expenses for its 15 candidates, which seemed a very reasonable outlay for the outcome. Two Labour men were successfully elected. One, the Railway Servants' Richard Bell, finally took a seat at Derby, while Keir Hardie was returned in the Welsh mining seat of Merthyr Tydfil.

Bell's progress to victory was relatively straightforward, but Hardie needed to be able to take advantage of the vagaries of the electoral system to win. He was invited to stand in both Preston and Merthyr; this was possible because legally they were two separate elections. He rightly had misgivings about Preston which, in spite of all Liberal and Labour hopes to the contrary, had elected Conservative MPs ever since 1852. When Hardie lost he had enough time to race down to Merthyr where the two Liberal candidates (Merthyr was a two-seat constituency) were in an uneasy alliance. Despite the reservations of the miners' union Hardie had been adopted as the candidate by the local trades councils, and two experienced ILP campaigners, one of whom was Joseph Burgess, had been running his campaign while he was in Preston. South Wales was one of the few places in which jingoism and imperialism were weak, and when Hardie weighed in against the war he attracted support. He won the second seat and was returned to Parliament on a wave of enthusiasm. He remained there until his death in 1915.

Ramsay MacDonald stood against Henry Broadhurst at Leicester but lost heavily, while Philip Snowden stood unsuccessfully in Blackburn. Fred Jowett, a veteran of the Manningham Mills dispute, was defeated in Bradford West while John Hodge of the Steel Smelters was beaten by the Liberals in Gower. The Gas Workers' leader Will Thorne, still an SDF member, stood as a union-sponsored Labour candidate in West Ham South, where he had supplanted Hardie as the candidate. He too was defeated. Nevertheless, the LRC could regard its election as something of a success. It had secured two MPs at very little cost, and had raised its profile quite considerably. It had demonstrated that it could mount a campaign on very few resources and take advantage of the opportunities that events offered.

For women, the 1900 election offered very little. The NUWSS had been split down the middle by the South African War and campaigning for the vote had almost come to a halt. Although the LRC manifesto included adult suffrage and sex equality there was no possibility of any Labour MPs being in any position to bring either of them about. Neither the Conservatives nor the Liberals fought the election on anything other than the war, and as a result much of the campaign was deeply unpleasant. A little band of socialist or pacifist women might oppose the conflict, but millions of others were caught up in the jingoistic excitement. Moreover, women could not vote and could not therefore vent their opposition at the ballot box. They could, however, campaign, although in most cases they did so in favour of the war rather than against it. In Leicester, Ramsay MacDonald noted that 'The lady in fine attire is no new thing

in Parliamentary elections. This time she has been especially busy ...
and [voters] went in twos and threes, poor miserable wretches, and voted
for her and against themselves.'[22] Even Liberal women such as Millicent
Fawcett took the pro-war side of the argument; Isabella Ford noted that
Millicent was 'most unspeakable during the Boer War – till she went to
the Camps'.[23] In many ways, the Khaki Election of 1900 marked a nadir
for women's campaigning voices.

The election did not offer much in the field of industrial policy, either,
with even the Labour manifesto offering only nationalisation. However,
even before it was called a series of events was in train which would bring
the whole issue of trade union funding to the fore and inadvertently
change the LRC's fortunes almost overnight.

In August 1900 a very ordinary strike broke out in South Wales. It was
sparked by a relatively commonplace event but within 18 months it had
become a cause célèbre of national importance. The union concerned,
the ASRS, was almost broken by it, but it gave the LRC an opportunity
which it seized with both hands.[24]

The ASRS had been fighting a long battle with the railway employers
over the issue of recognition. For a trade union to be able to negotiate
with an employer on behalf of its members the employer had to accept,
or recognise, its right to do so. In the mining industry the unions had
been recognised for many years, and as a result the miners had been
able to benefit from the strengths brought by collective bargaining.
In the railway industry, on the other hand, the employers were largely
intransigent, insisting that each company – of which there were many –
negotiated directly with its own workers. But this laid any man who dared
to challenge the employers open to victimisation with very little chance
of redress, since he could not expect much protection from his union.

The Taff Vale Railway Company operated lines taking people and coal
from the mining valleys of South Wales to Cardiff. It was a very profitable
business serving over 70 pits and their villages, and it had no intention of
dealing with trade unions or allowing a culture of collective bargaining
to develop. The demands of the South African War had boosted
coal production, which in turn had increased the company's profits.
Shareholders were doing very well, but the men and their families were
faced with rising food prices and serious inflation. By the time a signalman
called John Ewington was victimised for having tried to negotiate a wage
increase, feelings were running high and ASRS members came out on
strike.

Strikes were not illegal, but there were legal formalities to be observed. Workers intending to strike had to notify their employers in advance, and this the majority of the Taff Vale railwaymen did. As soon as the strike began the company contacted the National Free Labour Association to get strike-breakers in to run the trains, and took advice from the Employers' Parliamentary Council on the prevention of picketing. Initially about 800 men struck, bringing the trains to a standstill for a day until the Free Labour workers arrived. Unfortunately, and ominously given the company's determination to fight, the strikers included men who had not given the required notice of their intention as well as those who had.

The ASRS executive committee reluctantly backed the strike, which had started without their blessing. The secretary, Richard Bell, was very uneasy about it and advised the executive not to give the strike its support. He was fully aware of the fact that existing trade union legislation was regarded as weak, and that there were widespread apprehensions that the employers' new militancy could result in it being weakened even further. Bell went to Cardiff, where strike-breakers were met off the trains by pickets and handed leaflets inviting them to go back home again, which about a third of them did. There was widespread support for the strikers, but the railway owners held firm.

In fact, they chose to increase hostilities by prosecuting the men who had struck without giving notice and applying for an injunction to prevent further picketing. Bell knew that they were now in very deep waters and managed to get a negotiated settlement. The company agreed to take all the strikers back to work and to drop prosecutions against them, but the strikers won none of their original demands. They were back at work by 1 September. The strike had lasted just 12 days.

There the matter might have rested had the applications for injunctions against Bell, John Holmes (who had moved the resolution to set up the LRC at the 1899 TUC) and the ASRS itself been dropped. Instead, despite the fact that the strike was over, the injunctions were granted on the grounds that the actions of the pickets at Cardiff, particularly in relation to the content of the leaflet distributed to arriving strike-breakers, was unlawful and threatening. This opened up the possibility of the company claiming damages, but it also led to the clarification of an important point of law. The Trade Union Acts of 1871 and 1876, which were the principal pieces of legislation governing trade unions and their activities, were unclear about unions' legal status. They did not say that unions were corporations, and therefore liable for the actions of their members and officers, but neither did they say that they were not. On 5 September 1900 the judge decided that since the law expressly permitted trade unions to own property and act through agents they were indeed effectively incorporated.

Any hope that trade unionists had held that their funds were protected from legal action was now gone. The implications of this were serious. Most unions ran benefits funds for their members; indeed, in many cases access to unemployment, sickness and death benefits were the main reasons why people joined a trade union in the first place. But most unions did not separate their benefit and strike accounts. There was therefore a real danger that if damages were awarded against them they would be unable to protect their benefit funds and continue to make payments to their members. The ramifications of this were obvious; not only would poverty and destitution increase, but working people would lose faith in the unions to which they had entrusted their money.

In the event, all the unions' worst fears were realised. The case wound its way through the courts all the way up to the House of Lords, who ruled on 22 July 1901 that since the union had effectively chosen not to keep the benefit and strike funds separate both could be taken into account for damages. Further, if a union could own property, employ staff and inflict injury Parliament must have 'impliedly given the power to make it sueable in a Court of Law for injuries purposely done by its authority and procurement'.[25]

The legal position was now clear, and the Taff Vale Railway Company pressed home its advantage. It sued Bell, Holmes and the union for damages and won. The union had to pay £23,000 (the equivalent of about £2 million in 2018 values), a huge amount for an organisation dependent upon the small contributions of its members. It also, of course, had to find its own legal costs, which added several thousand more to the bill.

A couple of weeks later the law lords handed down a ruling in a case involving the boycotting of a butcher in Northern Ireland by the Belfast Journeymen Butchers' Association. The lords found in favour of the butcher, effectively making boycotting by trade unions illegal. The lawful limits of picketing were also the subject of judicial interpretation. Weavers on strike in Blackburn in June 1901 were summonsed and fined by the magistrates. The strikers employed a band to play near one of the mills; the band was also summonsed. Although there had been some crowd unrest in the vicinity of the pickets, the picketers themselves had been peaceful, and so far as anyone could see all the band had done was play music. In February 1902 the TUC Parliamentary Committee met the (Conservative) Home Secretary and the Chancellor of the Duchy of Lancaster who was also chairman of the Coal Trade Conciliation Board. When the question of the Blackburn pickets was raised the Chancellor said that in his opinion it was possible to sue legal pickets for damages. The constraints which the unions had feared for so many years now seemed to be closing in on them.

The TUC pursued various avenues to try to mitigate the judgments, protect unions' benefits funds, rescue picketing and promote compulsory conciliation in industrial disputes. Unfortunately, there was no clear agreement about how these things should be achieved. Views differed about what the Taff Vale judgment meant, what its implications for trade unions might be and even whether or not it should be resisted. The 1901 TUC meeting in Swansea was fractious and alarmed. Some men made their possessions over to their wives so that they could not be seized if they were sued. There were demands for increased parliamentary representation. It seemed self-evident that an independent voice in Parliament was necessary, but many unions had so far been unable to make the case successfully to their members. The leadership of the Amalgamated Society of Engineers had failed to get LRC affiliation through its membership, and it was by no means alone. There were other issues, too, on which trade union leaders could be at odds with their members. Some might have opposed the South African War, but most trade unionists were in favour of it and exhibited just as much enthusiastic jingoism as the rest of the population. Many peace candidates had been defeated at the election, and even at the TUC a delegate from the Navvies' Union who tried to move a resolution demanding an immediate cessation of hostilities and the granting of the Boers' demands was howled down.[26] Similarly, although the Taff Vale judgment exercised the TUC leadership to a considerable extent, there was relatively little evidence that grass-roots members shared their concern, or at least not until they understood that their benefits were under threat.

Attempts were made to find political solutions. The eight Lib-Lab MPs who had been elected in 1900 met the two Labour members (Hardie and Bell) for the first time to look at the legislative implications of Taff Vale, but the Liberal Party itself seemed lukewarm about the need for any change in the legislation, and the Conservative government was adamantly opposed. Yet for the unions and the LRC there was an important principle which urgently needed to be resolved. In July 1901 MacDonald pointed out that:

> Trade unionism is being assailed, not by what the law says of it, but by what judges think the law ought to say of it. That being so, it becomes necessary for the unions to place men in the House of Commons, to challenge the decisions which I have no doubt will follow this.[27]

At the beginning of August 1901 Hardie asked in Parliament whether the government would legislate to protect trade union funds. The Leader of the House, Arthur Balfour, said not. On the same day MacDonald wrote to the unions pointing out the necessity of labour representation and inviting them to affiliate and send delegates to the LRC conference to be held in Swansea where the whole issue would be debated. Slowly affiliations came in, and by June 1901 the LRC's membership had grown to nearly 384,000. Over the next 18 months it sprang up to well over 750,000, in no small part due to the unexpected outcome of a by-election in Clitheroe and a crucial change of political heart by the weaving unions.

The cotton weavers of Lancashire and Cheshire had remained Conservative-inclined, and although the experience of the Blackburn dispute had shaken that loyalty it had not dislodged it. The Conservative Party's anti-temperance, pro-religious education stances were attractive in areas which had large Catholic communities and no principled objection to alcohol. Unlike Yorkshire, Lancashire was not a stronghold of radical protestant Nonconformism, and the unions in its predominant industries had been relatively successful in gaining benefits for their members without supporting anything resembling socialism. In some parts of the cotton industry there was even rudimentary equal pay. But increasing confusion over the status of trade union legislation, coupled with alarm at the Conservative government's continued refusal to legislate, was beginning to weaken the faith of some union leaders, while the advent of a by-election in the constituency of Clitheroe offered an unusual opportunity for the LRC to flex its muscles.

Clitheroe was a Lancashire enclave of almost Yorkshire-style Nonconformity on the border between the two counties. It had traditionally returned a Liberal MP, and when the most recent incumbent, Sir Ughtred Kay-Shuttleworth, accepted a peerage it seemed inevitable that he would be succeeded by another Liberal in the same radical mould. The Conservatives had not contested the seat since 1892, and it was likely that whoever the local Liberal Party supported would be elected. Philip Snowden had been nursing Clitheroe for the LRC and, given his ardent support of temperance, would have been an ideal candidate for the seat, but he was persuaded to stand aside for David Shackleton. Shackleton was a popular weavers' union leader of stature in every sense. He had stood for Darwen Town Council as a Liberal, but after he had given the LRC assurances of his independence he was adopted by them as their candidate. Following some tortuous negotiations, during which the LRC steadily refused to support a Liberal candidate, the Liberals gave in and agreed not to run. Shackleton was elected unopposed in August 1902 and became the third Labour MP (although by this point Richard Bell was already well on his way to becoming a Liberal).

David Shackleton was not in any way a socialist, but he was a trade union man with connections across Lancashire. Not without reason, the ILP were deeply suspicious of him, and there were a series of incidents in which he had to be reminded of his obligations. Keir Hardie, who would have repelled Liberal voters with his socialist fire, stayed away from this and other by-elections, as did Bruce Glasier for the same reason. Other speakers were more welcome. Emilia Dilke of the Women's Trade Union League (WTUL) arrived to support the principle of working-class representation in Parliament, remarking that:

She was not a party politician. She had never yet set foot on any Liberal platform except her husband's, and she did not mean to … she went nowhere except where Labour called her. What the miners had done the weavers of Lancashire could do … It is now for Liberals to pay their debt to Labour, and to help Labour to that direct representation to which it has a claim.[28]

Shackleton's address to the electorate contained one or two nods to socialist policies but nothing to which Liberal voters could reasonably object. Once he was elected attempts were made by Emilia Dilke's husband, Sir Charles, and others to persuade him to accept the Liberal whip. Had he done this the LRC's coup in winning the seat would have been wiped out and the ILP's support for the LRC might have been withdrawn. In the event he was introduced to the House by Hardie and remained a Labour man until he left politics in 1910.[29]

The Clitheroe by-election was a turning point in another campaign, too. In order to pay Shackleton's expenses and (once he was elected) his salary, the weavers' union raised a levy of sixpence per member. This was common practice in mining constituencies, but in their case the members were generally men who could vote. In Clitheroe, however, the majority of union members were women, who found themselves being asked to campaign and pay for a candidate for whom none of them could vote. Early in the campaign the Manchester-based North of England Society for Women's Suffrage (NESWS) arrived to urge Shackleton to include female suffrage in his programme. Led by their secretary, Esther Roper, the women held public events to press the case. At an open-air meeting which attracted 18,000 people, Emmeline Pankhurst observed that:

> 60 per cent [of Trades' Unionists in the Clitheroe Division] were women. If that percentage had votes they would be able to return Trades' Unionists at the head of the poll. She moved: 'That any member of Parliament for the Clitheroe Division, as representative of a constituency containing so large a proportion of women textile workers, should put enfranchisement of women at the forefront of his political programme, and ask for its immediate enactment.'[30]

The women also approached Shackleton directly. The secretary of the Manchester and Salford Women's Trades Council, Eva Gore-Booth, later recalled that they reminded him that:

> before the Cotton Unions could subscribe £900 a year to the Labour Representation Committee, and before a candidate could be run and his salary paid as a Labour candidate for Clitheroe, a ballot had to be taken of the women who far outnumbered the men in the Unions.[31]

Shackleton took heed and came out for women's suffrage, but not with much enthusiasm, and once elected his record proved disappointing. Despite this the weavers' unions duly affiliated to the LRC, bringing a further 103,000 Lancashire cotton-workers, male and female, into Labour's orbit. Shackleton's perceived duplicity was a blow to suffragists, and helped widen the gulf that was already slowly opening up between the suffrage movement and the LRC. Eva Gore-Booth was particularly annoyed to receive a letter from the LRC after the by-election inviting the Manchester Women's Trades Council to affiliate. On 9 October she replied inquiring:

what benefits you consider would accrue to our members by joining your Society. We are convinced that the women workers do suffer severely in their trade interests through want of direct parliamentary representation, but we should like an assurance that the representation of female labourers is part of your programme.[32]

This assurance was never received, and the Women's Trades Council never affiliated.

Eva Gore-Booth and Esther Roper were leading figures in radical and trade union circles in Manchester. Esther was from working-class stock and had experienced a troubled childhood, but she had been lucky enough also to have a good education at a college in the city. From there she went on to work on female suffrage, in particular trying to develop a franchise campaign among trade union women in the cotton industries. Eva Gore-Booth, on the other hand, was a society lady from a wealthy Irish Ascendency family with radical tendencies. In the mid-1890s both Esther and Eva had separately suffered from poor health and gone to Italy to recover. There they met in a garden in Tuscany. 'Each,' wrote Esther later, 'was attracted to the work and thoughts of the other, and we became friends and companions for life.'[33] They spent their time in Italy together and after it were rarely apart. Eva left her privileged life and went to live with Esther in a small terraced house in Manchester. Their lives were spent working with and for women, either through trade unions, the suffrage campaign or the peace movement, and despite difficult times they remained devoted to one another. It was their influence which brought Christabel Pankhurst briefly into contact with working-class and trade union women as well as, more lastingly, into the suffrage movement.

However, the failure of either the LRC or the TUC to embrace women's suffrage meant that both Eva and Esther distanced themselves from the Labour Party and many of the women in it. Eva, in particular, detested it, once calling the LRC 'built in sin and founded in unright-eousness'.[34] Although they took a particularly extreme view, many others over the years came to share a certain degree of scepticism about the LRC's commitment to women's equality. The LRC's structures, its origins and its electoral focus all combined to push women to the fringes of its work for many years, and it would take the collective efforts of Labour women themselves to change that.

∞ 5 ∞

Women's Work

On 26 November 1867 a widowed shopkeeper called Lily Maxwell voted in a parliamentary by-election. Lily lived in Manchester, and as a Liberal she wanted to vote for the great Mancunian radical Jacob Bright. She was able to do so because of a little-known loophole in the legislation covering the registration of electors. The system put the onus squarely onto individual voters to make sure that they were on the list. As the franchise was gradually extended political parties began to employ agents to canvass door-to-door to make sure that their own supporters registered. But people could also object to anyone whose names they thought had been wrongly registered, and these objections would then be heard by a barrister. Anyone whose name was removed could appeal to the courts, but anyone who got past this stage remained on the list. Since no objection had been raised to Lily Maxwell's name, she could not be prevented from voting. On 26 November, accompanied by two other ladies, she went to the polling station and cast her vote for Bright; according to the newspapers, they were all three 'much cheered as they passed to and fro at the poll'.[1]

Bright won the seat, and Lily's vote was later declared illegal, but one of the women who had accompanied her, Lydia Becker, was the secretary of the newly formed Manchester Society for Women's Suffrage. She quickly realised that the legal anomaly could be put to good use, and in 1868 she led a group of women in a very successful national drive to get thousands of women to register. Barristers who might previously have heard only a few cases a year now found themselves hearing dozens and sometimes hundreds. Because the law was unclear, each barrister interpreted it differently and the conclusions to which they came varied considerably. Some simply removed all women from the list, while others fined them for time-wasting. Others still allowed women's names to remain, while in a few areas there were actually no objections at all so that all the women who had registered were theoretically able to vote.

Some of those whose names had been refused appealed against their exclusion and Richard Pankhurst and other radical lawyers argued in court that women had an ancient right to vote which could not be denied. They lost, and in the end only a small number of women remained registered for the 1868 local elections. The whole campaign had involved thousands of women, tied the electoral registration process up in knots for months, attracted much press coverage and drew attention to the confused and inconsistent state of the legislation. The Education Act of 1870 allowed some women both to vote and stand in elections for school boards, but the loophole Lily and Lydia had exploited was closed.

The mid-to-late nineteenth century was alive with campaigns on social issues, and women were involved to one degree or another in most of them. The suffrage movement had grown out of campaigns for women's legal and economic rights which themselves had drawn on the methods and successes of the anti-slavery campaign. Suffrage societies sprang up in a number of cities, but were particularly strong in London and Manchester, which had long been of a radical turn of mind. Groups lobbied MPs and Parliament, staged meetings and events and wrote pamphlets and articles. From 1867 onwards there were repeated attempts to get some form of female suffrage measure through Parliament. The multiplicity of societies, however, meant that the national campaign often lacked cohesion, until in 1897 the regional societies were reorganised and brought together to form the National Union of Women's Suffrage Societies (NUWSS). Led by Millicent Fawcett, it provided an umbrella organisation and a national voice for the campaign.

For socialists and trade unionists the issue of suffrage was rarely approached from a feminist perspective. It was often hard for women to get the suffragist point across successfully and, in any case, there was no agreement among women themselves about what the line should be. Women who had a Marxist economic analysis were likely to regard the vote as a gesture rather than a solution, and the suffrage movement's limited franchise demand – for the vote 'on the same basis as it is, or may be, given to men' – looked like a commitment to retaining property qualifications which was unacceptable to the majority of trade unionists. Moreover, for many socialists and trade unionists the idea of enfranchising middle-class women and then trusting them to do the same for their working-class sisters, or to promote legislation which would benefit them, was unrealistic. In a culture in which the idea of intersectionality was only rudimentary at best it was easy to cast the struggle for political power as a contest between sex and class.

In 1886 Eleanor Marx and her partner, Edward Aveling, published an essay called 'The Woman Question: From a Socialist Point of View' in which they said that:

> for women, as for the labouring classes, no solution of the difficulties and problems that present themselves is really possible in the present condition of society. All that is done, heralded with no matter what flourish of trumpets, is palliative, not remedial. Both the oppressed classes, women and the immediate producers, must understand that their emancipation will come from themselves. Women will find allies in the better sort of men, as the labourers are finding allies among the philosophers, artists, and poets. But the one has nothing to hope from man as a whole, and the other has nothing to hope from the middle class as a whole.[2]

In this scenario, allowing a limited number of middle-class women to vote was not going to help the great mass of working-class women who needed an economic revolution if their lives were to be improved. Middle-class women were fighting against men, but working-class women needed to combine with men in order to defeat their joint oppression. Eleanor agreed with the German Marxist Clara Zetkin that:

> A Socialist society alone can solve the conflict brought about to-day by the economic activity of women. When the family as an economic unit shall disappear to make way for the family as a social unit woman will become the equal of man, producing, striving side by side with him; will become his comrade, both living their lives as human beings.[3]

For most British socialists and trade unionists the answer lay in equal and universal adult suffrage to include women as well as men. This aim came to be generally known as 'adultist', and its supporters were much distrusted by limited franchise campaigners. They saw the adult franchise as a front for manhood suffrage, which would only benefit men, and feared that women would again be betrayed and left out. They believed it was essential to establish the *principle* of equal criteria for the vote so that if (or when) the property qualification was abolished, women and men would be treated equally. In the meantime, middle-class women would be able to represent the interests of working women in Parliament. However, this view was much easier to take from the relative comfort of the middle class; it was hard for working-class women to believe that the vote for somebody else would solve all their own problems when what they were desperate for was higher wages and more secure employment. But most women barely thought about it at all: in the struggle to feed their children and keep a roof over their heads, politics generally seemed irrelevant. The world was a harsh and hostile place, and children could not eat a vote.

In fact, the suffrage movement was often aware of the fact that it needed to broaden its appeal to working-class women, but it faced the same organisational problems that faced both the trade unions and the socialist parties. In Lancashire and Cheshire, however, the efforts of Eva Gore-Booth and Esther Roper did bring large numbers of working-class women into the suffrage fold. In the cotton textile industries women were often unionised, some had more or less equal pay and wages were often high enough to take them out of the most abject levels of poverty. Women living above the breadline, even if only just, were more likely to be able to take an interest in both politics and suffrage. As we have seen, these women were active in the Clitheroe by-election of 1902, but even before this Eva and Esther had been developing a working-class suffrage campaign. In 1901 they collected over 30,000 signatures from textile workers on a petition which they presented to MPs in March; the following year Isabella Ford collected a further 30,000 signatures from textile workers in Yorkshire for a petition which was presented in March 1902. She noted that the attitude of the MPs to whom they spoke 'rather opened the women's eyes ... to the size of the battle which lies before them. Their backs began to stiffen a little.'[4]

The first proposal at the Trades Union Congress (TUC) to support women's suffrage had been moved in 1880 by Jessie Craigen who, in a debate about the county and borough franchise, tried to amend the resolution 'so as to assert the right of women householders to the Parliamentary franchise'.[5] The chairman tried to rule her out of order, and she was asked to withdraw. It is not recorded whether or not she did.

Jessie Craigen had started work at the age of four as a dancer on the stage with her mother. Her theatrical training proved useful when she took to public speaking, initially in support of temperance, then of the suffrage campaign, Irish Home Rule and many other causes. She was reputedly a difficult woman to deal with, extravagant, temperamental and erratic. However, she had a beautiful oratorical style and a reach into communities far beyond that of most of the middle-class ladies, which made her a popular speaker and a valuable asset to a number of campaigns.

In 1881 Jessie tried again, pointing out that 'women wanted votes just as men did, to enable them to get rid of oppression'.[6] Again she was defeated. In 1884 the Liberal government introduced the Representation of the People Bill to Parliament with the intention of enfranchising all male freeholders and leaseholders; this would have the effect of extending the vote to about 60 per cent of men. Radical Liberals attempted to add female householders to the legislation, but the prime minister, William Gladstone, maintained that if they insisted upon this he would drop the Bill altogether since he would not be able to get it through the Lords, where there was in any case considerable opposition to enfranchising a 'a numerous and ignorant class' of men. At the TUC that year Maria Addis of the Dressmakers' Society moved a resolution to enfranchise women ratepayers which was debated at some length, with several men agreeing that if women had to pay rates and obey laws they should have a say in setting them. But Charles Freak of the London Boot and Shoe Riveters opposed her on the grounds that:

> If Miss Addis had moved that they should have universal adult suffrage, he would have been with her, but he would never agree to the principle at present acted upon that a woman or man paying rates should have a vote, while others who did not pay rates … should not, for he contended that every person that toiled in the country paid the rates and taxes of the country indirectly.[7]

Here was the adultist argument in a nutshell; the problem for Freak was not the discrimination on the grounds of sex, but of income and class. In the end the resolution was amended to read 'that the franchise ought to be extended to women on the same conditions as men'. This was passed with only three votes against and was the high point of TUC support for female suffrage.[8] The passing of the 1884 Representation of the People Act meant that by the time the Labour Representation Committee (LRC) was founded in 1900 most TUC delegates could vote and women's suffrage was no longer on the agenda. This partly explains why the enfranchisement of women was omitted from the LRC's election programme in 1900; there was a commitment to equality, but nothing more.

In 1901, however, the TUC's Parliamentary Committee set up a subcommittee to consider the franchise issue again. It consisted of five men and one woman, and was required to report back to Congress that year.[9] The woman,

Helen Silcock, was a cotton weaver from Wigan who was a member of the Social Democratic Federation (SDF), a full-time organiser for the Women's Trade Union League (WTUL) and a member of Esther Roper's Lancashire and Cheshire Women's Suffrage Society. She was at the TUC that year as one of the few women to represent a mixed union, and moved the Franchise Committee's report, which took the form of a resolution. It was not, however, the one she had wanted. She had tried to get the Committee to agree a limited franchise position, but they insisted on putting a universal adult wording to Congress which said 'That the time was ripe for the extension of the franchise to all adult men and women, on the principle of one adult one vote.'[10] Helen reluctantly did her duty by it but in her speech she observed that:

> [Women's suffrage] was not the idea of a few smart women desirous of getting seats in the House of Commons. It was advocated by women workers generally, because they thought better legislation was absolutely needed to improve their lot ... As to the wise exercise of their votes, she would say, 'Give us a chance, and if we cannot do better than you men, well, we cannot do worse.'[11]

Eleanor Whyte, the victor of the long fight for women factory inspectors who was attending her twenty-first TUC, seconded the resolution, and it was passed 'without further discussion'.

In 1902 Helen (now Helen Fairhurst) tried again, this time seconding a limited suffrage resolution moved by Yorkshire weaver Allen Gee. Gee was a long-standing supporter of the women's campaign and a friend of Isabella Ford, but even he, well-respected as he was, could not persuade delegates and the proposal was narrowly defeated. For various reasons Helen Fairhurst subsequently changed her own view to support the adultist position and thereafter concentrated on women's industrial issues. In 1903 Eleanor Whyte made a further plea for Congress to support women's suffrage, but there was no resolution and therefore no vote.

Meanwhile, the universal adultist point of view was finding its defenders among women trade unionists. In 1903 Margaret Bondfield engaged in a public debate with Isabella Ford, who was a great supporter of both trade unionism and the limited franchise. More than 20 years later Sylvia Pankhurst described Margaret's appearance on that occasion:

> Miss Bondfield appeared in pink, dark and dark-eyed, with a deep, throaty voice many found beautiful. She was very charming and vivacious, and

eager to score all the points that her youth and prettiness would win for her against the plain, middle-aged woman, with red face and turban hat crushed down upon her straight hair.[12]

This is an unusual picture of Margaret, who was generally speaking not, from all accounts, a woman likely to use her looks to win arguments. Sylvia Pankhurst's very readable memoirs are not always kind to women who disagreed with her, and she clearly disliked Miss Bondfield. But unfortunately the picture of her that she gives has stuck, and her allegation that 'Miss Bondfield deprecated votes for women as the hobby of disappointed old maids whom no one had wanted to marry' has been repeated over the years and used to attack both Margaret herself and adultists generally. However, it seems an extremely unlikely thing for Margaret to have said; apart from anything else she herself had, according to her autobiography, decided very early in life never to marry.[13] Moreover, her usual style, though often trenchant, tended towards courtesy rather than invective. It would have been out of character for her to have been quite so offensive when she was addressing a distinguished trade unionist of an older generation, especially one whom she most certainly must have known, at least by reputation, and very probably in person.

The LRC conference also discussed female suffrage, but not in its early years. The first few female delegates seem not to have spoken, though women attended from 1901 onwards. The first woman to attend was called Annie Lee. She lived in Openshaw in Manchester and in 1901 she was a delegate from the Workers Union. She had been secretary of Openshaw Independent Labour Party (ILP) for a number of years and was a member of the local trades council. In 1919 she was elected as a Labour member of Manchester City Council where she remained for nearly 20 years, campaigning on unpopular issues such as abolishing the marriage bar in teaching or providing birth control in municipal clinics. In 1936 she became the city's first female alderman. She was described as having 'fearlessness in the face of all opposition, and a passion for helping those she considers downtrodden – generally those of the female species'.[14] Despite this, however, she is not recorded as having spoken at the 1901 conference, and does not seem to have been a delegate again.

Indeed, the Labour conference had to wait until 1904 to hear a woman speak. Isabella Ford had attended in 1903, but although it would have been unusual for her to have stayed silent for two whole days while men discussed issues in which she was keenly interested, she is not recorded as having spoken. In 1904 she was again an ILP delegate, this time in company with Julia Varley from Bradford. Julia was later described by Margaret Bondfield as 'having a great spirit of adventure', on one occasion investigating workhouses by tramping:

> from Bradford to Liverpool after a hypothetical husband named Thompson, a dock worker, whom she was seeking … She would say that thousands of the poor had three existences – in the workhouse, in filthy lodging-houses, or in prison, so she learned about the insides of all three.[15]

It is hard to imagine a woman like Julia remaining silent throughout a conference either, but the report does not record her voice. Isabella Ford, however, did speak, becoming, so far as is known, the first woman to be heard – or at any rate minuted – at a Labour conference.

The resolution she seconded proposed the extension of the franchise to 'women on the same basis as that allowed to them for parochial purposes', and required LRC MPs to introduce a bill to Parliament to achieve this. Women were indeed able to vote in parish council elections, but only if they were ratepayers or married women who owned property separately from their husbands. This might have enfranchised a few working-class women, but would have excluded the vast majority of married women. It was moved by the Burnley weavers' union, and the record of the conference does not indicate whether or not it was passed.[16] Isabella's speech supporting it was brief; at the end of it she mildly observed that 'There was a feeling … that there ought to be a woman on the L.R.C. Executive.'[17]

The following year in Liverpool there were four female ILP delegates; Isabella Ford, Ethel Annakin (who would soon marry Philip Snowden), Selina Cooper from Nelson, who had been involved in the campaign in Clitheroe to get Shackleton to support women's suffrage, and Emmeline Pankhurst. Yet again, there were no women delegates from the trade unions, nor were any women elected to the executive, though Emmeline Pankhurst did head the poll for the Standing Orders Committee. This conference is notable for being the first occasion upon which the LRC discussed women's parliamentary suffrage, and it is worth considering the debate in some detail since it set the tone for the Party's attitude to female suffrage for nearly a decade to come.

On the eve of the 1905 conference the Women's Social and Political Union (WSPU) (then still a non-militant organisation), the Women's Trades Council and a couple of textile workers' groups organised a public meeting in support of women's votes. Speakers included Emmeline Pankhurst, Isabella Ford and Allen Gee, who had moved the unsuccessful suffrage motion at the TUC, as well as Philip Snowden and Keir Hardie. In her speech Isabella remarked that women 'did not want to use dynamite' and were 'accustomed to move slowly in this country'.[18] Support for women's suffrage in Liverpool was high, at least in part as a result of the work of Eva Gore-Booth and Esther Roper, and the large crowd at the meeting raised hopes. The following day in the conference hall the Engineers' union moved:

> That this Conference heartily approves of adult suffrage and the complete enfranchisement of both sexes, and endorses the Women's Enfranchisement Bill introduced into Parliament last session, believing it to be an important step towards adult suffrage.[19]

The Women's Enfranchisement Bill to which the resolution referred proposed simply to add women to the current electorate on the same basis as men. Crucially, however, it included married women, and thus it would have enfranchised a significant percentage of the female population, including many – though by no means all – working-class women. Suffragists generally backed it as a major step towards their objective, and campaigned hard to get others to support it, both within and outside the LRC.

Selina Cooper, who seconded the resolution, was a trade unionist, socialist and suffragist. She was involved with the Women's Co-operative Guild and had helped to organise the Lancashire and Cheshire working women's suffrage petition in 1901. The Clitheroe by-election had dented her confidence in the LRC, but she was prepared to give it another chance. In her speech she pointed out her background: 'She claimed to speak on behalf of thousands of women engaged in the textile trades, to whose class she belonged.' She rejected the idea that the vote would be simply a palliative. Finally she said that:

> In the Clitheroe Division alone 5,500 women had signed a petition in favour of women having the vote on the same terms as men and she would impress upon the delegates present that they should not think that women wanted the vote merely as women. They were as keenly

alive to the needs of the people as anyone, and if they had the vote they would be able to use it in the interests of reform.

An amendment was then moved by Harry Quelch, nominally the delegate from the London Trades Council but actually speaking on behalf of the SDF. The SDF had been one of the founding organisations of the LRC, but within a year their own internal wrangling led them to disaffiliate. Quelch was the editor of the SDF journal *Justice*, and although he was able, principled and moderate, his moderation was relative. The SDF generally was not keen on female suffrage. It also had control of the London Trades Council, and its amendment therefore reflected the SDF's view. It read:

> That this Conference, believing that any Women's Enfranchisement Bill which seeks merely to abolish sex disqualification would increase the political power of the propertied classes by enfranchising upper and middle class women, and leaving the great majority of working women still voteless, hereby expresses its conviction that Adult Suffrage – male and female – is the only Franchise Reform which merits any support from Labour Members of Parliament.

His speech supporting this began with the political, but he soon moved on to attacking women themselves, particularly middle-class women. 'There was none less charitable, less possessed of the milk of human kindness, none more bitter in the class struggle than the middle class woman,' he said, going on to add that if he 'had to meet a committee of employers, he would prefer that they should be men rather than women.'

The debate which followed was almost entirely about the effects of women voting rather than the principle itself. Probably the best contribution came from Philip Snowden, who confessed that a year previously he would have supported the amendment, but that during the last six months his opinion had changed. Given that six months was almost exactly the period during which he had known Ethel Annakin, this is perhaps not surprising. At the end of his speech he pointed out that 'if the Women's Enfranchisement Bill was passed ... the demand for reform would be enormously stimulated'. But the general mood of the hall was against him, and by the time Emmeline Pankhurst rose to speak she must have known that the debate was lost. Her speech was redolent with the anger which was beginning to pervade her thinking. She told delegates that:

> to her this question had resolved itself into a life and death struggle as far as women were concerned. The mover of the amendment ... had contended that the Bill would only enfranchise propertied and reactionary women. ... She and those associated with her spoke for those working women who would benefit under the Bill. ... She appealed to delegates to discard sex prejudice and to press for the removal of sex disability as the first step in franchise reform. Unless they could get a majority in the House of Commons, pledged to remove sex disability, they would have manhood instead of adult suffrage.

It was no use, however; when the amendment was put to the vote it was carried by 483 votes to 270.

When Emmeline described the suffrage movement as having 'resolved itself into a life and death struggle' she was encapsulating what had happened to her personally and to her thinking since her appearance nearly a decade previously on the platform at Boggart Hole Clough. Richard Pankhurst's death had plunged the family into a crisis on almost every front. His success as a radical lawyer with significant levels of pro bono work had restricted his income, and his later reputation as a socialist had deterred paying clients. The widowed Emmeline and her four children had to move from their comfortable house to a smaller one nearer the city centre.[20] She tried running a shop (which she had done before when living in London) and then took a post as a registrar of births and deaths in Chorlton. This had a salary attached, which made things slightly easier. In the meantime, however, the socialist networks to which she and Richard belonged had swung into action and two funds had been raised, one to build a hall in Richard's memory, and the other to provide an income for Emmeline and the children.

Both of these funds were to cause trouble in their own ways. All the trustees of the second one were men, and some of them humiliated Emmeline by treating her as the object of charity and forcing her to ask for money for basic necessities. But one of the biggest battles occurred when, at the end of 1902, the trustees suddenly reduced the amount of money she was receiving on the grounds that they needed to save for the education of her 13-year-old son, Harry.[21] Apart from anything else, this would have made it extremely difficult to educate the three girls, Christabel, Sylvia and Adela. Emmeline was incensed. One of the trustees, who was actually trying to be helpful, explained to her that the meeting which had made the decision thought that the fund 'should now be husbanded for the boy to give him the best possible start in life'.[22] Emmeline responded promptly outlining her plans for the education of all her children. 'I believe,' she wrote, '& my husband thought it too that it is quite as important to give opportunity of education to gifted girls as to boys. I am carrying out his wishes in what I am doing.'[23] It took her a year to get the decision reversed, and her daughters did indeed get their education, but it was an uphill fight.

It was the fund for the Memorial Hall, however, which precipitated the foundation of the WSPU. The Hall was being built in Salford, and was to house the local ILP branch. By and large, the ILP was in favour of temperance, and did not encourage the sale of alcohol in the Labour clubs springing up around the north of England. But there was no denying that selling drink attracted members and made money, and therefore the temptation for struggling local parties was strong. At some point during the late summer of 1903 it became clear to Emmeline that the Salford branch was going to sell beer. This in itself might not have been an issue, but the opening of a bar on the premises meant that women would be excluded. Given that the hall had been built in memory of Emmeline's feminist, pro-suffrage and pro-temperance husband, and decorated free of charge by her artist daughter Sylvia (like her mother, an ILP member) this was both distressing and infuriating. The hall was to be opened at a ceremony in October, and by the time John Bruce Glasier and Philip Snowden turned up for the opening Emmeline was so angry that she refused to speak to them. Christabel Pankhurst later reported her as saying to friends, 'Women, we must do the work ourselves. We must have an independent women's movement. Come to my house tomorrow and we will arrange it!'[24] It was this meeting, on 10 October 1903, which gave rise to the WSPU, the organisation which eventually became the militant wing of the women's suffrage campaign.

Emmeline's demand for an 'independent women's movement' has often been interpreted as a call for a feminist rather than a socialist group. In fact she meant both. Enid Stacy[25] had persuaded the ILP to agree in principle to set up women's organisations in 1894, but nothing much had been done about it, and while there were some local women's groups there was no separate, independent structure for Labour women. The LRC was an affiliate-based body with no provision for individual membership, and had no capacity for women's organisation either, although women were able to organise as adjuncts to local LRCs. But Emmeline had started her political life as a Liberal and, while living in London, had come into contact with the Liberal Party's women's organisation, the Women's Liberal Federation. In 1903 she had no intention of leaving the ILP, and was in fact still heavily involved in it, having been recently elected to the National Administrative Council (NAC) together with Isabella Ford. Her idea was to set up some form of socialist women's group which would be able to strengthen women's role and voice in the labour movement as well as change minds on female suffrage; it is very unlikely that at this stage she intended to actively campaign against the ILP which she and Richard had been instrumental in founding.

Both the Conservative and the Liberal parties had begun to co-opt women into their structures before either the ILP or the LRC existed. The Conservative Primrose League was formed in 1883 to foster activism among both women and men, and from the start women were allowed to join on an equal basis. In 1885 a group of women set up the Ladies' Grand Council of the Primrose League, which fundraised and campaigned for Conservative candidates. There was, in the upper echelons of the Party at least, some support for enfranchising propertied women, and some Primrose League women were also active in the suffrage campaigns.

The Women's Liberal Federation, which drew together a number of local and regional women's organisations under one umbrella, followed in 1886 under the auspices of Catherine Gladstone, wife of the Liberal leader. Although it was never as big as the Primrose League it included many influential women and a great many suffrage campaigners. Given the trade union movement's close relationship with the Liberal Party, many Liberal women were also involved with organisations such as the WTUL and the Women's Industrial Council (WIC). However, suffrage was a divisive issue and in 1892 it caused the Federation to split. About 10,000 members objected to the Federation's support for the women's suffrage campaign and seceded to set up a separate Liberal women's organisation. Liberal women, including Millicent Fawcett, were heavily involved in organising the NUWSS in 1897, and the NUWSS's structure followed the federal model adopted by the Liberals a decade earlier.

When Emmeline convened her meeting at Nelson Street she had in mind forming an independent group of Labour women along these lines rather than launching a new suffrage campaign. Composed almost wholly of ILP women (at this stage even Christabel was a member), the WSPU was a tiny group which saw itself entirely as part of the labour movement. It was initially intended to call it the Women's Labour Representation Committee, which would have mirrored the LRC's name and clearly indicated the group's function and connection, but Christabel, who at this time was infatuated with Eva Gore-Booth and was heavily involved in Eva and Esther's suffrage work, pointed out that this could cause confusion with the recently established Lancashire and Cheshire Women Textile and Other Workers' Representation Committee. As a result the name was changed to the WSPU. Rachel Scott, the first secretary, wrote to the *Labour Leader* to explain the new organisation:

> its objects being to secure for women complete equality with men, both social and political ... We ask you to publish this appeal to all women Socialists to join in this movement to press upon the party and the community the urgent need of giving to women the vote, in order that they may take their share in the work of social emancipation.[26]

For the first couple of years the WSPU sent speakers to ILP meetings around the north of England, held meetings and lobbied the movement. At the 1904 ILP conference Emmeline scored a significant victory by getting a resolution passed which demanded that Labour MPs introduce a private members' bill to give women the vote on a limited suffrage basis. This they did in August 1904, but the bill did not get past its very early stages. Private members' bills were (and are) a very uncertain way of achieving change, and the opportunity to bring them in was allocated, then as now, by ballot. Keir Hardie agreed to try to get another suffrage bill into the Commons but was not successful in the ballot. However, the Liberal MP John Bamford Slack drew the fourteenth place; his wife Alice and sister Agnes were both members of the NUWSS and he was persuaded to use his opportunity to introduce a bill 'To enable women to vote at Parliamentary elections.' This he duly did, listing Hardie and David Shackleton as supporters. From the fate of this bill suffrage campaigners of all complexions drew important lessons, and Emmeline and Christabel Pankhurst, in particular, began to think of new ways of pursuing the cause.

The Bill was discussed by the House of Commons on 12 May 1905. Hundreds of suffrage campaigners, including Emmeline, Eva Gore-Booth and Isabella Ford, gathered outside and in the lobby to await the outcome. But anti-suffrage MPs were determined that the bill should fail, and by talking at great length about the intricacies of the Vehicles' Lights Bill which preceded it they delayed the start of the franchise debate. When it did finally begin it was easily talked out. As this news filtered through to the crowd waiting outside there was rising anger. Keir Hardie came out to meet the women and, according to Sylvia Pankhurst, the police allowed them to hold a meeting in 'Broad Sanctuary by the Abbey Gates, where, as people with a grievance generally do, we passed a resolution of indignation against the government'.[27]

At much the same time there was a demonstration in Manchester of men protesting against the dropping of a bill to help the unemployed. This turned violent, and there were arrests. The government found a formula which enabled it to reinstate the bill without losing face. The lesson of this was not lost on the Pankhursts and their supporters, and Christabel, in particular, began to consider ways in which the suffrage campaign, which had rapidly become her sole focus, could be brought more forcefully to public attention.

◆ ◆ ◆ ◆ ◆

By the early years of the century, Margaret Bondfield was firmly established as a trade unionist of repute. She was still one of a tiny number of women union officials, and her union was small and organising in a difficult industry, but she worked hard and toured the country relentlessly to address meetings, support strikes and recruit members. Although still a member of the SDF, her energies were devoted almost entirely to fighting low pay and exploitative employers, and she was particularly concerned about the iniquitous living-in system used by most shops, which, she said, 'robbed the assistant, whether man or woman, of the sense of personal responsibility which is developed by ordering and controlling one's own life'.[28] She was a popular public speaker and much in demand at a variety of meetings, but the union always came first.

In March 1902 the Shop Assistants' Union conference was held in Newcastle. When Margaret arrived at the station she was met from the train by a 21-year-old woman with whom she struck up a friendship which was to change both their lives and have a major effect on the trade union and labour movements. Mary Macarthur was the daughter of a shopkeeper from Ayr. As a precocious teenager she had experienced a difficult time at school, clashing with authority and yearning after nameless ambitions. 'I must, I will, be famous,' she once wrote in her diary,[29] with no idea of what she would be famous for. In her late teens she was a member of the Conservative Primrose League. At the age of 20 she discovered trade unionism and from that point on devoted her life to the organisation and support of women workers. She had charm, intelligence and a charismatic personality, and Margaret was profoundly attracted. The journalist (and later Labour MP) Mary Agnes Hamilton said that Mary Macarthur was 'the romance of [Margaret's] life – and a very real romance'.[30] The exact nature of their relationship cannot now be known, but the impact of each woman upon the other was both immediate and lasting. In 1903 Mary left Glasgow and came to London, arriving at Margaret's flat over the union's offices in Gower Street where she would live for the first two years of her London life.

The most immediate task was to find Mary a suitable job and, as luck would have it, the secretary of the WTUL had just resigned. Emilia Dilke, as president, was faced with the task of finding a new secretary, and tried to persuade Margaret Bondfield to do it. Margaret was reluctant to leave the union, but suggested Mary. Emilia Dilke and her niece, Gertrude Tuckwell, who would shortly take over as the WTUL's president, were sceptical, but agreed to see her. When they did, they accepted her without hesitation. In her book about women and trade unionism Mary Agnes Hamilton recorded that they saw:

somebody quite out of the common … there was, when she lit up, a fire in her eye and a quality in her brain that were remarkable. Here was a crusader. Lady Dilke recognised her as Margaret Bondfield had done. This girl might make difficulties; in fact she did; but she would assuredly also make things hum; in fact she did.[31]

The WTUL spent a considerable amount of time lobbying MPs of all parties to try to get industrial legislation changed and improved. Part of Mary's job was to go through the reports of factory inspectors and find cases which would support the need for better protection or support for women workers. Margaret described her as:

storming down to the House [of Commons] or to the department and by the very strength of her indignation [getting] the necessary official investigation started. She put courage and life into those in a position to offer evidence, but who without her support would have been terrified to do so.[32]

Despite their passionate commitment to the advancement of women, neither Margaret Bondfield nor Mary Macarthur involved themselves in any of the female franchise campaigns. Both suffragists and socialists believed that the particular reforms they advocated would in and of themselves remake the world for whichever group of excluded people they fought. Emmeline Pankhurst, for instance, dismissed Keir Hardie's unfailing work for the unemployed by observing that 'when women had the vote such matters would be dealt with as a matter of course'.[33] But trade unionists such as Margaret and Mary were trying to right present wrongs, and were not prepared to defer redress until either capitalism had fallen or the franchise had been extended. This was one of the things which made trade unionism so attractive to radical or progressive middle-class women. The unions themselves often remained resistant to involving them, but both the WTUL and the WIC welcomed women of all classes and gave them the opportunity to use their skills in creative and constructive ways which could result in real improvements to working-class lives. They also understood that, as Isabella Ford said, 'the industrial woman must work out her freedom for herself … We cannot possibly know her needs as well as she herself can.'[34]

The WIC was the successor body to the Women's Trade Union Association (WTUA), which had been set up by Clementina Black in the wake of the 1888 matchworkers' strike. Emma Paterson's Women's Protective and Provident League (WPPL), which had become the WTUL in 1891, had worked to set up women's trade unions in a number of parts of the country, but had found very little success in the East End of London. The WTUA had been intended to rectify this, but all the usual problems of organising poorly paid women who were more afraid of losing their jobs than they were of anything else soon made themselves felt. Unions were started easily enough, but very few of them lasted for more than a few months. The depressed state of the economy in the early 1890s meant that unions generally were losing members, and there was very little support available for an organisation which seemed to be swimming against the tide. In 1894 the WTUA was converted into the WIC with a specific remit to educate, research and campaign. Middle-class women such as Margaret MacDonald, whose statistical brain was perfect for this type of work, were heavily involved, but so too were such working-class women as Margaret Bondfield, who understood the necessity of being able to convince decision makers with facts as well as rhetoric. Between 1896 and 1898 Margaret Bondfield researched shop conditions for the WIC, getting jobs in a variety of establishments ranging from fashionable stores in the West End to corner shops in the East End, and she remained an active supporter, years later helping to carry out research for Clementina Black's seminal report, *Married Women's Work* (1915).

Between 1894 and 1914 the WIC investigated nearly 120 different trades, campaigned on issues such as homeworking, sweated labour and technical education for girls, and was an early advocate for a minimum wage. Many Labour and trade union women worked with it or in it, themselves acquiring skills and experience which they transferred elsewhere. But the WIC also provided a meeting place for women from different campaigns: limited franchise suffragists worked with adultists, trade unionists with academics, socialists with Liberals. The WIC's reports and publications were submitted to parliamentary committees and inquiries and on more than one occasion forced changes in the law. It ran girls' clubs and educational projects, even offering childcare at a school it set up to provide women with technical skills.

One of the women who joined the WIC early in its life was Mary Fenton Macpherson. Mary is one of the many women whose impact on the development of the labour movement was considerable, but who has to be hunted through the diaries, letters and reminiscences of other people. She was born in Kent in 1859, and her father was a pilot of the Cinque Ports. She had a good education, attending Bedford College in London where, after her death, her husband founded an essay prize in her name.[35] She studied languages and later worked as a translator at socialist and trade union conferences. She joined the ILP and during the 1890s worked with Keir Hardie on the *Labour Leader*, effectively becoming his personal assistant and office manager. In 1897 she married Fenton Macpherson, a Scottish journalist and author who was then based in Paris. At this point, judging by the census records, she discreetly reduced her age by about seven years so as to obscure the fact that she was older than him. He went on to have a very successful career as a foreign correspondent, and the Macphersons were friends of both Robert Blatchford and Keir Hardie, no mean feat considering the degree to which Blatchford and Hardie disliked one another. Mary must also have had some local government experience, since in 1901 she was the author of a Fabian pamphlet, *Municipal Fire Insurance*.[36]

At about this time she started writing a 'Women's Corner' feature in the *Railway Review*, the journal of the Amalgamated Society of Railway Servants (ASRS). Although the railways did not directly employ many women the union did have an organisation for the female relatives of railwaymen called the Railway Women's Guild. This is usually quoted as the inspiration for Mary Macpherson's attempts to persuade the LRC to set up some kind of women's structure, but given her connections and background it seems much more likely that she knew about the WSPU and objected to its heavy focus on suffrage. Emmeline's success in persuading the ILP to adopt a limited suffrage position had led directly to the setting up in the autumn of 1904 of the Adult Suffrage Society, the prime movers behind which were the working-class activists Ada Nield Chew and Jennie Baker, and in which Mary was involved. Ada was particularly critical of the limited suffrage demand and had conducted a spirited debate with Christabel Pankhurst through the columns of the *Clarion*, during the course of which she maintained that a limited franchise would mean that:

> The entire class of wealthy women would be enfranchised, that the great body of working women, married or single, would be voteless still, and that to give wealthy women a vote would mean that they, voting naturally in their own interests, would help to swamp the vote of the enlightened working man, who is trying to get Labour men into Parliament.[37]

Christabel took issue with this and wrote putting the WSPU and ILP point of view, but Ada was not convinced, replying that she could only support legislation which would 'enable a man or woman to vote simply because they are man or woman, not because they are more fortunate financially than their fellow men and women'.[38]

Ada described the Adult Suffrage Society as 'Socialist women who are disgusted with the ILP's betrayal of working women's interests'.[39] The ILP's NAC, of which Isabella Ford and Emmeline Pankhurst were members, decided to counter this by demonstrating that the limited franchise would actually benefit many working women. They asked branches to assess the number of 'working women' on the municipal electoral roll; when the answer came back that the limited franchise could give the vote to over 80 per cent of working-class women they unsurprisingly felt themselves to be vindicated. But this survey was hardly scientific. Only about 50 of the ILP's 300 branches responded and, as Jennie Baker pointed out, each branch had been left to use its own definition of the term 'working woman' so that in some places shopkeepers and small business women had been included, while elsewhere they had not.[40]

Meanwhile Mary Macpherson had been thinking about the need for a Labour women's organisation which was allied to the LRC and which was not immersed solely in the suffrage struggle. She envisaged a body which would be able to provide support at election time, but she also wanted to get beyond the relatively narrow community of trade union and socialist women and reach women working in unorganised trades, or who were even, for one reason or another, out of employment altogether. This would have the effect, she hoped, of increasing male support for Labour as well as preparing women for the inevitable day when they, too, would have the vote.

Because Mary envisaged the women's organisation as working in tandem with, and in effect being an integral part of, the LRC, she was careful not to be precipitate, but to try to take the existing structures with her. In November 1904 she wrote to Ramsay MacDonald asking him to support and advise her on her proposal. She wanted, she said, to set up an organisation which would be 'for the purpose of assisting all Labour candidates, ... of furthering the interests of the Labour movement, and of spreading its principles among women generally'.[41] She also said that she had the support of Margaret Bondfield, and it seems unlikely that she had not also discussed the possibility with other Labour women, including Mary Macarthur and Margaret MacDonald.

The initial plan was to get a resolution through an organisation which was affiliated to the LRC's executive, whose formal approval would then give the new organisation some authority. However, this proved more easily said than done, and in the end it fell to Ramsay MacDonald to raise the matter at the LRC's executive. Not for the last time, the executive took a different view of how women should organise from that expressed by the women themselves. They were willing to countenance a local women's organisation where the LRC was standing a candidate in the looming general election, but not a national body in its own right acting independently of men. This recommendation was agreed by the 1905 LRC conference without debate.

Probably with a due sense of irritation, Mary Macpherson now went back to the women's trade unions where she had started, and the Railway Women's Guild passed a resolution which was clear in its intent: 'This Conference requests the national L.R.C. to take immediate steps to form a national Labour Women's Committee and directs our Secretary to send these resolutions to the L.R.C.'[42]

Mary duly sent this to MacDonald in his capacity as secretary of the LRC. Whether with her knowledge and agreement or not, he sent it to the ILP executive, followed by that of the LRC. Quite why he did this is not clear, but he may have thought that, as there was some overlap between the two executives, getting it through the ILP would mean that the LRC would follow. But this strategy was not quite as successful as might have been hoped. The ILP's reply to Mary in early October 1905 was distinctly unhelpful, and couched in terms all too familiar to women both before and since:

> [The Executive] desires to point out, however, that women are eligible for membership of all local LRCs and that they may be elected as representatives to its annual conference and may sit on its executive committee. Some of us think that women ought to make more use than they do of these opportunities to take part in our work.[43]

For the LRC's executive the priority was being better prepared for an election than they had been in 1900. For the moment, the matter was closed.

Meanwhile, Christabel Pankhurst had decided to take direct action to force people to recognise women's demands. On Friday, 13 October 1905, she and her friend Annie Kenney attended a Liberal rally at the Free Trade Hall in Manchester. The speakers were prominent Liberals and included Winston Churchill, who was fiercely opposed to women's suffrage. After the speeches had been made questions were invited, and Annie called out 'Will the Liberal government give votes to women?' The question was not answered, so Christabel repeated it. Both women unfurled a banner that said 'Votes for Women'. They were ejected from the meeting, but not detained. Christabel therefore spat at a policeman, and both were arrested, charged, and sent to prison, Christabel for a week and Annie for three days. The first phase of the militant campaign had begun.

∞ 6 ∞

Breakthrough

The 1906 general election was remarkable in a number of ways: the Liberal Party gained the last landslide victory of its history; the Labour Representation Committee (LRC) saw a record number of its candidates elected; the Leader of the Conservative Party – and erstwhile Prime Minister – lost his seat; and Councillor Thorley Smith became the first Women's Suffrage candidate in British history.

In July 1904 the catchily named Lancashire and Cheshire Women Textile and Other Workers' Representation Committee had announced its intention of finding and fielding a candidate at the next general election. Wigan was a Conservative seat whose 8,800-strong electorate (about 15 per cent of the total adult population) included cotton-workers, miners and railwaymen. Most Lancashire seats of a similar type were already being nursed by Labour candidates, but in Wigan there did not seem to be one. This made it an obvious choice for the Representation Committee. The Wigan Trades Council, which had not been consulted about Smith's candidacy, refused to back him, and he did not have support from the LRC nationally. Other Labour people did rally to him, with Emmeline Pankhurst and others speaking for him and Keir Hardie writing to the local paper to urge electors to vote for him.

Remarkably, Smith came in second, behind the Conservative candidate but ahead of the Liberal. Had either Smith or the Liberal not stood, their combined votes would have been enough to defeat the Tory in a seat he had held for 20 years. The absence of a Labour candidate in Manchester East, for instance, certainly contributed to the Liberal defeat of Arthur Balfour, the Conservative leader and former prime minister, who had represented it for 20 years. The absence of Liberal candidates in other seats unquestionably helped Labour candidates to win. In fact anyone looking at the pattern of LRC and Liberal candidates in some parts of the country could only admire their mutual self-discipline. In 31

119

of the 50 seats in which Labour candidates stood there was no Liberal candidate. Elsewhere, Liberal candidates appeared to have been given a clear run. It was all very neat.

Electoral neatness of this kind, however, does not usually happen by accident, and in this case it was the result of a mutually convenient deal and some patient back-room negotiation. In February 1903, Ramsay MacDonald had held a private meeting with the Liberal MP Jesse Herbert. Herbert was acting on behalf of the Liberal chief whip, Herbert Gladstone. MacDonald was acting on behalf of the executive of the LRC, most of whose members knew what was going on, but most of whom were also doing their best to pretend not to. They were pursuing a high-risk strategy which, if it failed, could destroy the LRC's credibility and jeopardise its electoral future. In the event, it paid off and led to Labour's electoral breakthrough in 1906.

The LRC had been set up very clearly as a vehicle, not only to get working-class representatives into Parliament, but also to get them to work together independently of the Liberals once they arrived. So far, however, they had found only limited success in getting MPs elected, and it was clear to both Hardie and MacDonald that they would need to find a new way of unpicking the electoral lock. Hence they embarked on a strategy which, at first sight, seemed a complete negation of everything the LRC stood for. This is often referred to as a 'secret' plan run almost as a lone-wolf project by MacDonald, but in fact the possibility of some kind of deal with the Liberals had been publicly discussed for years. In 1899, in a joint essay, Hardie and MacDonald had noted that 'independence is not isolation' and that, provided that the Independent Labour Party (ILP)'s freedom was protected, co-operation with 'kindred sections' could be possible.[1] In 1902 MacDonald observed in the *Daily News* (a paper owned by George Cadbury, who had funded some LRC by-election candidates' expenses), that:

> What Labour candidates have to strive for is to get the Liberal Associations to decide to stand aside … In that way Labour can draw votes from … that growing mass of electors known as the Tory working men.[2]

A pact on seats with the Liberals was one part of the plan; local organisations which were strong enough to mount winning campaigns and resilient enough to regroup when they lost were the other. Everything

MacDonald had learned, particularly from the long stream of by-elections in which Labour had found mixed success, had convinced him of the need both to build local capacity and to neutralise the Liberals.

The issue of party organisation was one which had been occupying the Liberal and the Conservative parties for some years. The system of employing barristers to challenge individual electors' rights to register had evolved into a system of professional agents, and in time these began to run election campaigns as well as manage registration. The Conservative Party had set up its Central Office in 1870, while the National Liberal Federation (NLF) had followed in 1877. By the end of the 1890s the Liberals had a very effective electoral organisation which was able to deliver results at every level. Both parties now trained and supported full-time staff to one degree or another, and both could generally rely on local networks and structures which knew how to run campaigns. It was during this period, as the franchise widened and more and more voters had to be signed up, that the concept of door-to-door canvassing emerged; the canvass cards that Ramsay MacDonald had sent Margaret during their courtship were principally a mechanism for registering electors.

Compared with the organisational resources upon which both the old parties could call, the LRC appeared to be in a very unpromising position. Trades councils and ILP branches were growing but they tended to be heavily focused on the local, and to be resistant to external influence or interference. As he travelled around the country and observed by-election outcomes, MacDonald came to understand the importance of developing strong Labour grass-roots organisation where the Liberals on the ground were frail. Immediately after the 1900 general election he and Hardie began to think about how the Liberals' internal problems over free trade and imperialism could best be exploited, and as a result in December 1900 the National Executive Committee (NEC) approved a report which proposed that the Party persuade other parties (in reality, the Liberals) to stand aside for them in one of the seats in two-member constituencies. The second prong of the plan was to ramp up the LRC's presence and organisation specifically in those constituencies where it had fielded a candidate in 1900, thus building upon work already done and making Labour look like a stronger electoral prospect by the time the next election arrived. The NEC approved this also, so that MacDonald and Hardie now had a mandate both to negotiate nationally and build locally. In the case of the first they took this perhaps a little further than the NEC intended, but almost certainly not without at least its tacit consent.

Indeed, it is because the strategy was being openly discussed that the Parliamentary Committee of the Trades Union Congress (TUC), still wedded to its Liberal affiliations, was able to engage in manoeuvres to try to thwart it. The Parliamentary Committee and the National Democratic League held a conference in July 1902 aimed at arriving at the 'allocation of an agreed number of constituencies to Labour nominees'.[3] Hardie declined to have anything to do with this enterprise, and not without reason. The National Democratic League was a curious alliance of radical Liberals and Social Democratic Federation (SDF) members, most of whom were associated with the London Trades Council or similar bodies. In fact neither this nor similar initiatives succeeded, and gradually over the next decade trade union allegiances were transferred to Labour, but relationships with the Liberals remained a thorny question. Meanwhile MacDonald worked hard to build up an election fund which would be able to guarantee independence for Labour candidates, and it is a measure of his success that in 1903 he was able to tell Jesse Herbert that not only could the LRC command the votes of a million men (undoubtedly an exaggeration), but also that it had an election war chest of over £100,000 (which indeed was probably more or less the case). Moreover, the NEC had agreed to pay its MPs £200 a year – not a fortune, but certainly enough to enable them to live. This would take the edge off the need to look for work elsewhere as well as enable the LRC executive to insist on a fair degree of loyalty to it rather than local groups or trade unions.

From the Liberal point of view also there were advantages to a deal. They did not yet see the LRC as competitors, much less as their nemesis. Most Liberal leaders thought that the LRC could provide a useful addition to their armoury, particularly when it came to helping to get more working-class men elected, an objective of which, at least in theory, they were broadly in favour. They assumed that most trade union men would retain their traditional loyalties, and that the LRC's contribution would be to bring through a wider range of men including the journalists and intellectuals of the ILP. Many trade unionists would have agreed with this analysis, and even as the 1906 election approached very few people expected the LRC to develop into a distinct political party in its own right.

During 1905 it had become increasingly clear that the Conservative government was in serious difficulties. When Christabel Pankhurst and Annie Kenney disrupted the Liberal rally in Manchester they did so because there was a general expectation that the Liberals would soon be forming a government. Arthur Balfour's Tory administration had managed to offend a wide range of people, and when it collapsed at the end of the year it was mourned by almost nobody. Balfour had hoped that an incoming minority Liberal administration would try to cling on to power despite its own internal differences, but instead the new prime minister, Herbert Asquith, chose to strike while the iron was hot and call an election immediately.

The key economic issue was free trade, a debate which had been going on for decades and was deeply polarising across the political spectrum. Free trade was favoured by Liberals and socialists on the grounds that it was believed to ensure cheap food. Britain had not been self-sufficient in food terms for many years, and relied heavily upon large imports from both its colonies and the Americas. The imposition of tariffs would increase prices for the poorest sections of society, and tariffs were therefore widely opposed. But businesses, employers and many Conservatives favoured tariff reform, which they thought would enable them to protect British interests against foreign competition. The Conservative government had only been able to remain in office because of support from the Liberal Unionists led by Joseph Chamberlain. In 1903, however, he suddenly announced a complete reversal of his position on tariff reform, and this caused a further upheaval, with many free trade Liberal Unionists returning to the Liberal fold. Some free trade Conservatives, including Winston Churchill, defected to the Liberals. The Conservative administration thus found its position untenable, although the unstable situation overall meant that there was some justice for Balfour's belief that the Liberals would not find government easy either. He certainly did not seem to anticipate the scale of the Tory collapse that was coming.

Had free trade been his government's only problem it might have survived, but it had managed to make enemies on other fronts, too. Its refusal to do anything to ameliorate the Taff Vale judgment had alienated Conservative trade unionists, of which there were many, particularly in cotton towns such as Wigan where the Tories were traditionally strong. The 1902 Education Act had introduced taxpayer support for religious schools which had infuriated Liberals, Nonconformists and socialists who believed that the state should not be funding sectarian education. The South African War had dragged on for much longer than anyone had anticipated, and the death toll had been unacceptably high. The frenzied jingoism of the first years of the century had given way to a more pragmatic imperialism. Moreover, the import of bonded Chinese labour into the South African mines had infuriated both Liberals (on the grounds that bonded labour was akin to slavery, and ought not to be allowed) and socialists and trade unionists (on the same grounds but also because they thought the jobs should have gone to free British workers as part of a solution to the unemployment problem). Balfour's hubris in simply handing the government over to Asquith rather than going to the country served to seal his party's electoral fate even more effectively.

The LRC's 50 candidates were almost all either in two-member seats where the Labour candidate was in harness with a Liberal, or in constituencies where there was no Liberal candidate at all. It had not been easy to enforce the discipline required to achieve this, and it proved impossible to prevent some Labour men from standing anyway as independents. Ultimately, the pact's success lay not in the numbers of candidates it facilitated, but in the electoral breakthrough it made possible. Labour's path to government in the 1920s was initially laid by the Liberal Party's complacency in 1906.

Polling day in Wigan was on 17 January, but the election as a whole was spread across a month between 12 January and 8 February. As in 1900, each constituency or town had its own polling day or days and results were declared as and when they were available. It must have been clear fairly early on, however, that what became known as the Gladstone–MacDonald pact was going to pay off. Hardie, Shackleton and Henderson were all re-elected. MacDonald himself won in Leicester, Philip Snowden in Blackburn and Fred Jowett in Bradford West. In all, 29 of the LRC's 50 candidates were elected. It was a remarkable achievement, and it remains the last occasion upon which a new political party broke through into the existing political system on such a scale within only a few years of its founding.

The LRC's election address was even shorter than it had been in 1900, and effectively claimed that Labour representation in Parliament would solve most of the most pressing problems of the working class. Its opening sentences were a clear challenge to the existing order:

> This election is to decide whether or not Labour is to be fairly represented in Parliament. The House of Commons is supposed to be the people's House, and yet the people are not there. Landlords, employers, lawyers, brewers, and financiers are there in force. Why not Labour?[4]

Problems (unemployment, housing, rents, unfair taxation and poverty in both childhood and old age) were clearly identified, but no solutions other than voting Labour were proposed. Towards the end of the 240-word document the LRC attacked Conservative economic protectionism, but otherwise the causes of the election were left more or less untouched. The text was intended to form the basis of each of the 50 LRC candidates' election addresses, and concluded with an appeal to the working class to 'forget all the political differences which have kept you apart in the past' and vote for the LRC. There was no mention of suffrage, either adult or female.

Not surprisingly, the Women's Social and Political Union (WSPU) considered this inadequate, and wrote to the LRC:

> [We] wish to protest to the LRC on account of the omission in your manifesto of the immediate necessity of giving the Parliamentary Franchise to women ... our Association will not work for any candidate at the coming election, unless pledged to support this measure.[5]

The LRC's assistant secretary, Jim Middleton, responded that the LRC conference had agreed to support the adult suffrage position, and that the limited franchise demand could not therefore be included in the manifesto. The WSPU, he said, was welcome to approach individual candidates, but 'it is now almost too late in the day for any effective services to be rendered to them in their fight'.[6]

The Conservative Party, which had won a landslide victory in 1900 with over 50 per cent of the vote, lost more than half of its seats in 1906, including those of the majority of the former Cabinet. Joseph Chamberlain's Liberal Unionists, who had kept the Tory government in power, lost almost two-thirds of their MPs and never recovered as a significant political force, finally merging with the Conservatives in 1912. The Liberals, on the other hand, despite not fielding candidates in over 30 constituencies, increased their seat tally by more than 200 and secured a majority of over 60.[7] The LRC's success was seen in some quarters as hugely significant; an anonymous writer in *The Times* remarked that 'the Labour Party has introduced into the organism of middle-class Liberalism, now perhaps for the last time triumphant, the seed of inevitable disintegration'.[8] It did indeed turn out to be the last election at which the Liberal Party won a clear majority of both votes and seats, and though Liberalism still had electoral successes to come, it never again achieved a victory of such crushing proportions.

Once the election was over, the newly elected Labour MPs had to form themselves into an official group in Parliament. This meant that they would have to elect someone to act as their leader, a role that had never been required before. Ramsay MacDonald wrote to Margaret during the election that 'there is a great log rolling going on about the leadership of the party, and I am rather afraid that personal jealousies combined with trade union exclusiveness may produce nasty feelings and unfortunate results'.[9] His apprehensions turned out to be fully justified at the first meeting of the new Parliamentary Labour Party (PLP).

The chairman of the PLP would effectively be the leader of the Party, and the MPs assembled on 15 February had the choice of two candidates. They were very different men, and presented the Party with a choice of both style and substance. Keir Hardie was an articulate and charismatic campaigner who had carried the parliamentary Labour banner more or less single-handedly through the lean years prior to 1906, and he could reasonably have expected to be elected without serious opposition. However, he was not well liked by the unions, and all but six of the new PLP were trade unionists. His opponent, David Shackleton, was the victor of the Clitheroe campaign who had a strong trade union background and was a careful, methodical man with an eye for organisation and detail. Presented with this choice, the PLP split down the middle and the result was a dead heat with one abstention. The ballot had to be run again, and this time the abstainer – believed to have been Ramsay MacDonald – voted. Hardie won by one vote.

Arthur Henderson was chosen as chief whip and MacDonald himself as secretary. The LRC conference, held a few days later, agreed to change the organisation's name to the Labour Party. Soon by-election victories began to add to the number of MPs, bringing in the Gas Workers' leader Pete Curran and the mercurial Victor Grayson, both of whom went on to present challenges to Hardie and MacDonald in different ways.[10]

Wigan was the only constituency in which suffragists ran a candidate of their own, but women were active throughout the campaign. The WSPU was still, at least nominally, an organisation of Labour women, and although Christabel Pankhurst had already begun to view the LRC as an enemy, her mother continued to regard many Labour people as friends and allies, spending much of the election helping Keir Hardie in Merthyr Tydfil. Other WSPU members enjoyed themselves energetically disrupting the campaigns of various Liberal candidates and, in particular, working against Winston Churchill in Manchester. The National Union of Women's Suffrage

Societies (NUWSS), on the other hand, had a policy of supporting any candidate, regardless of party, which supported women's suffrage.

Meanwhile Mary Fenton Macpherson had continued to pursue the question of setting up a separate, but connected, Labour women's organisation. The creation of the Women's Labour League (WLL) is sometimes explained as Ramsay MacDonald's idea for something which would give Margaret and other Labour wives something to do. However, it is rare for men to put the energy into creating women's organisations (though they may, and often do, seek to control or take them over once they exist) and, in any case, Margaret was not at all the sort of woman to add yet another layer of activity to her already busy life unless she believed in it. But there are a number of other reasons why she should have chosen to take it on. It must already have been clear by 1906 that the WSPU was not going to be able to serve as a Labour women's organisation for much longer. Some trade union women such as Mary Macarthur and Mary Macpherson also had a number of concerns about the activities of Eva Gore-Booth and Esther Roper in Lancashire and Cheshire and Sylvia Pankhurst in the East End of London. They thought that a working-class movement so heavily focused on suffrage as the solution to women's problems would distract from the question of working women's economic oppression. Both before and during the election there was discussion in a number of quarters about what to do next, including 'a long consultation with Mrs Macdonald [sic], [after which] the executive committee of the Railway Women's Guild called a preliminary meeting of women'.[11]

Margaret's contribution was important not just because of her husband. She was a powerful and influential personality who focused on action rather than endless debate. The feminist Ray (Rachel) Strachey described her as:

> a woman who combined in a remarkable measure the gifts of wisdom, sympathy and enthusiasm. [She] was one of those pioneers whose work for the women's movement was invaluable. She opposed the 'feminists' indeed on some points of policy, and devoted herself mainly to improving the conditions of working women, and to strengthening their position within the Labour Party; but she was one with them in her aims and ideals, and in her enthusiastic support of the Suffrage.[12]

For several years Margaret was a member of the NUWSS's executive, but her primary focus was on women's social and economic position, and, in particular, on alleviating conditions for the worst-paid, most-exploited women of all. By 1906 she had four children under the age of eight but this did not seem to slow her down. Every few weeks she and Ramsay held open house on Sunday afternoons, when anyone could come and meet whoever else happened to be there. Sylvia Pankhurst, who conceded that despite her private income Margaret was 'not exempt from the troubles encountered by mothers who busy themselves with activities outside their household affairs despite a growing family of small children', recorded that:

> On one occasion, when some of us were taking off our coats in a bedroom of the flat, we heard a slight cry from the bed, and found that the guests had been piling their coats on top of two little Macdonalds [sic] asleep.[13]

The little MacDonalds themselves had many tales to tell of the informal nature of their upbringing. Their parents do not seem to have believed in many of the normal Edwardian formalities of bourgeois child-rearing, and the children ran around the flat barefoot, travelled across London alone and played riotously in the green square outside the house. Since their parents believed that religion was a personal matter, none of the children was baptised. Unlike many middle-class families they had no bathroom, and the children were washed in a basin on the kitchen table. There were no live-in servants, either, although the charwoman, Mrs Gurling, doubled as a nanny sometimes when both parents were away. There also seems to have been a certain amount of shared responsibility for childcare, with Ramsay having some or all of the children with him when Margaret was busy. Years later their second child, Malcolm, recalled that:

> the Labour Representation Committee's executive meetings were held in our ... living room. We children were not banished from the place on these occasions. Provided we stayed silent, we could squat on the floor playing games, drawing and painting sketches or reading books, while the founders of Britain's Labour Movement conducted their serious discussions round a table in the middle of the room.[14]

Often one or other parent was absent for days or even weeks on political business: in the run-up to the 1906 election, while Ramsay was away campaigning in Leicester, Margaret observed that Malcolm 'can't quite get out of his head that his father is sleeping at the office just now and looked [in the Labour Party's headquarters in Victoria Street] for the bed'.[15]

Stories of Margaret's haphazard housekeeping were legion, as were tales of her lack of attention to her personal appearance. 'They were very untidy,' recalled one of MacDonald's secretaries, '– he wasn't, I think he wanted to be tidy, but she never.'[16] Other guests remembered having to clear tables of jumbles of papers, toys and hairbrushes before meetings could be held, and the MacDonalds' eldest daughter, Ishbel, remarked that she had been told that:

> the only person who could concentrate at some of these committee meetings was my mother; and we used to be crawling around under their feet, under the table, while they were sitting in committee. Or we'd be crying in the corner. And my mother just went on with the business.[17]

Sometimes the informality was too much even for people who were used to it: Margaret Bondfield at one stage invited Margaret MacDonald to meet at her rooms rather than Lincoln's Inn Fields since 'then I can be sure of getting your attention! What with babies, telephones and callers, etc. that is impossible at your home.'[18]

The MacDonalds' flat was the obvious place at which to hold the inaugural meeting of the WLL, which was set for 9 March 1906. Even then the business was not without controversy. The original calling notice said that the organisation would operate 'in connection with the Labour Party'. Ramsay MacDonald wrote on behalf of the executive to object; members did not want people to be under the misapprehension that the women would have any formal link with the main Party. Given that the meeting was to be held in the MacDonald dining room at the same table around which the LRC's executive had met for several years it is hard to know what the breakfast conversations on the subject between the MacDonalds might have been.

The women who attended this first meeting were a mix of LRC wives, trade unionists and suffrage activists. Many were already members of the WSPU. Margaret was elected as the president, Mary Macpherson became the secretary, and the WLL was formally founded. An interim executive was established which included Mary Macarthur, Margaret's friend Mary Middleton (the wife of James Middleton, the Labour Party's

assistant secretary) as well as suffrage campaigners Charlotte Despard
and Mary Gawthorpe. Membership was set at twopence a year for the
national organisation. Local branches were to be allowed to set their own
subscription levels, but the main aim was to make membership accessible
to as wide a range of women as possible. The League decided to ignore
the Party executive's objections and identified its purpose as 'To form an
organisation of women to work for independent Labour representation in
connection with the Labour Party.'[19]

Plans were laid to hold a conference in Leicester later that year, but
first there was a meeting to launch the Central London branch in April.
Speakers included Margaret Bondfield, Mary Macpherson, Ramsay
MacDonald and Keir Hardie. Sylvia Pankhurst later suggested that Hardie
actually opposed the formation of the WLL on the grounds that:

> He saw it as a rival to the WSPU, moreover he wanted the women
> to be in the Labour Party and the Socialist societies on equal terms
> with men. ... He approved the WSPU as a fighting body, created for
> obtaining the vote, and to raise the status of women.[20]

There is little other evidence for his opposition, however, and most
people referred to him as being positively supportive. Indeed, until the
WSPU split from the ILP many women were comfortably members of
both organisations, and the divisions between them which are seen now
with the advantage of hindsight were not necessarily obvious to contemporaries. The NUWSS supported the early stages of the militant WSPU
campaign: in 1906 Millicent Fawcett made public statements in support of
ten women – including Mary Gawthorpe and Sylvia and Adela Pankhurst
– arrested and imprisoned in Holloway, and in December she helped to
organise a banquet at the Savoy to mark their release. Once the more
violent phases of the WSPU's campaign developed, however, this support
weakened, although suffragists across the board opposed the use of forced
feeding against hunger-striking prisoners, and communication between
the various suffrage and women's groups was maintained throughout the
campaign.

In June 1906 the WLL held its first conference in Leicester. It was open
to all women who had joined since March, and 'about 150'[21] attended,
including a WSPU contingent headed by Isabella Ford and Emmeline
Pethick-Lawrence, who was the WSPU's treasurer and fundraiser. She
moved a resolution to add a commitment to the limited suffrage option

to the League's aims, but this was heavily defeated. Isabella then moved the addition of the words 'and to obtain direct representation of women in parliament and on local bodies'. This was passed.[22] Neither Isabella nor Emmeline Pethick-Lawrence remained involved with the WLL after this conference, although both retained a commitment to Labour itself. Isabella continued her political activism through the ILP, and Emmeline Pethick-Lawrence eventually became one of the Party's first female parliamentary candidates in 1918.

The WLL's original objectives had not committed it to being a specifically socialist body, but within a year the Central London branch – to which Margaret MacDonald belonged – put down a resolution to the League's 1907 conference to add the words 'By the education of working women in the principle of socialism, to endeavour to hasten the overthrow of the present capitalist system of production.'[23] Since many trade unionists were not socialists and, indeed, were actively hostile to socialism itself, this would have had the effect of distancing the WLL from a whole strand of the movement. Mary Macpherson thought the resolution unhelpful, writing to Margaret MacDonald that 'as our sole object is to work with the Labour Party, so we ought to keep in step'. Margaret, however, was inclined to try to get the branch to withdraw it; it had been passed in her absence, when she was on a tour of the colonies with her husband, and she may well have felt irritated by it. Mary Macpherson thought that 'it would be a pity if it passed … but it is always dangerous to stifle resolutions'.[24] In the end Margaret wrote to Mary Middleton, who was soon to take over from Mary Macpherson as secretary, that:

> we may as well let it go as it stands. Of course, I do not mean to stifle
> it in any case, as it would be on the agenda, and would be discussed
> by branches and anyone could move it, even if the Central London
> Representative did not … I daresay we shall worry through.[25]

To the extent that the proposal was withdrawn they did, but it flagged up the problem that there was not entire agreement about what kind of political animal the WLL should be. Its leaders and members were wholly committed to the Labour Party, and saw it as the working classes' only hope of changing the system through democratic processes, but they also wanted to remain independent. The experience of setting up the WLL had shown them very clearly that male sympathy did not always translate into action, and they were strongly of the view that the WLL should remain separate, exercising influence, organising for victory, but not being subsumed. Identifying the League too closely with any one of the different elements which composed the Party would lessen that influence, and would leave the League more vulnerable to the inevitable shifts of power and opinion.

In 1907 Mary Macpherson stood down as secretary, although she remained a member of the executive. The new secretary was Mary Middleton, the wife of the Party's assistant secretary and Margaret MacDonald's closest friend. Between them, these two women represented both of the main strands from which Labour in its early years was drawn. Margaret was a middle-class intellectual who had received every advantage in life; Mary was a Scottish miner's daughter whose formal education had been cut short before her teenage years. Although she had been a clever child, and had thought of being a teacher, there was not enough money to allow her to stay at school, and after her family moved to Workington in Cumbria she went into service as a housemaid at the age of 12. Despite this, however, she continued to educate herself for years afterwards, reading anything she could lay her hands on and attending local clubs and societies on her days off. In 1900, at the age of 30, she married Jim Middleton, a journalist on a local paper and a member of the ILP. They moved to London, where Middleton found work with the LRC and Mary met Margaret MacDonald. When she took over the secretaryship of the WLL she had no administrative experience, but her eye for detail, coupled with the skill with which she dealt with difficult people, 'piloted [the WLL] through difficulties which threatened to swamp it'.[26] Outside her research Margaret had no eye for administrative detail and she could be intimidating, but Mary was both efficient and approachable, and she appreciated the range of women's activity in a way that perhaps the more high-profile members did not.

Together, Margaret MacDonald and Mary Middleton presided over the WLL's early years. It thrived at least in part because they nurtured rather than controlled it, and in this Mary's firm hand on the administrative tiller, efficient but not intrusive, set the tone.

Many women saw the WLL almost as the Labour Party's social conscience, particularly when it came to issues of particular concern to women. The first conference passed resolutions on, among other things, the inspection of dangerous trades, old age pensions, the abolition of sweated labour, the treatment of indigenous South Africans, and free school meals, while Katharine Bruce Glasier, chairing the 1908 WLL conference, observed that:

> the League could teach the men of [women's] needs as women, of the needs of the children, and of the needs of the homes of the people if they were really to be homes and not merely work kitchens and sleeping dens.

The separate nature of the League meant that it could be more welcoming to a wider range of women than the Party itself could. Both the Party and the trade unions believed that they treated women equally, but the absence of an individual membership scheme, coupled with the very masculine nature of organised labour and the difficulties of organising women workers, meant that in practice they did not. As Lisbeth Simm noted in 1908:

> some old trade unionists are afraid we shall spoil the homes by taking women out to meetings ... the great answer up here is 'women's place is in the home' – women have heard it so often that they have begun to believe it now.[27]

The question of the League's affiliation to the Labour Party was considered at the 1907 conference, and a request was sent to the Party's executive. In what may have been seen as a humorous move, the Party executive had decided to send to the WLL conference the one member who had voted against sending a fraternal delegate. John Hodge, who was secretary of the steel smelters' union, protested vigorously in terms that will be familiar to activists everywhere – it was his only free Saturday for ages, and wouldn't someone else be better suited?

Once he got to the conference he declared himself a supporter, although he was bound to advise them that they would not be able to affiliate unless the Party's constitution was amended to allow it. Nevertheless, they duly wrote to the executive requesting affiliation, and pointing out that the League provided 'a channel for the expression of the special knowledge and experience of women of the Party'.[28] The executive ducked the problem by replying that it 'declined to comment on letters from societies not already affiliated'.[29] By 1908 this position seemed to have softened, perhaps partly because the League had worked hard in by-elections, but also perhaps partly because there was now less dual membership with the

WSPU, which by then had finally cut its ties with Labour. For whatever reason, the WLL and the executive agreed to recommend rule changes to the Party's conference. By this time the League's own executive had learned a thing or two about dealing with the Party, and its conference was held in Hull at the same time and in the same venue as Labour's. This gave them the opportunity to network and lobby, so that by the time the resolution got to the floor of conference there was general support for it. Unfortunately, however, the Central London branch had convinced the WLL to accept affiliation from women's organisations who were not eligible to affiliate to the Labour Party, which left the door open for either the WSPU, or the breakaway Women's Freedom League, to affiliate at some future date. This seriously weakened the WLL's position with the Party, so that the constitutional amendment which was actually passed represented a pale imitation of what affiliation should have been. The WLL would not be able to vote on questions concerning the use of the political fund (including candidates), nor participate in the election of the NEC. There was no intention of giving women a representative of their own: they could send a delegate to conference, but would otherwise be restricted to a support role for the men. Should the WLL bring itself into compliance with the Party's rules (i.e. cease to accept affiliations from non-Labour organisations), it would be allowed to reapply on the same basis as a trades council.

This fudge was far from ideal but it was also partially self-inflicted, and the WLL accepted it. At least it had now been recognised by the Party, and it also had the freedom to develop along its own separate lines. Meanwhile the Labour Party had done the minimum that could be required of it, and could continue to focus on the problems posed by its new status as a parliamentary organisation.

◆ ◆ ◆ ◆ ◆

Keir Hardie had been chosen to lead the new PLP but his dislike of Parliament was well known, as was his disinclination for the more tedious parts of political life. He often found it hard to find common ground with people he disagreed with, and although he, MacDonald, Philip Snowden and John Bruce Glasier (known as the 'Big Four') worked together and were friends for years, they also had a considerable capacity for rubbing one another up the wrong way. On public platforms Hardie was inspirational, but in the corridors of Westminster, as the leader of a disputatious party, his touch was less certain. The 30 members of the PLP were not accustomed to operating as a team,[30] and Hardie was not by nature always a team player himself. The new MPs had come from different parts of the movement, and had different objectives, and while they could unite around issues such as Taff Vale they were more fluid in their approach to other issues. There was no tradition of parliamentary discipline, and Arthur Henderson, as the first chief whip, was more or less having to invent the role as he went along, adopting a style of avuncular coercion which earned him the nickname 'Uncle Arthur'. The government's large majority, and the relatively small number of Labour MPs, meant that getting anything done required negotiation and persuasion as much as impressive speech-making. Labour members such as David Shackleton still held strong Liberal sympathies, while others were more socialist in their approach, and a few even managed to adhere to both. Keeping all the elements of the Party together, as well as achieving some of its core objectives in Parliament, was going to be challenging.

Despite all this, Labour did score some successes in the first session in 1906, most notably in relation to the Trade Disputes Act. The Liberal Party had promised to deal with the Taff Vale problem and, following debate in the Cabinet, produced a Bill intended to do that. However, its contents were the result of a fudge between the prime minister, Campbell-Bannerman, who understood that Taff Vale was driving Liberal trade unionists into Labour arms, and the home secretary, H. H. Asquith, who saw them more from the employers' point of view. To the annoyance of the Labour Party the Bill still allowed employers to sue trade unions for damages following a strike and, while it would have mitigated some of the more drastic effects of the Taff Vale judgment, it did not in any way give the unions as organisations the rights they had been seeking. David Shackleton promptly went to work to produce an alternative Bill which Walter Hudson, the MP for Newcastle-upon-Tyne and former senior official of the Amalgamated Society of Railway Servants (ASRS), introduced as a private members' bill. The government's Attorney General was scathing about it in his advice to the government, and was therefore astounded when Campbell-Bannerman rose to his feet to support it. Despite further arguments within the government, Labour's Bill got through the legislative process more or less intact, even surviving the expected mangling in the House of Lords, then still a body with considerable legislative teeth. For the first time in history the right to strike was enshrined in law.

The Trade Disputes Act of 1906 constitutes the Labour Party's earliest significant parliamentary hit, and demonstrated to critics both inside and outside the Party that it was possible to achieve real progress within a democratic system, even when the Party had no real power. Certainly the infant Labour Party had some luck when proposing it which it did not subsequently encounter with other legislation: the Cabinet was divided over what should be done, while the House of Lords, which might have been expected to be more hostile, was distracted by limbering up exercises for its forthcoming battles with the Commons and did not pay the Bill the attention it might otherwise have done. Despite this, however, the Act represented a significant triumph, and an exemplar of what the detailed work of people such as Shackleton, combined with the oratorical skills of Hardie and others, could achieve.

The success with this Act served to demonstrate to the trade unions that the Party was worth supporting, and affiliations again began to increase. There had been a view in some quarters that only socialist organisations should be allowed to seek affiliation, and, then as now, very few unions would have met this criterion. Clearer heads at the top of the movement understood that this purist line would be problematic. Ramsay MacDonald, whose pragmatism was unpopular in some quarters, saw co-operation and compromise as a necessity if there was to be any progress. Others believed adherence to socialist principles to be more important than electoral or parliamentary success. MacDonald and Hardie were beginning to think that despite its success in 1906 the Liberal Party's days were numbered, and even some Liberals were starting to oppose any extension of the franchise on the grounds that working-class men, in particular, might vote Labour. Even if Labour could not form a government it might be able at some point to hold the balance of power, but to do that effectively it needed both to survive and have functioning parliamentary relationships.

Thus it was disappointing that, despite the strong start, cracks soon started to appear within the PLP. The government produced very little legislation for that session, which gave Labour scant opportunity for influencing government policy – or, more to the point, to be seen to be influencing it. Worse, some of the issues which did come to the surface were hugely divisive for socialists, and none more so than the fraught question of education.

For decades, education had been seen as one of the most fundamental issues when it came to improving the lives and opportunities of

1.   Emma Paterson. This picture hung over Mary Macarthur's
desk at the National Federation of Women Workers.

2. The inaugural Independent Labour Party National Administrative Council, Bradford, 1893. Katharine Conway is seated behind the Secretary, Shaw Maxwell.

3. Clementina Black.

4. Margaret MacDonald.

5. Margaret Bondfield.

6.   Women's Labour League Conference, Hull, 1907. Front row: (l to r) unknown, Margaret Bondfield, Katharine Bruce Glasier, Margaret MacDonald, Mary Middleton, unknown. Second row: Mary Gawthorpe (third from left without hat), Charlotte Despard, Ethel Snowden, Mary Macarthur, Minnie Nodin, unknown.

7.   Isabella Ford.

8. Mary Macarthur addressing a strike meeting of box-makers in Trafalgar Square, 1908.

9. Women chain-makers at work in the Black Country, 1910.

10. Mary Middleton, Mary Macarthur and Margaret Bondfield on the platform at the Women's Labour League Conference, Newport, 1910.

11. Katharine Bruce Glasier speaking at a Women's Labour League meeting, c.1910. (L to r) Katharine Bruce Glasier, Mary Middleton, Minnie Nodin, Sister Kerrison, Marion Phillips, Mary Macarthur, Marion Curran.

12.   Marion Phillips at work in the Women's Labour League office (*c*.1913) under a photograph of Margaret MacDonald.

all sections of the working class. There was a certain degree of political consensus about this, but considerable disagreement on how to put good intentions into effect. In 1902 the Conservative government had passed a highly controversial Education Act, one of the effects of which was to fund denominational religious education in schools. Opposition to this was a contributory factor in the Conservative defeat, and Campbell-Bannerman's Liberal government came in committed to changing it.

Soon after the election the Liberal government duly published an Education Bill which provided that public funds could only be used to provide non-denominational education. Predictably, there was substantial opposition from some of the churches and the Conservatives, and argument rumbled on for months until the House of Lords finally killed the bill off. But the controversy provided one of the earliest instances of the PLP being at odds with much of its membership, and much of the membership being at odds with itself. Even within the PLP there was not complete agreement: James O'Grady, the MP for Leeds East, had many Catholics among his constituents and fought strenuously for them to retain the right to subsidised education. Across the north of England working-class Catholic communities from Liverpool to Sunderland objected to the Labour line, and in the north-west this spilled over into seat losses when Labour did badly in local elections as Catholic voters went back to the Conservatives. Local ILP branches and LRCs blamed the PLP in London for their troubles.

Parliamentary by-elections were also a source of conflict. Between February and December 1906 alone there were 22[31] and close to a hundred between 1906 and 1910. However, the Labour Party stood candidates in relatively few. This was partly because resources were limited, but also because the leadership was still wary of forcing direct electoral confrontations with a resurgent Liberal Party. Local ILP branches and LRCs did not always agree with this strategy, however, and within months of the general election there was a dispute in Colne Valley in Yorkshire when, despite the NEC's decision not to support a candidate, local members insisted on running Victor Grayson. Grayson was a gifted and charismatic public speaker with little regard for authority, and his election and subsequent parliamentary career, though meteoric, widened rather than narrowed the points of difference, particularly over issues such as unemployment.

MacDonald and his assistant, Jim Middleton, spent much of their time trying to resolve various local rows over candidates. Often one or other of them had to go in person to try to resolve matters: for example, in 1908

MacDonald went to mediate in Newcastle taking his four-year-old son David with him. 'The meeting decided by 21 to 7 to fight,' he wrote to Margaret, 'and its resolution has to be confirmed or otherwise tonight … [David] and I have solemn afternoon walks and many parcels are being made up for Londing [sic]'.[32]

But it was the by-election in Cockermouth in 1906 that sparked the major row within the ILP which led to proposals to expel the Pankhursts. The Labour candidate, Robert Smillie, was not particularly supportive of women's suffrage and clearly unprepared for the advent of the WSPU, who, in the persons of Christabel Pankhurst and Annie Kenney, not only took him to task but also refused to support him. It was not a seat Labour was likely to win, and in fact they did not, but the WSPU's stance caused huge controversy. Christabel was persuaded to agree not to repeat the offence, and the Manchester and Salford branch of the ILP voted against expulsion, but suspicion now followed the WSPU at every election. In May 1907 there was some controversy over their attitude in a by-election in Wimbledon, and Edith How Martyn rather tartly informed the ILP that she 'should like to point out even if your view of our action were correct, that [the WSPU] exists not to carry out any particular policy, but to do whatever we think best to remove the sex disability'.[33] The whole relationship was now very strained, and though Emmeline would probably have preferred to keep it going for as long as possible, Christabel was made of sterner stuff and a rift became inevitable. Ever the peacemaker, Isabella Ford tried to heal the breach but by the end of the year it was clearly a lost cause.

In April 1907 both Emmeline and Christabel resigned from the ILP. Sylvia and her youngest sister, Adela,[34] remained members with Sylvia in particular continuing to organise working women, a class from which her mother and older sister were becoming ever more alienated. Worse was to follow. Emmeline and Christabel's autocratic leadership demanded an almost military level of obedience, as well as loyalty to the WSPU and to them personally above everything else. When Emmeline unilaterally abolished the WSPU's democratic structure and cancelled its annual conference it was a step too far for some Labour women, and Charlotte Despard, Teresa Billington-Greig, Edith How Martyn and others left to form the Women's Freedom League (WFL). The debate over the split was played out at length in the columns of the *Labour Leader*. The Middlesbrough socialist and feminist Marion Coates Hanson, who had run the independent Labour candidate George Lansbury's election campaign in the town (in the process converting him to the suffrage cause), wrote:

> The future action of women with respect to candidates for Parliament seems to me to depend entirely upon the amount of enthusiasm of political parties for the reform which women demand. So far no political party has shown the necessary amount of enthusiasm. We disagree with Mrs Pankhurst purely on the ground that she, like the Liberal government, has taxed us, and would prevent us from being represented. We favour a democracy, she, an autocracy. We wish to hear the voice of our branches; she desires that the few shall rule despotically. We have suffered so under manmade laws, we do not intend to permit a section of women to stand in the same position towards us. ... We merely ask Mrs Pankhurst to carry into effect amongst our women what she asks the Government to do with respect to women generally.[35]

The new WFL was also a militant group, but it was more flexible about the question of support for political parties. Some WSPU women such as Emmeline Pethick-Lawrence remained Labour supporters and even ILP members, but the WSPU as a whole became increasingly hostile. Other Labour women began to reduce their involvement in the Party because of its resolutely adultist stance. Isabella Ford stood down from the ILP's National Administrative Council (NAC) and got herself elected instead to the executive of the NUWSS on the grounds that 'we who are in the Women's Suffrage Party have all agreed to put our cause before everything else and to fight for it first'.[36]

The WFL might have been less hostile to Labour, but its dislike of the adultist campaign was as great as the WSPU's. In December 1907 a public debate was held between Margaret Bondfield and Teresa Billington-Greig, a Lancashire teacher and founder member of the WFL. She was an able public speaker and put the limited suffrage case with eloquence. She contended that 'the gravest bar to real democracy, to true national self-government, exists in the sex disability, and that this should first of all be abolished'.[37] Women had no power to alter the existing property-based franchise and would only be in a position to abolish it when they had the vote. Moreover, the women who would be enfranchised by the vote on the same basis as men were 'entitled to the vote now, and no-one has the moral right to deny it to them'. Finally, she believed that although 'the number of women [who would be enfranchised] is non-essential, luckily it happens that the great majority would be working class women'.

Margaret Bondfield agreed 'absolutely on the main principle – that women should be allowed to vote; we are both agreed that women should be allowed to vote at the earliest opportunity', but pointed out that the current franchise legislation was unsatisfactory, and that married women would not get the vote under the limited franchise proposal then before Parliament. But what made her truly indignant was the often-made suggestion that:

> we merely bring forward our proposals in order to block the way for the removal of the sex-equality bar. Of course, you are all entitled to your own opinions, but as one who has worked strenuously for Adult Suffrage, I absolutely and emphatically deny that. I work for Adult Suffrage because I believe it is the quickest way to establish real sex-equality.

Teresa Billington-Greig had suggested that even if only six women were enfranchised, they would be able to enfranchise the rest. Margaret rejected this on the grounds that:

> Mrs Billington-Grieg [sic] … goes on to say that we have no right to stop these six women enfranchising themselves. I say we do not. What we do oppose, and what we must emphatically protest against, is that these six women should use the bulk of working-class opinion to enfranchise themselves. I have always said in my speeches and in my conversation that these women who believe in the 'same terms as men' Bill have a perfect right to go on working for that Bill, and I say good luck to them, and may they get it! But don't let them come and tell me that they are working for my class.

When a vote was taken Teresa Billington-Greig's position won the day, but not by a great margin. The wider debate – between different suffrage positions, and within both the Labour and the suffrage movements – was to go on for another 20 years until equal voting rights were finally achieved in 1928.

❀ 7 ❀

Suffrage and Sweating

In 1908 both the Labour Party and the Liberal government found themselves with new leaders. Both were significant and in different ways both ushered in new phases for their parties.

In Labour's case, the change followed Keir Hardie's resignation as chairman of the Parliamentary Labour Party (PLP). His increasing restiveness in the post had been accompanied by rumbling dissatisfaction on the part of many of his colleagues. Ramsay MacDonald was irritated by his failure to take the parliamentary responsibilities of leadership more seriously, while Hardie himself felt that his views were ignored and that his real work lay outside the House of Commons. Even Independent Labour Party (ILP) colleagues such as Philip Snowden began to feel that some kind of crisis was inevitable. Hardie's leadership, he wrote privately, was 'a hopeless failure' because 'He seems completely absorbed with the suffragettes. I can assure you there is intense dissatisfaction amongst the ILP members. I doubt if he would get two votes if the leadership were voted upon today.'[1]

The PLP was proving tricky to manage on a number of levels, but that was not the only problem the leadership faced. Hardie's support for Victor Grayson in the Colne Valley by-election had been seen as unhelpful while, fairly or otherwise, there was a belief in some quarters that, had he wanted to, he could have prevented or mitigated the Women's Social and Political Union (WSPU)'s actions in Cockermouth. It was all too easy to see why people thought that he was disproportionately committed to the limited suffrage cause, and this came to a head at the Labour Party conference in Belfast in 1907. One of the major issues discussed – controversial then as now – was the degree to which MPs should be bound by Conference decisions. The parliamentary leadership had a very clear line: Conference decisions were advisory only and the PLP had to have the freedom to act as it saw fit. Given that the Party was made up of two separate socialist and trade unionist strands, Hardie argued, there had to be some give and take. 'There must,' he said, 'be some free play between the two sections. Otherwise they were in for a spill.'[2] Delegates agreed with him, and the leadership's position was passed by a comfortable margin. There was also a victory for them on the question of whether the Labour Party should be a specifically socialist organisation, on which Conference agreed a neutral position. Delegates even decided against making it compulsory for all members to join trade unions.

But the debate on suffrage turned into a major row, with Hardie strongly opposing a move to mandate the PLP to vote against a limited suffrage bill. Not only did he argue against the principle of being bound by Conference, he also put a positive case for a limited suffrage based on a property qualification. Not surprisingly, he was forcefully opposed by women delegates as well as men: Mabel Hope of the Postal Telegraphs Clerks' Association, who was also a founder member of the Women's Labour League (WLL) and a member of its executive, told him that although she had some respect for the campaign for women's suffrage 'they had created a sex antagonism instead of a class antagonism and it was contrary to the spirit of socialism'.[3]

Hardie's position was comprehensively defeated, and the Party retained its commitment to universal suffrage. At the end of the conference he made a closing speech as leader and shocked delegates by threatening to resign from the Party if they insisted on binding him to vote for universal suffrage. He said that he 'could not be untrue to his principles, and he would have to [resign] in order to remove the stigma of women being accounted unfit for political citizenship'. This was a staggering announcement and not surprisingly served to reinforce the general impression that he was committed to suffrage over socialism. In the event the PLP arrived at a compromise by which they agreed that suffrage was a matter of conscience and members should therefore be allowed a free vote. This was the first time that such a device had been used and formed the precedent upon which the current rules around conscience votes are still based. Embarrassment on this occasion had been avoided, but the whole episode was an indication of how little wedded Hardie was to formal leadership of the Party.

During the rest of 1907 things continued to unravel. Hardie himself reconsidered his position on suffrage and by March had come around to the view that there was, after all, something to be said for the adultist case. Unfortunately, he chose an appearance on a platform with Emmeline Pankhurst to announce this, and she was predictably furious. Then a few weeks later there was another pitched battle at the ILP conference in Derby. The ILP agreed to stick with its support for limited suffrage, but when Hardie wanted to send a telegram of congratulation to Christabel Pankhurst on her release from prison, women such as Margaret MacDonald were incensed because it seemed that he was supporting women who were undermining the Party against those who worked hard for it. Soon after this Hardie was ill and went home to Scotland to recuperate. In July he departed for a tour of the colonies, writing late in the year to say that he would not be standing for re-election as leader. He wanted to be free to speak out on the issues he cared about, and did not believe that he could do that as chairman of the PLP.

Despite a view that David Shackleton should take over, it was Arthur Henderson who stepped into the breach. In some ways he was as unlike Hardie as it was possible to be, but this turned out to be a mixed blessing. Hardie had (usually) been able to take the ILP with him even if the unions were suspicious; in Henderson's case it was the other way around. ILP members, already unhappy over the Party's parliamentary performance, thought Henderson was too close to the Liberals, too prone to compromise, and too much in the unions' pocket. Since his salary was paid by the Friendly Society of Ironfounders this was hardly surprising, but at a time when MPs were not salaried most were paid by their unions as well as receiving a small stipend from the Labour Party. Payment of MPs from the public purse would be a step towards opening politics up to more working-class men but no government had shown any sign of bringing it in, and in the meantime the unions and the Party had to find the money with which to fund their representatives themselves. Complaints about Henderson's closeness to the Liberals were voiced within months of his election: John Bruce Glasier wrote to Ramsay MacDonald that Henderson 'should appear to lead the party as a fighting force, and he cannot do that if he is always side by side with Liberals on virtually Liberal platforms'.[4]

Henderson had begun his life as a Liberal and had in fact been the agent for the Liberal MP for Barnard Castle, before being elected to Parliament as an Independent Labour candidate in the by-election following his employer's death. But it was also the case that the PLP was new, inexperienced and sometimes chaotic, and it had real difficulty finding its parliamentary feet in its early days. It also faced a considerable threat in that the Liberal government was using its huge majority to move the Liberal Party leftwards onto Labour's territory. This began with Campbell-Bannerman's support of the Trade Disputes Act and the passing of the Workmen's Compensation Act in 1906, but soon moved on to other, more contentious areas. After the change of prime minister in 1908 the challenge increased, and throughout this period both Hardie and Henderson encountered problems when it came to establishing the Labour Party as a separate and distinctive political force.

A few months after Hardie's resignation the Liberals also changed their leader. In early April Henry Campbell-Bannerman resigned on health grounds and was succeeded as prime minister by H. H. Asquith.[5] Asquith was inclined to the reforming wing of the Liberal Party in some respects, but since he was also a cautious and pragmatic Yorkshireman he constructed a Cabinet which aimed to balance the various wings of his party. David Lloyd George became Chancellor of the Exchequer and the 33-year-old Winston Churchill President of the Board of Trade. Promotion to the Cabinet meant that Churchill had to seek re-election to Parliament, and a by-election was duly held in the Manchester seat he had represented since 1906. His opposition to women's suffrage was widely known, and the suffrage movement turned out with enthusiasm to campaign against him. The Manchester and Salford Women's Trades Council, led by Eva Gore-Booth and Esther Roper, also worked hard to get him defeated, this time over the question of whether or not women should be allowed to work as barmaids. This seemed an unlikely issue to motivate an all-male electorate, but for different reasons it had become a cause célèbre among both feminists and temperance campaigners. Lancashire was a temperance heartland, and Churchill was even more opposed to temperance than he was to women's suffrage. Help for the campaign to defeat him came from a variety of quarters, including Eva's older sister, Constance (Countess Markievicz). Much more ebullient and outgoing than Eva, she was already involved in Irish nationalist politics as well as the suffrage movement, and she knew how to make an impression. She drove a carriage around the constituency from the roof of which, at appropriate halts, she, Eva and others made speeches. The carriage was drawn by four white horses, and Constance was a skilled driver. At one point a man in the crowd shouted out to her, 'Can you cook a dinner?', to which Constance replied, 'Yes, can you drive a coach and four?'[6] Churchill lost the election to the Conservatives but rapidly found another seat in Dundee which allowed him to take up his cabinet post.

Historically, the Liberal Party had always believed in individual responsibility. This meant that there had been a long-standing resistance to state interference in either industry or the provision of charity or relief for the poor or unemployed. They shared the general view that people who worked hard and looked after their own families should not then be taxed in order to look after those who did not. Self-help was seen as the goal, and poverty as a choice. The more the state intervened to alleviate society's problems, the less chance there would be of individuals taking responsibility for themselves and their children. But since the 1880s there had been tension between this and a more collectivist view, and socialists, social reformers and people such as the Fabians had begun to produce some new thinking. This was accelerated by the shock discovery during the South African War that many young working-class men were unfit for military service. There was a panic about the general health of the nation and a growing realisation that if people were underfed and overworked as children they would be unlikely to make vigorous adults. But although inquiries and commissions were set up to investigate, there was very little actual progress towards acting on their findings.

For the left, individualism became code for class-based self-interest. John Bruce Glasier's remark in his diary about the 'miserable individualism'[7] of Emmeline and Christabel Pankhurst is usually quoted as an example of his opposition to women's suffrage, but it may be that he already detected their drift to the right. Collectivists were socialist; individualists were not. Collectivists saw the state as a possible provider of both economic and social solutions; traditional Liberals and, to an even greater extent, Conservatives, regarded state provision as an interference. For different reasons many working-class people were also opposed to state intervention. They were suspicious of middle-class people's philanthropy, and legal reductions in hours or other restrictions often also meant loss of income. Many industries were not unionised and could not therefore benefit from collective bargaining and trade agreements. Paupers and workers living on starvation wages were at the mercy of almost everyone, including well-meaning but often judgemental charities which constantly tried to change the behaviour of the poor by the application of more stick than carrot.

By the first decade of the twentieth century the Liberal commitment to individualism was beginning to break down, and in 1906 the incoming government had some modest proposals for a more collectivist approach. These included supporting legislation for the provision of school meals for underfed children, a measure which had been the subject of debate for decades.

There were already many small-scale charitable schemes feeding hungry children, although it was in Bradford that the first steps had been taken towards state provision. Margaret McMillan was a gifted

ILP speaker and propagandist, but her main cause was that of children's welfare. In 1894 she had been elected to the Bradford School Board and, together with Fred Jowett, had begun pioneering work to improve the health and well-being of the working-class children attending the local schools. They had brought in medical inspections, home visits, and the novel idea of encouraging teachers to communicate with parents so as to involve them in their children's education. They had also, illegally, introduced a free school meals system. The alarm engendered by the discovery of the scale of childhood malnourishment among the working classes had led to a concession in some quarters that the state might have some responsibility. In 1906 the incoming Liberal government passed the Education (Provision of Meals) Act.

Like the Old Age Pensions Act a couple of years later, what became known as the School Meals Act was a fudged attempt to resolve a deep-rooted problem without costing anyone a great deal of money. It began life as a private members' bill introduced by Tyson Wilson, a newly elected Labour MP who proposed a discretionary scheme which would allow local authorities to provide meals to needy children and to raise a halfpenny rate to cover it. The government supported it, but the Conservative Party, the House of Lords and the Charity Organisation Society, which considered itself (and was in some quarters considered) expert in matters of poverty, all opposed it. Even the national Board of Guardians opposed it, largely on the grounds that it would encourage men to abdicate their responsibilities for their children. Some peers went so far as to want to disenfranchise fathers if their children received free school meals. Many Labour members, on the other hand, wanted the scheme to be compulsory. In the end Wilson's bill got through more or less unscathed, largely because of government support. The principle of free school meals provided by the public purse had been agreed, but getting the Act implemented would prove to be much more of a challenge.

For the WLL, this was an ideal campaign. Many members were themselves engaged in local government and some were serving as Poor Law guardians and understood the problems. Once the Act was operative the League began to campaign on two fronts: first, to make the provision of free meals compulsory; and second, to get local authorities to implement a voluntary scheme. Perhaps unsurprisingly, councils were not enthusiastic. Raising a rate, however small, to cover expenditure which many people considered an interference with the normal rights and responsibilities of parents was not an attractive prospect, and there was substantial resistance. WLL branches began to try to persuade councils, particularly those with Labour members, to take action. They met with some success: Birmingham implemented the Act, as did the London County Council, and Leicester after a campaign led by Margaret MacDonald. But overall implementation was patchy and the criteria being used to determine eligibility inconsistent and sometimes discriminatory. The WLL therefore decided to launch a national campaign to amend the Act, which it did in the form of a petition, backed up by literature and lobbying. This campaign ran right up to the start of World War I, and while it was not successful in changing the law it did secure the implementation of the 1906 Act in a number of authorities and keep the issue to the forefront of Labour members' minds.

In fact, one of the major obstacles which stood in the way of progress was not the School Meals Act but the Poor Law which covered the relief of destitution generally. This dated back to 1601 but had been amended in 1834 to bring in the workhouse system, which was based on the theory that the more unpleasant destitution was made the less likely people were to allow themselves to fall into it and, as a result, the lower the burden would be for the rate- and taxpayers. Workhouses were therefore made very unpleasant indeed, and although by the end of the nineteenth century there had been some improvements, these were relative and not very effective. Families entering the workhouse were often split up so that children might have the double dislocation of losing both their home and their parents. Elderly couples were also separated, in some cases rarely seeing their spouses again before they died. Rations were limited and the work provided hard. Periodically there were horror stories in the press about the near-starvation conditions in some workhouses, but improvements were marginal and slow. In 1838 Charles Dickens' picture of workhouse life in *Oliver Twist* had shocked people, but 60 years later children were still being fed inadequate food and made to work long hours. In the 1890s a number of ILP members, including women, were elected to boards of guardians and were outraged by the conditions they found. The spectre of destitution haunted poorly paid workers, who were prepared to endure even the worst excesses of the notorious sweating system of employment rather than enter the workhouse gates or allow their children to do so.

By the turn of the century there was general agreement that something needed to be done, but very little as to what that something should be. The Labour Party wanted to see the Poor Law repealed altogether and

replaced with something much more humane and effective. In the sixth
League Leaflet the WLL explained that:

> Women are working with the Labour Party in order to secure for the
> disinherited some of those advantages in society to which their labours
> for the community fully entitle them … there need not always be men
> and women who toil all the best days of their life, and have nothing for
> themselves in their old age – widows who have to neglect their children
> in order to earn a crust of bread for them – children who are starved
> with cold and hunger.[8]

In 1905 the Conservative government set up a Royal Commission – by
no means the first – to look at the operation of the Poor Law. The commissioners included Beatrice Webb and the charity expert Helen Bosanquet,
who, between them, represented the difference between collectivist and
individualist approaches. Many Labour and Fabian women had begun
with charitable work, as had Beatrice herself, but the intractable nature of
the underlying problems had driven them to seek a more comprehensive
explanation and solution. Helen Bosanquet, on the other hand, was
active in the Charity Organisation Society which saw private giving as
capable of meeting the need and did not wish to challenge either social or
industrial systems. Her view was that:

> the one fundamental cure for poverty is to make the poorer wage-
> earners more efficient in the widest sense of the term – more efficient
> as producers, as consumers, and in all the relations of life. They could
> not then, I hold, fail of greatly increased economic prosperity. But
> that prosperity would not be at the cost of any other members of the
> community, all of whom would benefit in their degree by the greater
> efficiency of the class in question.[9]

However, Helen did think that the charity 'sector' itself was disorganised and sometimes dysfunctional. To remedy this she advocated
training for charity workers which would include an understanding of
politics and wider social and economic issues as well as the management
of casework, the relief of poverty, and basic organisational and financial
management skills. Helen was both a suffragist and a feminist, while by
1906 Beatrice had only just publicly recanted her earlier opposition to
women's suffrage and never described herself as a feminist. Helen was

a Liberal, while Beatrice had been a socialist since about 1890. Helen had been one of the first women to gain a first-class honours degree at Cambridge, while Beatrice, though widely read even as a child, had received very little formal education. Despite a mutual antipathy, it was the powerful views and obvious expertise of both women which would inform the debate about the relief of poverty and ultimately feed together into the development of the welfare state and the professionalisation of the charity sector.

The concentration over the years on the suffrage campaign has tended to mask how important campaigns around poverty were for many women at this time. Indeed, for most Labour and trade unionist women the great question was not so much the vote as the eradication of sweated labour. Millions of women (and a smaller number of men) lived on starvation wages, underpaid and exploited, living and working in conditions that were dangerous for both them and their families. Some sweated workers were employed in factories, but many worked at home, making a huge range of articles. The cheap clothes and consumer goods which were readily available in Victorian and Edwardian Britain were possible only because they were produced by women who were lucky if they earned enough to reach the breadline. Their one- or two-roomed homes – usually in overcrowded slum houses and tenements – were also their workshops. Conditions were often unhealthy and sometimes dangerous: some trades, for instance, resulted in fibres in the atmosphere which could choke the lungs of the children who had to breathe them even in their sleep. Homes were hard to keep clean and even harder to keep safe. Workers were often paid by the piece and had to buy their own tools and materials, not infrequently at an inflated price from the middleman who paid them. There was no factory inspection for homeworkers, so child labour was still common, with children coming home from school to work long hours or even missing school altogether. There were no trade unions for these women, and no possibility of collective bargaining with the hundreds of thousands of individual employers and middlemen.

The campaign to outlaw sweated labour was as old as the campaign for the women's vote, and had achieved about as much success. From time to time there had been a public outcry, but there was little political will to take on the vested interests involved. One of Margaret MacDonald's first pieces of work for the Women's Industrial Council (WIC) had been an investigation into homeworking which went on to form the basis of the Home Work Regulation Bill of 1902. Even more than a century later, the account of it still makes grim reading. As a report of the inquiry (probably written by Clementina Black) noted:

> Even the historical strikes of unskilled labourers, of dockers and seamen, difficult as they are to conduct, leave unstirred the lower depth of daily work; rank behind rank stand masses of helpless women, generally too poor and ignorant to organise, to struggle, or even to remonstrate, mere slaves to the imperious necessity of starvation wages.[10]

A decade after the report was published there had still been virtually no progress. Many people, including Beatrice and Sidney Webb, had long been of the view that a minimum wage of some kind was the only answer, but there was not entire agreement about this and there was some uncertainty about how it would be enforced. Advocates of a legal minimum believed that many employers were unlikely to do the right thing of their own accord, and that there would therefore need to be an element of compulsion. A basic level below which wages could not fall would enable more men to maintain their own families and would have the added benefit of improving children's health, too, since they would not be brought up in workshops and would have the full attention of their mothers. Opponents thought that an enforced lower level of pay could both interfere with collective bargaining and actually tempt more married women into employment. Unscrupulous employers might try to reduce male wages to the legal minimum and it would be difficult to inspect and monitor what was happening. It would be particularly difficult to inspect the huge number of small and domestic workshops, which was where the majority of sweating took place. There was also, despite periodic outbursts of guilty revulsion on the part of the public, no general will to take action. The cost of higher wages would be dearer consumer goods; clothing prices, in particular, would rise if the women who made garments were paid more. Some people thought that, since the cheapest products of sweating were consumed primarily by the poorest in society, the result of an enforced minimum wage would actually be increased poverty. Part of the problem was finding a way of convincing people that the price would be worth paying.

The Women's Trade Union League (WTUL), under the continued presidency of the formidable Emilia Dilke, had campaigned for years for an end to sweating, and her husband, Sir Charles Dilke MP, had introduced an anti-sweating bill into Parliament every year since 1900. Each time it had fallen for lack of support. Something was needed to push the genteel guilt people felt about sweating over into action, and Mary Macarthur believed she had the answer. In 1904 the German trade unions had held a very successful exhibition in Berlin to bring the evils of sweated labour home to the buying public. Mary thought that this could be replicated in London, but it needed some high-profile backing. According to her biographer, Mary Agnes Hamilton, she:

> rushed off to see the editor of the *Daily News* ... She broke in upon Mr A. G. Gardiner, who had never seen her before, and, white-faced, with burning eyes, poured forth her story and appealed for his help ... When, however, he began to suggest some difficulties ... she disarmed and alarmed him by bursting into tears.[11]

This story may or may not be apocryphal, though Mary did sometimes tend towards the dramatic. Whatever the spur, Gardiner was taken with the idea of an exhibition sponsored by his paper, and once he was on board matters moved quickly. The Sweated Industries Exhibition took place at the Queen's Hall in May 1906 and was a huge success. It was visited by over 30,000 people who, for a small fee, entered a hall laid out in a manner described by the *Daily News* as resembling a bazaar. 'But,' added the paper, 'when one looks at the price tickets it will surely seem a bazaar belonging to Dante's Inferno.'[12] At each stall real workers carried out their trades, demonstrating all the skills for which they were so grossly underpaid. Placards gave details of each individual, the trade, the rate of pay and the household expenses it had to cover. Visitors could talk to the workers and ask them questions. The exhibition was opened by royalty and attended by almost every politician of note. Lectures were given by experts such as Margaret MacDonald and Mary Macarthur; over 1,500 people turned up to be harangued by George Bernard Shaw. A handbook was produced giving harrowing details of the lives of the workers accompanied by atmospheric photographs. The National Anti-Sweating League (NASL) was established with a committee composed of a mix of people including Mary Macarthur, Clementina Black, Margaret Irwin (the erstwhile secretary of the Scottish Trades Union Congress), Keir Hardie and the Webbs, as well as the Liberal Herbert Gladstone, and Emilia Dilke's husband, Charles.

However, now that there was the prospect of real progress a serious division of opinion between Labour and trade union women came to the surface. There were two basic approaches. One was for a minimum wage to be established for each trade by means of a wages board. This idea had already been implemented in the Australian state of Victoria, where its supporters believed it had met with some success. Its opponents thought that such a scheme would be impossible to implement effectively and instead favoured a system of licensing for homeworkers which would enable the inspection of domestic as well as industrial premises. Margaret MacDonald favoured a licensing system, while Mary Macarthur supported wages boards. In 1906 she spoke in support of a resolution at the Trades Union Congress (TUC) supporting the minimum wage and calling upon Labour MPs to 'press forward this proposal in the House of Commons in the next session of Parliament'. In her speech, Mary conceded that 'the question of a legislative minimum wage really bristled with difficulties' and that they should have a scientific and properly researched basis. The resolution was passed unanimously.[13]

In the ranks of the WIC, however, there was no unanimity. Clementina Black, now in her 50s and hugely experienced, was an advocate of the minimum wage. Margaret MacDonald, who had been a WIC stalwart almost since its inception, and who very well understood what was required in terms of proper research, became more opposed the more she investigated. In late 1906 she had travelled to Australia to examine the operation of the Victoria Wages Boards for herself and she returned convinced that they were not the answer. She agreed that they would discourage women from working but, given that she tended to defend women's right to work (if not always the desirability of their exercising that right), she did not necessarily regard this as a good thing. She also thought that what was possible in the small setting of the state of Victoria was not automatically transferable to the East End of London or the back streets of York. As the anti-sweating campaign gathered pace so too did the disagreement, and in 1907 the *Labour Leader* gave Margaret MacDonald and Mary Macarthur the space to debate the issue at some length over several editions.

Margaret's case rested on four basic factors, all of which Mary Macarthur roundly rebutted. Margaret believed that the minimum wage was 'diverting our energies from the direct fight for Socialism in order to advocate a palliative which, in my opinion, would not only be ineffective, but in some cases positively harmful'.[14] Mary replied that this was effectively saying that 'the same argument must apply equally to all factory legislation … and, if we follow this line of reasoning to its logical conclusion, Socialism must be further off now than it was fifty years ago'.[15] Secondly, Margaret contended that it was not possible simply to replicate the Victorian Wages Boards in the larger and much more complex economy of Britain. She cited figures which gave the number of industrial workers in Victoria as 112,610 men and 32,669 women, while in Britain 'returns for 1899 of persons employed in factories and workshops give 1,528,881 females and 3,077,108 males'.[16] This, she argued, would make the Victorian model, where both employer and employee members of wages boards were elected by their relative sides, impossible to set up, and would thus give the Secretary of State, who would be appointing the board members, a significant power which his counterpart in Australia did not have.

Mary's response was to sweep these difficulties rather imperiously aside. Despite being very familiar indeed with the problems of organising the lowest-paid workers, she maintained that 'The Trade Unions, which, if not already in existence could, I believe, be formed, would almost certainly – as in Victoria – prove the determining factor in the election of the workers' representatives.'[17] She went on to say that wages boards would in fact encourage the development of trade unions, and that this was one of their principal attractions. The legal minimum would be underpinned by the extension of collective bargaining and the strengthening of workers' rights.

Margaret's remaining objections were about the outcomes rather than the process. She did not believe that wages boards would result in higher pay, and she thought that, since the legislation would apply industry by industry and district by district, the inconsistencies would enable unscrupulous employers simply to move their businesses to an area where it was not operative. Mary was particularly scathing about this, pointing out that this kind of thing was always said whenever any industrial legislation was proposed, and that it could always be resolved by extending wages boards as and when necessary. But on the question of whether or not the proposed system actually worked, she and Margaret were in flat disagreement. Mary wrote:

> In her concluding article, Mrs Macdonald states that Victorian experience is that the Wages Boards do not raise the average standard of the trade. This is absolutely incorrect. ... the *average* increase in the wages since the application of the Act ... was 4s 4d weekly. In no single case had there been a reduction.[18]

Given that this was not only tantamount to an accusation of dishonesty, but also a challenge to her credibility as a researcher and statistician, it is hardly surprising that Margaret took exception to it. Having seen the operation of the Victorian system at first hand she considered herself to have a level of expertise that Mary did not possess; Mary was an experienced trade union organiser who believed that she knew more about the practicalities than any researcher could, however well qualified.

The NASL was four-square behind the minimum wage and was attracting high-profile support. In June 1907 the government appointed a Select Committee on Homework which, though narrow in remit in that it did not include industrial workshops, was still an advance. Margaret gave evidence to it on behalf of the WIC, opposing wages boards and supporting a licensing system. As president of the WIC Clementina Black gave evidence supporting precisely the opposite conclusion. Clearly this split was not sustainable, and Clementina resigned soon afterwards. Mary Macarthur also gave evidence, particularly to point out that sweating was not simply an issue for homeworkers, but also for women such as the Cradley Heath chain-makers, who were so badly paid that they could not afford to join a union and therefore could not benefit from collective bargaining mechanisms. In July 1908 the Select Committee reported in favour of legally compulsory wages boards for both homeworkers and in factories and workshops. Winston Churchill, as President of the Board of Trade, was made responsible for seeing the measure through Parliament, and the Trade Boards Bill became law in 1909. It was the usual Liberal fudge; despite Labour attempts to broaden its scope it covered only four industries – bespoke tailoring, cardboard box-making, lacemaking and chain-making. The theory was that boards would develop in other industries as experience of them grew. This did indeed happen, but progress was very slow and vast swathes of industry remained untouched by minimum wages for decades to come.[19]

In the course of the debate on wages boards, considerable damage had been done to relationships between Labour women. The debate over suffrage had been temporarily resolved in 1907 with an agreement at the WLL's conference (moved by Mary Macarthur) which said that, given that there was disagreement between adult and limited suffragists, the WLL should agree to differ, leaving women:

> free to agitate the question on whatever lines appear to them best, but reaffirms the necessity for the recognition of the equality of men and women as citizens and the direct Labour representation of women in Parliament and on all local bodies.[20]

When it came to wages boards, however, no such room for manoeuvre existed. Mary Macarthur's position was heavily defeated, leaving the WLL committed to Margaret MacDonald's licensing plan. Since the first of her *Labour Leader* articles had appeared the day before she could justifiably feel pleased with the outcome. As time went on, however, and it became clear that licensing was not going to be the way forward, she became more and more entrenched in her views. In 1908 Mary Macarthur resigned temporarily from the WLL executive. An anti-sweating exhibition which the WLL had been proposing to mount did not take place, probably because the scale and now personal nature of the disagreement made it impossible.

Clementina Black's absence from the WIC did not last for long, and when she returned it was to more controversy. Margaret was already considering resigning, though Ramsay wrote to her that 'I always feel that to talk of resignation as a reason why one's opponents should not do something or another is objectionable.'[21] At this stage Margaret remained, but by July 1910 relationships had deteriorated so badly that the organisation had become a battleground. Eventually differences over the treatment of the report on married women's work,[22] combined with proposed changes to the WIC's structures, gave Margaret the opportunity she had perhaps been looking for and she resigned. Almost all of the considerable number of WLL women who were also members left with her, including Margaret Bondfield, Mary Fenton Macpherson, Mary Middleton and the WLL's treasurer, Minnie Nodin. Later the breach seems to have been healed to some extent, and in terms of the WLL was overtaken by other events, but it remained a source of sadness to Margaret for the rest of her life.

The Royal Commission on the Poor Law would eventually produce both a majority and a minority report, but it would take four years to do so and Asquith, Lloyd George and Churchill were not prepared to wait. They began to bring in the kind of legislation the trade unions and the Labour Party had been calling for for years. For Labour MPs this posed challenges; they could hardly be seen to oppose the new bills, but few of them went anywhere near as far as most of them would have liked. On the other hand, taken together, the proposals effectively began to bypass the antiquated Poor Law provisions and to introduce the idea, however hesitantly, of collectivist state responsibility for the welfare of citizens.

The first measure was the Old Age Pensions Act, which had been promised before Campbell-Bannerman's demise but was now enacted.

Although revolutionary in its way, it fell well short of a comprehensive solution to the problem. Pensions were only to be available from the age of 70 and were to be means tested. They were also hedged about with criteria and caveats. However, they were available to women as well as men, were funded centrally and, crucially, were not contributory. Ramsay MacDonald believed that 'Governments are not afraid of Socialist speeches; they are very much afraid of successful criticism in details',[23] and it was in this spirit that the PLP approached the debate. But applied to one piece of legislation after another it tended to leave Labour looking more like the left wing of the Liberal Party than a political player in its own right. ILP members, in particular, became angry and disillusioned. They thought that, given the Liberal government's huge majority, it would do the PLP no harm at all to take a properly socialist line and oppose legislation on that basis. In 1908 Ben Tillett, who had been one of the leaders of the 1889 dock strike and was now moving towards Marxism and the Social Democratic Federation (SDF), published a pamphlet called *Is the Parliamentary Labour Party a Failure?* To his mind the answer was a resounding affirmative, a view at least partly influenced by visits to Australia where Labour was perceived as having had more success. Tillett disliked Hardie, Henderson and Ramsay MacDonald and considered many members of the PLP to be of average quality at best. He accused the leaders of having 'stumped the country, subservient to the Nonconformist-Temperance-Liberal Party ignoring the great tragedy of starvation as represented by the millions unable to find work or food'.[24] Given that Hardie regarded the unemployed as his special concern, ultimately even above female suffrage, this was rather unfair, but Tillett was not alone. Victor Grayson also attacked the leadership over unemployment, and in November 1908 even refused to appear on a platform with Hardie at Holborn Town Hall. Philip Snowden and Katharine Bruce Glasier were shouted down at a meeting in Liverpool by an audience described by her husband as 'anarchists, SDP-ers, secularists, Clarionettes and Graysonites'.[25] He reflected in his diary: 'Egotism, mere self-assertion, disloyalty rampant. Its main motive is individualist – the hope of getting. Are we feeding wolves? I wonder ... I wonder ....'[26]

Matters came to a head in Edinburgh in April 1909 when the wolves gathered for the ILP conference. It was a very bad-tempered affair on all sides, although at points the leadership's groundwork beforehand seemed to be paying off. Delegates agreed by a huge margin that the ILP should remain affiliated to the Labour Party. They then agreed that ILP branches should not be allowed to run candidates without ILP and Labour Party support. Ramsay MacDonald was coming to the end of his three-year term as chairman and delegates gave a good reception to his valedictory speech. He, Hardie, Snowden and Bruce Glasier were all re-elected to the National Administrative Council (NAC), despite Bruce Glasier having resigned as editor of the *Labour Leader* in something of a huff. But then things started to go wrong. Conference effectively expressed approval of Victor Grayson's action in refusing to appear with Hardie in Holborn. The leadership was outraged. Overnight there were consultations and the following morning Hardie, MacDonald, Snowden and Bruce Glasier all resigned from the NAC to which they had just been re-elected. Appalled delegates begged them to stay and passed a resolution expressing 'emphatic confidence, personal and political'[27] in the four. They even reversed their decision on Grayson but it made no difference. The ILP's drift away from the Labour Party was beginning to accelerate.

A couple of weeks later the Chancellor of the Exchequer, David Lloyd George, introduced what would become known as the 'People's Budget'. It was, in fact, not quite as radical as he would have liked people to believe, but it was more than radical enough for the Conservative Party, the House of Lords and even some sections of the Liberal Party. It was effectively the first significant attempt by a British government to use the taxation system to redistribute wealth, and it caused a storm of protest. It included a land tax, a supertax on higher incomes, and higher death duties which were to fund welfare reforms including a state insurance system for workers. Employers of domestic servants were horrified to find that they would be required to buy national insurance stamps for their skivvies, and landowners were, for the first time, to be compelled to contribute to the national purse. Introducing it, Lloyd George said, 'This is a war Budget. It is for raising money to wage implacable warfare against poverty and squalidness.'[28]

The House of Lords refused to pass the budget on the grounds that almost none of it had been in the Liberal manifesto in 1906. Asquith and Lloyd George maintained that it did not need to have been, and that democratically elected governments had the right to govern as they saw fit, with or without the House of Lords. The inevitable result of the clash was a general election in which the 60 per cent of men who could vote were invited to decide who governed Britain. The election was to take place in January 1910, but at the end of 1909 the House of Lords dealt Labour a blow at least as serious as the Taff Vale judgment, and with even more far-reaching consequences.

The originator of the action was Walter Osborne, a railwayman, trade unionist and Liberal. His union, the Amalgamated Society of Railway Servants (ASRS), had moved the resolution at the TUC which had led to the founding of the Labour Representation Committee (LRC), but Osborne, a former Marxist, was now aggressively opposed to socialism. He particularly objected to the fact that the union imposed an extra membership levy which it gave to the Labour Party. In 1909 he sued his union to get this political levy stopped, and on 21 December the House of Lords duly obliged. It ruled that trade unions could not levy money for political purposes, and that they could not hand such monies over to the Labour Party. This effectively wiped out the Labour Party's funding stream and prevented the affiliated unions from underwriting Labour's election campaigns or organisation. It was impossible not to suspect that the Lords were acting from political malice given their opposition to what many of them regarded as a 'socialistic' budget. Even the Liberal home secretary, Winston Churchill, normally no friend to the trade union cause, later observed that:

> It is not good for trade unions that they should be brought in contact with the courts, and it is not good for the courts … where class issues are involved, and where party issues are involved, it is impossible to pretend that the courts command the same degree of general confidence. On the contrary, they do not, and a very large number of our population have been led to the opinion that they are, unconsciously, no doubt, biased.[29]

In the short term, however, nothing could be done to reverse the decision. Labour now faced a general election with the remnants of the Gladstone–MacDonald pact on seats still in place, but without the resources to back it up. Both parties were going to fight the January 1910 election on much the same ground, with only the Conservatives defending the House of Lords' position. If the Liberals could replicate their 1906 success and at the same time force Labour back from its 1906 gains, they would have a free hand to deal with the House of Lords and implement the People's Budget.

≈ 8 ≈

Changes

When the dust finally settled on the election in February 1910 it was apparent that matters had not gone well for the government. Far from having gained support for their strategy, Asquith and Lloyd George's Liberals had lost 123 seats and found themselves the largest party in a hung parliament. They now had just two seats more than Balfour's Conservatives, and would be unable to pursue the budget or the clipping of the House of Lords' wings without support from either Labour or the Irish Parliamentary Party (IPP).

Labour had done well, increasing its tally of seats to 40. There had been losses in Jarrow and in Colne Valley, where the electorate had put an end to Victor Grayson's short parliamentary career, but gains elsewhere had been encouraging. All of the party's parliamentary leaders had been re-elected, and the pact with the Liberal Party had largely held, with many Labour men being elected for two-member seats or in constituencies where there was no Liberal candidate. The Party's manifesto had been uncompromising in its demands, which included land reform, the abolition of the Poor Law, the introduction of a legal right to work and the extension of the franchise to all women and men. 'Vote for the Labour candidates,' it concluded. 'The land for the people. The wealth for the wealth producers. Down with privilege. Up with the people.'

Despite the encouraging results, however, the new Parliamentary Labour Party (PLP) was immediately plunged into a leadership election as Henderson resigned. Following some manoeuvring, the trade union leader George Barnes was chosen to replace him. The possibility of electing MacDonald was discussed, but he preferred the party-wide power of being secretary to the chair of the PLP. Besides, even before the election was over he and Margaret had been struck by a family tragedy which must have influenced his decision to some extent.

159

In late 1909 they had travelled to India to investigate various aspects of colonial rule. With the advantage of hindsight, MacDonald later said that this was the only one of their foreign travels during which Margaret felt anxious about leaving the children, and she was relieved when they were summoned home by the impending election. Ramsay was easily re-elected in Leicester in January but at the same time five-year-old David contracted diphtheria, dying on 3 February. Within days MacDonald had to go up to Scotland where his elderly mother, Annie, was ill; she died on 11 February a day after the election ended. Annie's death was a grief but not entirely unexpected; David's was devastating. A year later, on what would have been the child's sixth birthday, Ramsay wrote: 'Sometimes I feel like a lone dog in the desert howling from pain of heart … I [still] feel his warm little hand in mine.'[1] Replying to Katharine Bruce Glasier's letter of condolence, Margaret said:

> These statistics of mortality among children have become unbearable to me. I used to be able to read them in a dull scientific way, but now I seem to know the pain behind each one. It is not true that other children can make it up to you, that time heals the pain. It doesn't, it just grows worse and worse. We women must work for a world where little children will not needlessly die.[2]

The twenty-first-century view of what are often defined as 'women's issues' is that they are somehow softer than the more 'masculine' ones. Whether or not this is true now is debatable, but in the early twentieth century they were anything but. The death rates for children were horrifying, and hardly a family in the country, whatever its social or economic status, was untouched. When the very high levels of miscarriages and stillbirths are added to the toll it becomes even worse. Mary Macarthur's mother had three stillborn boys before Mary arrived, and Mary's own first child was also a stillborn boy. Margaret Bondfield and Beatrice Webb had both seen siblings die, Keir Hardie had lost a two-year-old daughter to scarlet fever, one of Emmeline Pankhurst's sons died at the age of four and the other at 20. For women living in the depths of poverty the chances of rearing living children were much lower, and *Married Women's Work*, the research for which began in 1910, lists one woman after another who had lost some or even all of her children to disease, malnutrition, the effects of pollution or industrial accidents.

Suffrage was important, but a minimum wage and cleaner air could save untold numbers of lives.

Neither the Liberal nor the Conservative Party manifesto had made any reference to suffrage, but Labour's, on the other hand, said that 'Restrictions upon the franchise, including the sex bar, must be swept away.' This essentially retained the commitment to universal adult suffrage but recognised that women were subject to an additional exclusion which should be addressed. The Conservative Party was largely (though not entirely) opposed to any extension of the franchise, while the Liberals were split, with Asquith opposed to female suffrage and Lloyd George generally disposed towards it. Labour, therefore, was slowly starting to emerge as the only party with a coherent policy on the issue, even though that policy was not the one that Hardie had favoured, and was regarded with varying degrees of disfavour by both militant and non-militant campaigners.

Meanwhile, women in the wider labour movement had come together to found the People's Suffrage Federation (PSF), which supported universal adult suffrage (now renamed the 'democratic franchise' in an attempt to mitigate the hostility many female suffragists felt to the term 'adultist'). The PSF brought together women trade unionists, the Women's Labour League (WLL) and the Women's Co-operative Guild (WCG), and tried to make the link between sectional demands for the vote and a wider commitment to the development of representative democracy and the setting of both as part of the class struggle. The WCG was one of the largest working-class women's organisations, but since the co-operative movement had not been present at the foundation of the Labour Party, and had not affiliated since, the WCG had had little direct involvement with the Party's development. However, many individual women were members of the WCG as well as the Independent Labour Party (ILP) and the WLL, and the spirit of the co-operative movement was a strong element in Labour's character. Led by the remarkable Margaret Llewelyn Davies, the WCG had a long history of involvement with the suffrage campaign, and had been looking for allies for its democratic slant on it. The PSF attracted support from all sides of the Labour and trade union movement, and its members included almost all Labour MPs.

When the February 1910 election was called the Women's Liberal Federation extracted from Asquith a promise to the effect that he would allow a free vote on the question of women's suffrage if it appeared as an amendment to a wider reform bill, and if there was public support. The National Union of Women's Suffrage Societies (NUWSS) launched a petition for which it collected signatures at polling stations;[3] over 300,000 male electors signed which, at least in the view of the NUWSS, demonstrated widespread support. The loss of the Liberal majority was therefore a blow, since although there were over 300 MPs who, during the election, had committed themselves to reform of one kind or another they could not all be relied on, and the government itself was dependent on the IPP and, to a lesser extent, Labour, to stay in office. Labour would not support a measure which did not include adult suffrage, and the IPP was generally speaking unreliable on female suffrage. It seemed unlikely, therefore, that there would be a government reform bill of any kind.

After the election a cross-party Conciliation Committee was established to draft a new Bill, which it duly produced in June. During this period, and while the Bill was under discussion, the Women's Social and Political Union (WSPU) was persuaded to halt militant action and the NUWSS continued to apply pressure to the Liberal leadership. H. N. Brailsford, a Liberal MP and supporter of women's suffrage, was the moving spirit behind both the Committee and the First Conciliation Bill which resulted. In order to secure Conservative support this proposed to enfranchise about a million mainly unmarried women on the basis of a property qualification. There had been Labour members on the Conciliation Committee and in the House the first reading of the Bill was moved by David Shackleton. Despite this, official Labour Party policy remained committed to universal suffrage, if only because the Bill would not have enfranchised many Labour women. Notwithstanding opposition from Lloyd George and Churchill, who maintained that the proposals would simply add a million Tory votes to the register, the Bill passed its first and second readings by sizeable majorities. However, Asquith then refused to give it any more parliamentary time, prompting a 300-strong delegation from the WSPU to the House of Commons on 18 November. When the women attempted to enter Parliament they were attacked by the police. Many were beaten and sexually assaulted, and there were numerous arrests. The date entered the suffragette calendar as 'Black Friday', and marked another turning point for the campaign, with the WSPU returning to militant tactics and Christabel Pankhurst, in particular, beginning to treat all men, even those who were supportive, as the enemy.

After Black Friday, Asquith announced that if the Liberal government were to be returned at the second 1910 election (due to take place at the end of the month) it would again support an extension to the franchise which would be open to amendment to include women. This was no longer enough for the WSPU, who smashed the windows of Asquith's car in Downing Street and assaulted another cabinet minister. MPs who had hitherto been supportive now distanced themselves, and communication with Asquith was curtailed. Millicent Fawcett was infuriated, writing to a colleague:

I do think these personal assaults perfectly abominable and above all extraordinarily silly. The P.M.'s statement ... was at any rate good enough to make the *Times* say the next day that it had made [women's suffrage] a question definitely before the country at this election and that if there is a Liberal majority it will be a mandate to grant suffrage to women. And then these idiots go out smashing windows and bashing ministers' hats over their eyes.[4]

When the general election at the end of 1910 produced almost the same result as that at the beginning, a new Conciliation Bill was introduced which was also duly passed by the House of Commons. Since it was basically the same Bill it was vulnerable to the same arguments, even if the people making them, such as Winston Churchill and David Lloyd George, were doing so only to wreck it. Following the Commons vote Asquith announced that although, effectively, there would be no further time available in the current session on Parliament, he would introduce a Bill to enfranchise 4 million men in the next one, and it would be possible to amend it to include women if the House wished. Millicent Fawcett and the NUWSS still thought that something might be achieved, but the Pankhursts had lost patience and organised a massive campaign of window-smashing in November. 'The argument of the broken pane of glass,' said Emmeline Pankhurst, 'is the most valuable argument in modern politics.'[5]

During the course of the debate over the Conciliation Bills the NUWSS had acquired a new secretary. Marion Phillips was an Australian who had arrived in London in 1905 at the age of 23. Despite her youth she already had a glittering academic career behind her, and had come to Britain to attend the London School of Economics (LSE) and write a doctoral thesis on colonial administration in New South Wales. She had a strong sense of both personal and social responsibility, a formidable intellect and boundless energy which was constantly looking for outlets. These she found in both academia and politics.

In 1905 the LSE was still only a decade old, but already it had begun to make a name for itself. Then as now, it focused on social sciences, economics and politics, and had begun awarding its own degrees in 1901. In 1905 it had not yet moved to its current Holborn site, but was in Adelphi Terrace near Charing Cross. This was within easy walking distance of the Houses of Parliament, and Marion took to going to hear debates in the Commons chamber. She was not favourably impressed, regarding both the Liberal and the Conservative parties as politically and morally bankrupt. At the LSE Marion had met Beatrice Webb, and in 1905 Beatrice employed her to help with research on conditions for children and widows for the Royal Commission on the Poor Law. This very quickly convinced her that socialism was the only answer to the problems, and since she liked much of what she had seen of Labour from the public gallery of the House she joined the ILP, the Fabian Society and the WLL. She also joined the NUWSS; having had a vote in Australia it must have seemed absurd to her that she should not have one in London, and she quickly became a committed campaigner. In 1910 she was about to turn 30 and was looking for a worthwhile job. She shared a house with Dr Ethel Bentham, who was a member of the WLL's executive, and by 1911 had come to support the adultist view, resigning as NUWSS secretary and accepting a post as organising secretary for the Women's Trade Union League (WTUL) to work with Gertrude Tuckwell and Mary Macarthur.

For many Labour women, and for trade union women in particular, 1910 and 1911 were to be remembered for a series of landmark strikes rather than Black Friday or Conciliation Bills from which they were excluded. One of the most famous of these was the Black Country chain-makers, but the lacemakers of Nottingham and the confectioners of the East End, as well as box-makers, glue-boilers, sweet-makers, pram builders and dozens more, were involved at one point or another. Men also took industrial action, and there were strikes on the railways, in the mines and in the printing and cotton industries among many others. Ramsay MacDonald estimated that 'In 1910 more people were on strike than there had been since the miners' dispute of 1893, and the aggregate duration of the strikes was three times the average of the preceding nine years.'[6] The strikes had various causes, and were often the culmination of a series of unresolved grievances as much as about pay itself, but there was no doubt that in many cases pay was the spur.

The struggle to organise women workers had not become any easier over the years, and by 1906 Mary Macarthur had come to the conclusion that something more effective was needed than the endless churn of small, unsustainable women's unions which continually came in and out of existence. This led to the setting up of the National Federation of Women Workers (NFWW) in 1906 to bring many different trades and workers together under one umbrella. Unions like this already existed for the men, but although some did admit women, women's interests were generally not well catered for. The NFWW was an instant success, gaining 2,000 members within the first year and absorbing small unions in a variety of trades, including the tiny women's branch of the Cradley Heath and District Hammered and Country Chainmakers' Association. Mary toured the country recruiting, advising, negotiating and supporting strikes; the trade unionist and secretary of the Anti-Sweating League, J. J. Mallon, observed that:

> Breathlessness is her dominant characteristic. She is always at top speed. She whirls from meeting to meeting, strike to strike, congress to congress; the street shouting behind the dust and rattle of her car ... She loves movement for itself, and deeds for themselves.[7]

Not surprisingly, membership of the NFWW rose rapidly until it reached somewhere in the region of 20,000 women. Precise figures are not available, and Mary was sometimes vague towards the point of mild exaggeration about the total, but there was no doubt that it was attracting women who were otherwise hard to organise and who benefited from the support it offered.

Mary's dual role with the WTUL meant that the possibility of a clash was avoided. Gertrude Tuckwell acted as president of both organisations and provided stability and a calming influence on Mary's more volatile outlook on life. Gertrude was Emilia Dilke's niece, and had worked with her for years. When Emilia died in 1904 Gertrude took over the WTUL, but she was also involved in many other industrial and social campaigns, including the Adult Suffrage Society and the fight for equal pay. Between them she and Mary made the NFWW a real powerhouse, giving it a much louder voice than its size necessarily warranted. One observer noted that 'Mary Macarthur and Miss Tuckwell wrought miracles ... they were no more than a stage army, but they said they were the women workers of Great Britain, and they made so much noise that they came to be believed.'[8]

Once the NFWW was affiliated to the Trades Union Congress (TUC), Mary attended as a delegate. Several times she had to deal with attempts to exclude women from trades where they were seen as being in competition with men. In 1909, moving an amendment to change such a resolution into one in support of equal pay she said that:

> The question is not, 'Shall the women be allowed to work in this particular trade or not?' It is, 'Shall this Congress take a sane and scientific view of the problem?' Are you going to handicap women? If you pass this resolution [to exclude women] you will not abolish the women; but you will put a weapon in the hands of those who are fighting us in our attempts to improve the women's conditions.[9]

Mary's amendment was accepted, and within a year the men found themselves confronted with the opportunity to make good their commitment to supporting women workers in what became a celebrated industrial dispute.

The 1909 Trade Boards Act, which had earlier caused so much controversy in the Women's Industrial Council (WIC) and the WLL, provided the spark for one of the earliest of a wave of strikes. It legislated for trade boards to be set up in four industries to negotiate a minimum wage appropriate to each. One of these trades provided the test case for the Act's implementation and became almost as well-known as the matchgirls' strike of over 20 years previously.

Chain-making was a Black Country industry which employed large numbers of women. As long ago as 1887, when Richard Juggins had taken on Clementina Black over the issue at the TUC, the male trade unions had wanted women excluded from it, but to no avail. Heavy chain and higher-quality small chain was made in foundries and large workshops, and did indeed largely employ men. These workplaces were unionised, paid rates achieved by collective bargaining and were covered by the relevant Factory Acts and inspection regimes. Lighter and lower-quality chain, on the other hand, could be made in small lean-to workshops using what was little more than a domestic hearth. It was hot, hard, heavy work, and women were bred to it from childhood. Mary Macarthur described babies lying in wooden boxes under the anvils screaming as they were showered with sparks. Older children huddled in the corners out of the way. Children still learned the trade, working before and after school and at weekends. Heavy work and inadequate food stunted their growth and made them prone to disease. Boys might in time graduate to the big unionised workshops, but girls would work at their domestic anvils for life.

Most women and girls toiling in these conditions were sweated labour in every sense. They worked through middlemen who brought the orders and collected the completed chain. In some cases they also supplied tools, though most women had to buy and maintain their own. Middlemen were much hated in the fight against sweating; Beatrice Webb referred to them as 'the maggot that appears in meat after decay has set in. [They are] not the cause, but one of the occasional results of the evil.'[10]

When the Trade Boards Act was passed the Black Country chain-making industry as a whole accounted for over 90 per cent of British production, making everything from the chains for the anchors on the *Titanic* to much smaller chain for use with horse traces or gate fasteners. Women chain-makers had no other skill and no other source of income; they were also paid substantially less than the men. Chain-making, however, was one of the four industries covered by the 1909 Act, if only because the owners of the large factories had lobbied to be included. This was not for any benevolent reason, but because they were concerned that the low level of sweated pay meant that there was always a danger of undercutting, which threatened profits. Combined with a depression in the chain trade in 1908 and the tendency for the chain made by sweated labour to be of poorer quality, this led to the employers hoping that the enforcement of a minimum across the industry would help them as much as their workers. They therefore set up the Chain Manufacturers' Association (CMA) to represent their interests and lobby for the industry's inclusion in the Act.

Once the Act was in force, the question of what the minimum wage should be had to be answered, and here the employers proved less enthusiastic. The Chainmaking Trade Board was established with members representing both the employers and employees and chaired by an independent person. In her capacity as secretary of the NFWW, Mary Macarthur was elected to represent the workers.

Even before the Chainmaking Trade Board first met early in 1910, the employers had begun to prepare for a fight. They had been stockpiling chain and continued to do so as they prevaricated their way through the early meetings of the Board. Mary Macarthur found this intolerable. After one particularly difficult meeting, one of the employers offered to drive her to the station to catch her train. She refused in no uncertain terms, and then had to run all the way, getting there only just in time. J. J. Mallon, with whom she was travelling to Nottingham to speak at a meeting of lacemakers, described her bursting into inconsolable tears at the injustice of the situation. 'Something like hatred moved in her for the people who, comfortable themselves, had no imagination to see the sufferings they were perpetuating.'[11]

By May, however, a rate had been agreed; at 2½d an hour it represented a significant increase for almost all of the women. There was then a three-month waiting period before the rate could be implemented, and during this time the employers 'persuaded' many women to sign forms contracting themselves out of being paid it. Many women made their mark rather than signing; despite education having been available since 1870, girls brought up under the showering sparks of their mothers' anvils had had hardly any time for school. Many were appalled when it was explained to them what they had agreed to, and very angry.

At the end of the waiting period the NFWW demanded that all the women be paid the new rate immediately. The employers promptly locked them out and the strike began. Within days more than 800 women had struck, many of whom were not actually union members. Strike payments were made immediately; one Conservative-leaning newspaper noted that it was 'pitiable that many of the women are actually better off than when they were working, for those who are members … receive 5 shillings a week'.[12] There were also handouts of food, and a milk ration for those with children, although in some cases people passed babies up and down the queue in order to claim more than they were strictly due.

As soon as the strike began, Mary Macarthur's considerable talent for publicity went into overdrive. She used every outlet available to her to raise awareness and funds, even making a little film for the new medium of the cinema. Donations, both in cash and kind, flooded in, and the strike fund reached £3,000 within weeks. People were moved by the dreadful conditions in which the women lived and worked, but they also felt that there was a principle involved. Mary Macarthur and the NFWW were trying to get the law implemented, and the employers were clearly trying to evade their responsibilities under it. On this basis even Conservative newspapers supported the strikers, and the employers found themselves isolated on the wrong side of public opinion.

The NFWW put considerable resources into Cradley Heath, including permanent organisers to support the strikers and distribute money and food. Among these was Julia Varley, whom Margaret Bondfield had described tramping from one side of the country to the other to see for herself what destitution was like. Julia had also been organising women in the Cadbury factory at Bourneville, and was the first woman to be elected to Birmingham Trades Council. After World War I she became the first

Chief Woman Organiser of the Transport and General Workers' Union (now part of Unite).

A month into the strike the annual TUC meeting was held in Sheffield, and a group of women chain-makers was invited to appeal for support from the platform. Interestingly, this is sometimes reported as the women simply silently holding up the chains they made: Mary Agnes Hamilton, for instance, observed that this 'spoke more eloquently to the silent assemblage of their better paid fellow-workers than any words could have done'.[13] In fact the TUC report records that the group was introduced by James O'Grady, the MP for East Leeds, who asked delegates to 'give this representative, Miss Nutt, who was not used to public speaking, their careful attention':

> Miss Nutt ... stepped to the front of the platform holding aloft the chain, the ends of which her companions grasped. She said 'We wish to thank you for the help you have given us, and to plead with you to help us get our price – 2½d per hour. If you only stand beside us we shall be successful. These are our friends and they all help make the chains ...'[14]

Congress expressed its full support for the women, and a collection was taken which raised over £11.

The strike lasted eight weeks, and the women won their 2½d. The strike fund had a huge surplus, which was used to build a workers' institute as well as help other strike funds, including the men in the Black Country metalworks when they themselves struck later. Mary and J. J. Mallon moved on to the lacemaking industry in Nottingham, which was also covered by a trade board and where the same kind of fight had to be gone through to secure the minimum wage. But the chain-makers had set a precedent; it was the first industry in which a legal minimum wage was set, and the first which elevated a female trade union organiser to celebrity status far beyond the Labour and trade union sphere.

◆ ◆ ◆ ◆ ◆

In Parliament, George Barnes' time as leader of the PLP was not proving a great success. As usual, the PLP was difficult to manage, resistant to discipline and divided as to what its strategy should be. Many followed MacDonald in believing that while the Liberal government was pursuing legislation which would benefit the working class it should be supported, or at any rate not actively opposed. Others took the view that Labour members were there to prosecute a form of class war and to resist all reformist legislation on principle. This divide ran through both the trade unions and the ILP, venting itself in angry exchanges at conferences and irate pamphleteering. Ben Tillett's 1908 *Is the Parliamentary Labour Party a Failure?* had been bad enough, but in 1910 four left-wing members of the ILP published a pamphlet called *Let Us Reform the Labour Party*, which argued for revolution rather than revisionism and largely blamed MacDonald for the Labour Party's perceived drift away from the socialist principles of the ILP's former years. The so-called 'Green Agenda' urged Labour MPs to oppose the Liberal government at all points. 'It is not statesmen we want in Parliament at present,' argued Russell Smart some years before co-authoring the pamphlet, 'but agitators, who will use Parliament as a platform.'[15] The authors also wanted a more aggressive approach to by-elections, with more general election candidates, and thought that if this happened Labour could be in government within eight years. They wanted more robust Party policy on unemployment and poverty, and more internal democracy in the Party itself. In one short document they articulated many of the demands that are still made in one way or another, and posed in concrete form the challenges the Party faced in turning itself into a parliamentary party rather than a pressure group.

As the year progressed it became clear that Barnes was not the man for the job. The debate over the People's Budget was now turning into a titanic constitutional battle between the Liberal government and its supporters on the one hand, and the Conservative Party and the House of Lords on the other. It was not possible for Labour MPs to stand aside from this without looking muddled. Since they had included abolition of the House of Lords in their manifesto in January they could hardly now oppose the clipping of the upper house's wings. Moreover, they actually agreed with the principle of many of the reforms the government was proposing, and knew that failure to pass them would not help the people they represented. The problem was how to support the government while remaining – and being seen to remain – separate from it, and Barnes did not possess the intellectual or political subtlety for this. Both MacDonald and Henderson did, and, although the relationship between them was usually uneasy, they took much the same view of what was needed if the Party was to survive.

Arthur Henderson, who would go on to become Labour's first cabinet minister during World War I and win the Nobel Peace Prize in 1934, was the son of a servant and a textile worker. He had started work in a foundry at the age of 12, becoming a trade union official in his 20s and moving from the Liberal Party to Labour in 1903. He combined an acute political brain with impeccable working-class credentials, but he was also a cautious and practical man with an eye for power and a strong ruthless streak. Like MacDonald, he understood that the post of Party secretary was the key to far more power than most people imagined, and like him preferred the levers of the bureaucracy to leadership. Between them they would lead the Party for 18 of the 24 years between 1908 and 1932, and their joint view would, until 1931, determine the Party's direction.

Henderson and MacDonald thought that the Liberal government should be supported when it did the right thing and opposed when it did not, and unfortunately it was in the area of opposition that Barnes failed. 'He has no energy and no grasp of policy,' wrote MacDonald in his diary. 'Our action in the House is consequently feeble, and this has a very bad effect outside the House.'[16] Others were also dissatisfied, including Philip Snowden and Will Anderson, the chair of the ILP. Pressure on MacDonald to replace Barnes began to build, but MacDonald resisted. In the autumn of 1910, as another election loomed, Barnes wrote to MacDonald to say that he was prepared to hand the chairmanship over, provided that it was to him. Ramsay wrote to Margaret:

> The Barnes message is a difficult one to answer. ... Our best men seem to be very doubtful of the future and as I can influence things in other ways I am not going to cut myself off from them ... Barnes has certainly made a mess of things – even a greater mess in the country than in Parliament. Hardie too seems to be plotting and planning and will probably put himself at the head of some movement. ... If it had been after consultation with some of us, that would have been alright, but as usual it is off his own bat. He wants to be Chairman again. Then the Secretary-ship of the party is involved. I cannot be Secretary inside and Chairman outside.[17]

By this time it was clear that there was going to have to be another general election to resolve the crisis caused by the Parliament Bill. The People's Budget had finally got through the House of Lords in April, but the Liberal government and its Labour and Irish Parliamentary Party (IPP) supporters now wanted to stop the unelected Lords being able to frustrate the will of the elected house again. The Parliament Bill would have the effect of doing this, but the problem was how to get it through the Lords, which was adamant in its opposition, and how to get the Conservative Party, also opposed, to consent. Prolonged negotiations failed to produce an agreement. As so often the sticking point was the issue of Home Rule for Ireland. The Conservatives and the Lords wanted it to be exempted from the Bill on the grounds that it was a constitutional issue, but the IPP knew that neither the Tories nor the upper house were ever likely to vote for Home Rule and therefore refused to come to an agreement on anything else unless Home Rule was included. Talks failed completely in November, and the inevitable election was scheduled for December.

For this election the Labour Party produced one of the shortest manifestos in its history. 'You are again being asked,' it began, 'to return a majority pledged to remove the House of Lords as a block in the working of our Constitution. Do it, and do it emphatically.'[18] It went on to demand action on the Osborne judgment, which was still in force, as well as on issues such as the right to work, sickness insurance, land reform, adult suffrage and Poor Law reform. It concluded:

> Let all petty differences go to the four winds. Now is the time to unite.
> The poverty of one is the poverty of all. Let those who suffer join to
> remove their suffering. It can be removed in no other way.[19]

It also made reference to the question of the payment of MPs, which had been a labour demand since Chartist times, and which had been included in the Parliament Bill. This was seen as one of the most important issues to be resolved if working-class MPs were to be able to get elected in any real numbers without being dependent on either trade unions or somebody else paying their wages.

The election began on 3 December and ran for the next three weeks. It was the last election to be held over such a period and, although nobody at the time knew it, the last to be held before the outbreak of the Great War. It resulted in virtually no change in the composition of the House of Commons, but the parties supporting the Parliament Bill did have a clear majority. The Liberals lost two seats and Labour, still under George Barnes, gained two. The Conservatives lost one and the IPP gained three. When the House of Commons reconvened in January 1911 it was to resume the debate with positions fundamentally unchanged.

What did change, however, was the leadership of the Labour Party. Partly because he believed that MacDonald was the answer to the problem, and partly because he wanted to be Party secretary, Henderson wrote to Ramsay:

> I can appreciate your position especially as opposition to any change is sure to come from Hardie and the I.L.P. members. We must face the difficulty or the Party will be broken. You ought in spite of all the drawbacks to throw yourself into the breach and accept nomination.[20]

Margaret was not enthusiastic. 'There will be more publicity, more attacks, more claims upon you,' she wrote. 'But we are doing the work of our destiny, and how silly of me it is to weary of the labour. I am not really weary; but it is heavy and one wants peace and happiness in work.'[21] At this stage she herself was not well; she was still grieving for David, her last two pregnancies had been difficult and her closest friend was suffering from a terminal illness. The prospect of having to deal with Ramsay in the throes of the inevitable troubles that leadership would bring was probably not attractive to a woman already tired and overburdened with her own work.

In mid-January 1911, MacDonald announced that he was prepared to stand. By the time of the PLP meeting on 6 February there was general agreement that he should lead, and at least a tacit view that this should be for more than a year. The constant changes in leadership had not helped to stabilise either the PLP or the Party in the country, and MacDonald insisted that he should be given time to do the job. Barnes did not stand, and MacDonald was the only candidate. He was unanimously elected and he immediately resigned the secretaryship to Henderson.

◆　◆　◆　◆　◆

In 1909, Mary Middleton had been diagnosed with cancer. This was one of the many diseases for which there was virtually no cure, and during 1910 and early 1911 she became increasingly ill. This did not deter her, however, from continuing as the WLL's secretary, and even when too weak to move from the house she maintained both interest and activity. But by the spring of 1911 it was clear that the end was coming. Margaret MacDonald took over some of the secretarial functions which, given her rather haphazard approach to administration, was not entirely successful, but she visited Mary every day that she could, bringing her new baby, Sheila, with her and discussing the League and its activities. In early 1911

the WLL conference was held in Leicester, but Mary was much too ill
to go. She wrote a letter of apology for absence which turned out to be
her valediction, and at the same time stated her philosophy of political
activism. She said:

> I think our success in the past has been achieved by the harmonious
> working together of the rank and file with what I might call the more
> brilliant intellects of the movement. To run a social successfully may
> be as useful for bringing in new members as a well written pamphlet;
> just let us all give what service we can. It may be small, but who can
> tell its usefulness.[22]

She died on 24 April 1911 at the age of just 40.

Mary Middleton had been a strong, reassuring presence among some
of the more mercurial characters in the Labour women's movement, and
her loss was felt very deeply. A commemorative booklet was produced and
plans were begun to found a mother and baby clinic in her memory. In
the booklet Mary's husband, Jim, wrote a short biography which contains
almost everything that is known about Mary; without it she would remain
just one of the many women about whom almost nothing was recorded.
Margaret MacDonald wrote of her 'courage, her conscientious drudgery
at details, and her cheery tact',[23] and affectionate tributes from Margaret
Bondfield and Katharine Bruce Glasier were published in the *Labour
Leader* and other papers.

The proposed clinic was a new, almost revolutionary idea which
ultimately fed into the creation of the National Health Service in 1948.
Dr Ethel Bentham, who was a member of the WLL executive, was
convinced that the very high death rate among working-class babies and
children was preventable. She thought that, although the provision of
medical inspection and (some) treatment for schoolchildren was desirable,
the trouble really started at birth. By the time the children who survived
started school they were already suffering from tooth decay, damaged
hearing, rickets and many other conditions which should have been
remedied or avoided. North Kensington, where poverty was endemic, had
the highest infant mortality rates in London, and it was here that the
WLL, led in this project by Ethel, decided to set up its clinic. It was to
be the first one of its kind and to set a model for what might be done in
the rest of the country. Fundraising was begun, and premises were found
in Telford Road. Once it had decided to do something the WLL tended

to move quickly, and it was planned to open the clinic by the end of the year.

For the WLL itself, there were also practical problems arising from Mary Middleton's death. It was clear that Margaret MacDonald could not continue as WLL secretary, and different arrangements were required. The answer to the problem – at least temporarily – turned out to be Margaret Bondfield, who had left the Social Democratic Federation (SDF) in about 1908 and joined the ILP. In 1909 she was elected to the WLL executive for the first time, and in April 1911 she accepted the job of organising secretary, which had been created as a permanent, salaried post.

That she was free to do this was due to changes in her personal circumstances. By 1908 she had spent a decade working for the Shop Assistants' Union and, even though she was only in her early 30s, she was almost burned out. She described herself as 'drained of vitality' and recognising 'the need for a complete change; the decision was made at once. It was like a grief and a deliverance.'[24] She and her friend, Maud Ward, went on holiday to Switzerland where Margaret was able to recuperate and regain her strength. She returned to many offers of work, but what she chose to do was become a lecturer for the ILP, a well-trodden path for socialist women but also one which could be as exhausting as trade union work. But Margaret did not leave trade unions behind; she was involved with the WTUL and the NFWW as well as the WLL and the Adult Suffrage Society. When the WLL decided to set up a paid post, Margaret was available and probably glad of the income, small though it was. She and Maud were living in lodgings at the time, and Maud was also making her living from itinerant lecturing. In 1910 they had spent five months touring the United States, speaking at meetings, factory gates and street corners to support women's trade union organisation there. They returned at the end of 1910 and were plunged straight into the general election campaign. By the spring of 1911 they were both back to lecturing, and a small but steady income must have had its attractions. From the WLL's point of view, Margaret was an ideal appointment. She was well known, had proven skills and expertise, and could lay claim to a wide network of contacts in the Labour and trade union movement. She started work immediately.

Within months, events robbed the WLL of the second of its leaders. On or about Thursday, 20 July, Margaret MacDonald cut her wedding ring finger. That day she went to Leicester as part of an investigation into the working of industrial schools, and the following morning found her back in London at a meeting of the Anglo-American Friendship Committee. From there she went to the House of Commons to meet Ramsay and together they went down to their cottage in the country for the weekend. By then her finger was throbbing and starting to swell. As they walked through summer fields towards their house she held her hand up to him and joked that it was 'protesting at its burden'.[25] Ramsay was worried, but she brushed it off. She had always been notoriously heedless about her health. The birth of her fifth child, Joan, seems to have been difficult, and after it the veteran socialist Amie Hicks had written to her: 'I do think you ought to take more care of yourself than you generally do, you must not forget your life does not belong only to yourself now ... but I must not give a lecture under the circumstances.'[26]

By Saturday night Margaret could not raise her arm to brush her hair. By Sunday morning she 'had to admit that she was ill', and Ramsay took her straight back to London. She was diagnosed with what was then usually called blood poisoning, but is now known as sepsis. For six weeks the doctors fought to save her, but without antibiotics it was more or less hopeless. She died on 8 September, aged 41.

This death, coming as it did so hard on the heels of that of Mary Middleton, was devastating, but it was also shocking because of what Margaret represented, and the outpouring of grief was considerable. Commiserations flooded in, not only from the labour movement but also internationally. At a time when death was common, this particular death seemed unusually arbitrary, and the cruelty of so small a thing as a cut finger depriving five children of their mother and Ramsay MacDonald of the wife he adored touched people across classes and political divides.

A commemorative booklet was produced for her as it had been for Mary Middleton, and the planned mother and baby clinic was renamed to celebrate them both and to commemorate 'the love they had for the small and weak and their passion to save from the wreck of life every living creature that was in danger of being crushed'.[27] In November 1911, only two months after Margaret's death, the clinic was officially opened under the aegis of Ethel Bentham and a small all-female staff to provide free preventative health care to babies and toddlers.[28] On its first day it had five patients, but this number grew rapidly. It was an instant success and WLL branches up and down the country were encouraged to campaign for similar provision in their area.

Margaret's funeral was a very public affair; her daughter Ishbel later recalled that 'The kerbs in Kingsway were lined with people standing limply to watch us pass.'[29] She also remembered being 'frightened and overawed' by Ramsay's grief, while her brother Malcolm wrote that, 'At a single blow my father was transported from infinite happiness to inconsolable sadness. I can never forget the terrible anguish which he suffered at her departure.'[30]

Ramsay commissioned a memorial seat to stand in Lincoln's Inn Fields,[31] and also wrote a memoir of Margaret which was still popular more than a decade later and which remains the principal source for the details of her life, if not her politics. Her loss was mourned among academics, researchers and social reformers as much as socialists and feminists, but it was particularly keenly felt among Labour women, who wrote many tributes to her. Katharine Bruce Glasier wrote an obituary in the *Labour Leader*, while Margaret Bondfield in the same paper said that the WLL had 'lost a leader of great personality, courage and charm; those of us who were privileged to work with her loved her dearly'.[32] Some dwelt on her domestic virtues, but many talked about her intelligence, the value of her work, and her ability to involve and engage people in the labour movement. 'Perhaps her greatest work,' wrote Mabel Bode in *The Times*, 'was to be what she was.'[33] She had not been entirely an easy or an uncontroversial figure; she was capable of great obstinacy, and sometimes exercised a Victorian moralistic streak which got her into trouble, as when the feminist and socialist Dora Montefiore sued her for libel in 1899.[34] But overall she had been an attractive and inspirational character who believed in the role Labour women had and could have. 'She wanted,' said Margaret Bondfield, 'to build up the League as her special contribution to the wider Labour movement.'[35]

The year 1911 marks a significant break in the development of the WLL, and ultimately determined the future of the organisation in 1918, when some women became able to vote. As the Labour Party grew and changed so too did the WLL, and after World War I the relationship between the Party and its women members changed decisively. But that point lay in the future and, in the meantime, some turbulent years lay ahead.

∞ 9 ∞

The Great Unrest

During the long, hot summer when Margaret MacDonald lay ill, Mary Macarthur and Marion Phillips, who was now working for the Women's Trade Union League (WTUL), found their hands full with a series of strikes. These were not isolated incidents, but part of a four-year period of stoppages, lockouts, demonstrations and riots that had started in 1910 and which, together with developments in Ireland and escalating Women's Social and Political Union (WSPU) militancy, came collectively to be known as the 'Great Unrest'.

The hundreds of industrial disputes which swept the country in the years before the war affected almost every industry. They arose from a number of causes, including falling wages, rising prices, poor working conditions, and the government's repressive reaction to the escalating conflict. It has been estimated that between 1911 and 1912 alone up to 41 million working days were lost to strikes and, as the situation worsened, the British middle and upper classes became very apprehensive that revolution was in the air. But many people were also bemused. This was the same period in which welfare provision was improving. The working classes appeared to have no gratitude for the old age pensions, health insurance and unemployment benefits which the Liberal government was initiating. In Germany the Chancellor, Otto von Bismarck, had introduced the first state-run welfare system in Europe in the 1880s, not because he shared socialist views, but because he believed that relieving some of the insecurity of working men's lives would make them less inclined to revolution. This was one of the ideas behind the Liberal government's programme of reform but, as industrial action spread, doubts began to creep in. It was almost as if the more the government did, the angrier the workers became.

The economic and social conditions were major factors, but the weather also played a part. The years before the outbreak of World War I

178

saw some idyllic summers which became the food of postwar nostalgia, but for people toiling for poverty wages in sweltering workshops and factories the heat was a torment. July 1911 had been very dry, and as a result there were both water and food shortages. In the north of England, textile workers were laid off as water ran out. Dock and transport strikes in London and Liverpool left food rotting at ports, thus increasing shortages. Without refrigeration, what food there was went bad very quickly, but many poor people had no option but to eat it anyway. It was estimated that about 2,000 babies and toddlers in London alone died in August as a result of drinking bad milk or eating contaminated food.[1] In the first couple of weeks of August the temperature in London reached 98°F (36.5°C). At night it was too hot to sleep and people took to the streets in search of cooler air. In the East End, and in the crowded alleyways of Southwark, where people were crammed together in insanitary housing, conditions were appalling. For women working in the factories making jam or baking biscuits, the level of heat in which they were expected to work for up to ten hours a day was intolerable.

Thus, on one of the hottest days of all, Mary Macarthur and Marion Phillips were summoned to Bermondsey by news of a strike. When they got there they found thousands of women and girls milling about in the streets in high spirits but without focus, a plan or any leaders. The strike had started in a sweet factory, where the workers had walked out and marched down the road gathering friends and relations as they went. Soon every factory and workshop they passed was emptying and, by the time Mary and Marion arrived, women from almost every trade were on strike. Mary set up her headquarters in the Labour Institute in Fort Road and began sorting out the different trades and trying to establish what had happened. The women refused to go back, and each trade had to have a separate agreement negotiated. Huge strike meetings were held, and on one occasion over 15,000 people crammed into Southwark Park to be addressed by Mary Macarthur, Ben Tillett and other Labour leaders. As the dispute ran into weeks the strikers also had to be fed, and at a time when food was in short supply this was challenging. Mary wrote to the press to ask for donations, explaining that:

Many thousands of women are on strike, many more are locked out, the pawnshops are closed and outdoor relief refused. ... The plight of the children is pitiable. We want at least a thousand loaves of bread ... if possible by noon on Monday. Who will send them?[2]

Money, bread, herrings and milk arrived in large quantities. Women had to queue up in baking temperatures to collect their rations; as at Cradley Heath the year before, babies were passed up and down the lines so that desperate women could claim more children than they actually had. Marion Phillips organised contingents to march through London with collecting boxes, and socialists and trade unionists poured in to help. Trade by trade, Mary and her colleagues negotiated agreements to get the women back to work. By the middle of September they had won increased rates in 18 out of the 21 industries involved. This was a significant achievement, wrested out of a situation which had begun in considerable confusion. So, too was the 'new sense of self-reliance, solidarity and comradeship ... making it certain that, whatever the difficulties and dangers of the future they will never again be, like those of the past, without hope'.[3]

Within days of the end of the strikes, and just two weeks after Margaret MacDonald's death, Mary Macarthur married Will Anderson. The son of a Banffshire blacksmith, he was largely self-educated and had met her in Ayr at the first Shop Assistants' Union meeting she attended. They became close through her early union work in Scotland, and he proposed to her in 1903 before her move to London. She turned him down; the woman who only a few years before had written in her diary that she had to be famous knew that she would not achieve a career and a life of her own if she married young. Eventually Anderson also went to London as a national officer for the union, a post which he left a few years later to pursue journalism and politics. They remained friends, and by 1908 were both members of the Independent Labour Party (ILP)'s National Administrative Council. In 1911 he was chairing the ILP, while Mary was a national figure in her own right, a charismatic and gifted leader who had won major industrial battles. She had no intention of retreating into domesticity and Anderson luckily had no intention of asking her to. They were married at the City Temple in Holborn and she was sufficiently famous for the press to write about the colour (brown) of her hat and dress. The couple had a brief honeymoon in Paris and then returned to rejoin the great battle over Lloyd George's National Insurance Bill, which was at one and the same time offering hope to millions of working-class people and splitting the labour movement.

On the face of it, the National Insurance Bill seemed like a real break-through, and initially that was how it was greeted. It was published in the same month in which the House of Lords finally agreed to pass the Parliament Act, which it did only after Asquith persuaded the new king,

George V, to threaten to create 400 new Liberal peers in order to get it through. Lloyd George had been working on the National Insurance scheme for several years and had based it on the scheme already operating in Germany, which he and many others had looked at very closely. If implemented, it would protect millions of working people from destitution caused by sickness or temporary unemployment, keeping them out of the workhouses (and thus reducing costs), and keeping families together. The problem, however, was that as with almost all Liberal social reform legislation in this period it was to some degree a fudge, with many exclusions and caveats and a complicated structure. It was also based on a contributory principle which was anathema to many socialists and trade unionists.

The legislation involved two separate schemes, one of which was much more contentious than the other. The first part of the Bill proposed a health insurance scheme which would enable those covered by it to get medical treatment (including medicines) without running up huge doctors' bills. Membership of it would be compulsory for everyone earning less than about £160 a year (the income tax threshold). It would be administered not by the state but by 'approved societies', who would have to be registered and who would deal with claims and payments while also collecting the contributions on behalf of the government. These societies could be insurance companies, charities or friendly societies; during the passage of the Bill trade unions were added. Part II of the Bill contained a less controversial unemployment scheme which would cover workers in cyclical trades subject to temporary lay-offs (mainly building, shipbuilding and related employments). Recipients of payments would get them for up to 15 weeks in any one year and would collect them from the Labour Exchanges set up by Winston Churchill in 1909.

Both schemes were to be funded by contributions from workers, their employers and the taxpayer. For the health scheme the contributions would be 4d a week for working men (3d for women), 3d from employers and 2d from the government. For unemployment payments, workers and employers would pay 2½d each, and the taxpayer 3d. Both schemes constituted a complete break with the ideas behind the antiquated Poor Law, and both were controversial because of the state's involvement, which alarmed Conservatives and some Liberals. But some Labour people also opposed them, for very different reasons.

For decades, the Labour and trade union movements had been campaigning for free services, especially for the poorest, and now it seemed as though Lloyd George was intending to introduce back-door taxes for those who were paid the least. The income tax trigger of £160 a year represented about £3 a week; most workers covered earned considerably less than this and if they were in both schemes they would have to find an extra 6½d a week. This was the cost of half a dozen eggs or two loaves of bread, which represented a considerable loss for families whose total income might be as low as £1 a week. The 1911 ILP conference had supported a non-contributory scheme, as did the Fabian Society; Beatrice Webb reported Sidney as being 'on the whole' in favour of the Bill but herself opposed. She referred to it as 'Lloyd George's rotten scheme of sickness insurance'[4] and thought it would lead to bad administration by the approved societies as well as a sense of entitlement and malingering among the recipients. 'I cannot,' she said, 'dismiss my rooted prejudice to relief instead of treatment.'[5] She thought that the root causes of poverty should be addressed, and that what was being proposed was effectively just an extension of outdoor Poor Law relief.[6] Nor did she think that requiring a forced contribution from those least able to afford it made sense. Keir Hardie was by no means alone in describing the scheme as a poll tax on working people.

There were also other concerns. Neither the health scheme nor the unemployment insurance took account of dependants, so that children were entirely excluded, as were married women who did not work. Women who did work earned less than men, and threepence was a much greater proportion of a woman's income than fourpence was of a man's. Mary Macarthur initially wanted all women earning less than 15 shillings a week to be excluded from having to contribute altogether, but the administrative challenges of having to contract out such a large number of women, combined with the arbitrary nature of effectively designating 15 shillings as a minimum living wage, meant that almost nobody agreed with her. But a great many Labour women did agree that the Bill was in effect discriminatory, and Labour and trade union women came together to lobby for changes on issues such as maternity pay. On the other hand, many women who employed servants were outraged at the thought that they would have to buy National Insurance stamps for their skivvies and campaigned to get domestic servants excluded. Public meetings were held at which feelings ran high. On one occasion, at a 'Mistresses' and Servants' Protest' in the Albert Hall, Mary Macarthur demanded of the Countess of Desart: 'What will be the position of servants if excluded?'

With a magnificent disregard for reality, Lady Desart replied, 'They will be in the position of being the most independent class of workers.'[7]

The Women's Labour League (WLL), the National Federation of Women Workers (NFWW) and others eventually took the view that, while a non-contributory scheme would have been best, a contributory one was all they were likely to get. The weaknesses in the Bill so far as women were concerned were so great that they could not be allowed to go unchallenged. Single women who were compulsory contributors before they married could not opt to be voluntary contributors afterwards if they gave up work, nor would they be eligible to receive benefits. In effect they would lose their money. Single women would not receive equal benefits with men and the proposed maternity benefit would be paid to husbands.[8] A Special Committee to Safeguard Women's Interests was set up which included a dozen MPs as well as a variety of women's organisations. The Fabian Women's Group (FWG) held a conference in May which brought together 19 groups and societies. The FWG had been founded a few years earlier by Charlotte Wilson, once the anarchist thorn in the Fabian side but now, having renounced anarchy, a member of the Women's Industrial Council (WIC) and the Women's Freedom League (WFL) as well as once more of the Fabian Society. She, Marion Phillips and Maud Pember Reeves produced a list of proposed amendments to the Bill which the *Fabian News* said had been drawn 'from the suggestions of Mr and Mrs Sidney Webb, together with demands put forward by various women's organisations'.[9]

Not all women were in favour of taking this approach: the WSPU and some members of the National Union of Women's Suffrage Societies (NUWSS) opposed the Bill altogether on the grounds that it was legislation about women made by men and should not therefore be countenanced at all. But there was some overlap between this and the opposition to domestic servants being included in the provisions. Sylvia Pankhurst, who took the view that since the Bill was likely to go through it should be as favourable to working women as possible, reported that '"I won't lick stamps!"; "Regimenting the workers"; "Burden on industry" – all the conflicting catch cries of the factions opposing the Bill were heard on suffrage platforms.'[10]

In June 1911 a joint deputation of women's organisations met Lloyd George to lay their concerns before him, but he was dismissive. Gertrude Tuckwell later reported that he took a particular dislike to Mary Macarthur, 'rating her like a schoolgirl' and maintaining against all the evidence that the position of women in the legislation was excellent and that Mary did not know what she was talking about.[11] When the next deputation met him in July it was without either Margaret MacDonald, who was by then ill, or Mary, and was headed instead by Marion Phillips.

Most working-class women had relatively little knowledge of how the Bill's provisions would affect them, and the WLL set about trying to inform them. In July, Margaret Bondfield led a door-to-door canvass in Birmingham, distributing leaflets and talking to people about what was being proposed. The gulf between well-informed middle-class women's lives and those of the poorest struck her yet again as pitiful and outrageous. Writing about the canvass afterwards in the *Labour Leader* she said:

> At 11 a.m. a few members who had risen early and finished their housework and I started to canvass. The shyness soon wore off, and each took a separate section of the streets. Reinforcements arrived in the afternoon. We visited a small number of courts. Oh! The lonely lives of these women, hidden away at the back of a network of small, mean streets![12]

Gradually improvements for women were secured by means of an exemption here and a small increase in benefit rates there. Keir Hardie was one of those opposed to the Bill in principle, but he could also see that if it was going to be passed it needed to be amended, and worked with Sylvia Pankhurst and others to get amendments. The issue of maternity benefits was particularly contentious, with women on the left arguing that they were inadequate and moral campaigners wanting the mothers of illegitimate children to be excluded. Through detailed committee work, Labour members were able to improve provisions for married women and low-paid workers, and clarify the position of trade unions acting as friendly societies, a role which they had played since they began. There had been some fears that, if they participated as approved bodies in the administration of National Insurance, their freedom to take industrial action might be compromised. However, despite these changes the principles underpinning the Bill remained the same, and this still rendered the whole scheme unacceptable to some MPs.

As soon as he became leader, Ramsay MacDonald had written to the Parliamentary Labour Party (PLP) in terms familiar to many leaders since. He called for more unity and less public dissent. He reiterated that 'Party meetings are the place to discuss differences' rather than the press, and he expected Labour MPs to vote together.[13] Given that Hardie was notorious for operating as a 'party of one' and had already voted against the proposal to pay MPs £400 a year since he objected to it on principle, MacDonald cannot have held out much hope of being able to enforce the whip across the board, and so it proved in the vote on the National Insurance Bill in December. Most Labour MPs voted for it, but Hardie abstained. Philip Snowden, Fred Jowett, Will Thorne, George Lansbury and James O'Grady all voted against. The PLP under MacDonald was proving as difficult to manage as ever.

◆　◆　◆　◆　◆

Margaret MacDonald's death had left the WLL at something of a crossroads. Margaret Bondfield had worked well in the post of organising secretary and had been there for long enough to be able to provide some continuity. But, as so often, she was heavily overworked, relentlessly touring the country to speak at meetings and encourage local organisation. In November 1911 she 'collapsed in the middle of a speech with a mind perfectly blank. It was a terrible experience. I felt lost.'[14] She was diagnosed with nervous exhaustion and instructed to 'live like a cabbage, not to read, or write, or talk'.[15] In January 1912 she tried to resign from her post, but the WLL executive refused to let her go. In April she tried to go back to work but found it impossible. She continued to offer her resignation, and the executive still refused to accept it. In her absence, Marion Phillips took over, ostensibly on a temporary basis, leaving her post as organising secretary of the WTUL. There was some friction between Margaret and Marion and this cannot have helped Margaret's recovery. In addition, the committee seemed markedly reluctant to have to offer Marion the secretaryship permanently. Maud Ward, with whom Margaret lived, was a member of the executive at this time, so Margaret must have heard the details of the debates. Since Ethel Bentham, who was Marion's landlady, was also a member Marion must have heard them too.

Katharine Bruce Glasier had joined the WLL executive in 1908. She and her husband and children lived in Lancashire, which made her one of a decreasing number of women from outside London who sat on the executive. Like Margaret MacDonald, she did not employ live-in servants, but relied on friends for help with childcare. In other respects, however, she was very different, taking much more pleasure in household duties and sometimes talking about them in the women's column she wrote under the pseudonym of Iona for the *Labour Leader*. She remained a popular and effective speaker, and was the public face for many years of a long campaign to get the government to compel mine owners to provide pithead baths. Despite their different approaches to domesticity she had been close to Margaret MacDonald, and exchanged letters with Ramsay for some years after Margaret's death.

Ramsay had allowed the WLL to continue to be run from the flat in Lincoln's Inn Fields with Ethel Bentham guaranteeing a rent of £25 per year, and Katharine tended to regale him with the WLL's problems. She did not much care for either Margaret Bondfield or Marion Phillips, writing to MacDonald that:

> I wish I had Margaret Bondfield's confidence or quite understood her: but her friendship with Miss Ward which your dear wife dreaded got right between us. These violent attachments don't seem to help, or to be good servants of the commonwealth. They have in them all the disproportionate heats and chills – and passionate and impulsive actions against outsiders who touch one of the beloved one's supposed interests or dignities that belong to lovers.[16]

Of Marion she wrote: 'The personality of Dr Phillips is a real difficulty … she is as hard and cold as glass. Brilliant as diamonds are, *none* of us can love her except Dr Ethel Bentham.' Though she came to appreciate Marion rather more as time went on, there is something rather unattractive about these observations, but Katharine was of her time and tended very much towards the conventional. Neither Margaret Bondfield nor Marion Phillips lived lives which were in any way orthodox by accepted standards, either in personal or professional terms, and Katharine's view of them would have been shared by many.

Margaret Bondfield herself was aware of the fact that her own character might be part of the problem, writing to MacDonald that:

> I have decided not to hold office in the League. I shall be a member of the executive committee only. For the first time I have met with people with whom I *cannot* work … At present my attitude divides the Executive Committee and is frightfully bad for the League. … I do not choose to be the nominal head without any real power.[17]

The position remained unresolved until September 1912, when the executive finally let Margaret go. Even then Marion's position remained temporary, not being finally made permanent until early 1913.

Marion Phillips was a gifted administrator and organiser and, despite Katharine Bruce Glasier's opinion, well liked by many people. But her style was very different from that of Mary Middleton and Margaret MacDonald, and this made the WLL into a different kind of organisation. Where Mary and Margaret had allowed a fairly loose structure to develop, with the emphasis on local activity and an interest in what was going on around the country, Marion had a strong centralising tendency which concentrated both power and activity in London and discouraged independent action elsewhere. As a result the WLL's national voice grew stronger, but that voice was more metropolitan than provincial, and more middle-class. Marion developed a firm grip on both the executive and the League's conference, and although this was generally accepted as working well, it had its consequences in the long run, particularly since Marion's view of what women needed differed to some extent from Mary and Margaret's.

One major difference was in the relationship that developed between the WLL and the Labour Party. Almost from the beginning, the WLL had hoped for some financial assistance from the Party, but this had not been possible, partly because the National Executive Committee (NEC) had not been particularly enthusiastic about the formation of a women's organisation, but also because the Osborne judgment, coupled with two general elections in one year, had made funds scarce. But the WLL too had its problems: subscriptions were kept purposely low to enable women to join, but that had meant a considerable reliance on individual donations and, in particular, funding from Margaret MacDonald herself. After her death the League found itself in even deeper difficulties, and the NEC came to the rescue with a grant of £100.

The Party's own financial straits were lessened over the next couple of years by two events: the introduction of an official salary for MPs, and the 1913 Trade Union Act. The Act effectively overturned the Osborne judgment and made it legal again for political parties to maintain political funds and to make political donations. Unions had to ballot their members and make provision for those who objected to the outcome to opt out. Not all unions chose to ballot their members, and not all of those who did so managed to persuade their members to support Labour, but the Party could now feel that it had a secure funding stream with which it could, among other things, field increased numbers of candidates and support local organisational development.

Inevitably, as the League's activities under Marion Phillips grew, so too did the need for funds, and the Party's grant was gradually increased. After the passing of the Trade Union Act in 1913 it was doubled. But the corollary of this was that Arthur Henderson, as Party secretary, felt able to intervene in its activities. In 1914 the Party decided that the WLL was not being run efficiently enough and retrenchments were made. This was a point at which many Labour women across the country were involved in either industrial action or suffrage campaigning or both, with some branches maintaining their own strike funds and others contributing to the NUWSS's Election Fighting Fund (EFF) or to election campaigns at local level. In 1914 there were over 80 local WLL branches and, although few new ones were opening, this was in line with the Party's own rather stagnant position in the pre-war years. It is hard, therefore, to see quite what the NEC might have meant by suggesting that 'branch organisation of the League, so far as it has come to the notice of members of our committee, was not as efficient or as strongly developed as it could be',[18] except that possibly there were different views between the men and the women about what form women's political activity should take. The net effect of the Party's significant level of WLL funding was that Henderson now had a degree of influence over its activities, undoubtedly helped by Marion Phillips's view that women were not yet ready for politics, and would need to be educated before they could play their full part. This approach worked when it came to providing training and support for women to prepare them for the time when they had the vote, but much less well when, a few years later, that vote arrived.

That time had not come yet, however, and following the failure of both the 1910 and 1911 Conciliation Bills the WSPU had returned to its militancy. In November 1911, Lloyd George met a deputation from the People's Suffrage Federation (PSF) and officially informed them that there was to be a government Reform Bill in 1912 which would propose adult male suffrage, but would be open to amendment to include women, and that if it was so amended the government would not oppose it. His intention was that this Bill should be introduced before the planned Third Conciliation Bill, which would be a private members' bill but could provide a fall-back in case the Reform Bill failed. In the event, Lloyd George could not get his Reform Bill through the Cabinet and the Conciliation Bill was therefore voted on first. It was lost by just 14 votes. There had been a significant loss of parliamentary support for women's suffrage, partly because of the resurgence of WSPU militancy but also because a number of previously supportive Irish MPs had changed sides in order not to jeopardise Home Rule.

Millicent Fawcett did not agree with the WSPU about much, but she now came to accept their view that the Liberal Party was simply playing with women's suffrage and would never deliver it in any form. Although this did not incline her more favourably to militancy, it did lead her to reconsider what the NUWSS's parliamentary strategy should be. Many NUWSS members were Liberals, but there was rising frustration with the perceived perfidy of Asquith and Lloyd George in particular, and the lack of effective Liberal action in general. There were resignations from the Liberal Party, and one woman spoke for many when she wrote:

> I am throwing my whole energies and substance into the support of the new development of the NUWSS policy – viz., the providing of a Labour candidate in all constituencies where either Liberal or Unionist has not proved himself a supporter of our cause not only in name but in deed.[19]

This 'new development' of NUWSS policy had been made possible, not only by the government's inconstancy, but also because of a small but perceptible shift in Labour Party policy. Over the years, the Labour Party conference had seen many debates on the franchise issue and had held fast to its support for adult universal suffrage. This had not been by any means uncontroversial, and in 1909 Margaret Bondfield had run into what she described as 'a storm of criticism' over her handling of the WLL's proposed addition to the electoral reform resolution being discussed.[20] The resolution demanded 'The enfranchisement of all adults, male and female' as well as a range of other measures to which the WLL proposed to add that:

> the inclusion of women [in any Reform Act] shall not be left to the chances of an amendment, but that it shall become a vital part of the government measure; and further declares that any attempt to exclude women will be met by the uncompromising opposition of organized labour to the whole Bill.[21]

The problem with this was that it tried to mandate Labour MPs to vote against male suffrage if the women were not included, and Margaret probably thought it was unlikely to be passed. Moreover, as president of the PSF she did not actually agree with it, and neither did Arthur Henderson, now Party secretary. Margaret said that he pointed out to her the 'technical difficulty' of such a demand, and that she therefore deleted the words 'to the whole Bill' before she moved the amendment. The WLL executive accepted her action but not without an understandable degree of irritation. This did not prevent them from appointing her as organising secretary a couple of years later, but her high-handed approach may have been one reason for her later difficulties with Marion Phillips.

In January 1912 the Labour Party conference gathered in Birmingham and once again discussed suffrage. This time, however, Arthur Henderson had changed his mind about the 'technical difficulties', and the resolution he piloted through was almost identical to the amendment which the WLL had proposed in 1909, including the requirement for Labour MPs to vote against any Reform Bill which did not include women. The resolution did not meet with universal support: the miners' unions, who had by now affiliated, voted against. The miners' leader, Robert Smillie, had been the Labour candidate in the ill-fated Cockermouth by-election a few years earlier, and had 600,000 members to use as a block vote against women's suffrage. Mary Macarthur was scathing, pointing out that:

> We have often been told that we women adult suffragists were being misled. We have replied that we trusted our Labour men, and yet the miners now say they will take manhood suffrage and leave the women out.[22]

Henderson's support, however, was enough to get the resolution through, and this sent a signal to the NUWSS that there might be some mileage in a closer connection with Labour. Millicent Fawcett wrote to MacDonald that she wished 'you were double your present strength in the House of Commons'.[23] H. N. Brailsford, the Liberal MP who had instigated the Conciliation Committee in Parliament, now acted as intermediary between Henderson, who was keen to preserve the Labour Party's cherished independence, and Millicent Fawcett and the NUWSS, who were equally keen to preserve theirs.

Henry Brailsford had started his political life as a Liberal, but in 1907 he joined the ILP in protest at the government's policy in Egypt. His wife, Jane, was an active member of the WSPU, and Brailsford made several attempts to reconcile the different wings of the suffrage movement. He was also a prominent member of the Men's League for Women's Suffrage.

In 1909 he had resigned from his job at the *Daily News* because of that paper's support for the forced feeding of hunger-striking suffrage prisoners, and as a result he had a reputation as a man of principle. By 1912 he was broadly trusted by both sides and, since the ILP had always had policy in favour of women's suffrage, was able to position himself as both a socialist and a suffragist.

The plan which emerged was one which would secure funds and, just as importantly, workers for Labour candidates in selected seats whilst ensuring that those candidates would overtly and wholeheartedly support women's suffrage. The NUWSS was to set up an election fighting fund which would be kept entirely separate from its other funds, and contributions to which would not be made by those who did not want to support it. Candidates would be run by Labour against Liberals who were not supportive of the women's cause, and the seats to which this criteria was applied would be chosen by the Party. The Labour Party's NEC set up a subcommittee to examine the proposals, and in April this met with the NUWSS officers. Among other things the meeting discussed the wording of the resolution which was to be put to the NUWSS's special council meeting in May. Henderson did not really want there to be too much publicity around the deal, prompting Brailsford to write angrily that:

> You will not be surprised to hear that there is a good deal of doubt and opposition to the scheme ... I leave you to guess the effect on these critics of the news that the Labour Party while apparently quite glad to take the women's money refuses to accept their support publicly. If the officers [of the NUWSS] have to convey that message to the Council, the plan is killed and incidentally all who have been urging that the Labour Party scheme should be trusted and helped are made to look ridiculous.[24]

When it came to the council meeting the officers presented the proposal as merely a continuation of the NUWSS's usual policy of supporting the best option for women at each election. There was considerable debate and strong opposition from both Liberal and non-aligned women, led by the social reformer Eleanor Rathbone. Nevertheless, the resolution was passed and the EFF established, and from this point on Labour became the party of both women's and universal suffrage.

It is striking that these negotiations were carried on entirely without any formal reference to the WLL or to any other Labour women except those already involved in the NUWSS. Marion Phillips, whose NUWSS connections must have been good, might have expected to be involved, or at least consulted, and perhaps she was behind the scenes. Ethel Bentham was the president of the WLL for much of this period, but neither woman seems to have been either officially a party to discussions or invited to meetings. On the other hand, there does seem to have been a general feeling that the agreement was a good thing, and that it opened the door for rapprochements between women whom the suffrage issue had separated. Isabella Ford and Selina Cooper, both of whom had been concentrating on the NUWSS in recent years, now became more active again in the Labour interest, with Isabella sitting on the EFF's committee and Selina organising for it in by-elections. Isabella was particularly encouraged by the new understanding between socialists and feminists, writing to a friend that 'I feel comradeship, the real thing, is growing fast just because of this battle. I never felt anything like it sometimes and it's growing amongst our sort of women ... I feel like bursting with joy over it at times.'[25]

The WFL, which included a significant number of Labour women, re-established friendly relations with the WLL. It had split from the WSPU in 1907, and members were perhaps now particularly keen to return to their Labour roots since the WSPU was actively campaigning against individual Labour politicians, even where, as in the case of Philip Snowden, they supported women's suffrage. As a result the League demanded that women choose between them and the WSPU, and the WSPU lost even more of its socialist connections. Similarly, at the beginning of 1914, Emmeline and Christabel Pankhurst forced Sylvia to decide between them and the working-class women she organised in the East End. Christabel was then living in exile in Paris, and Sylvia described travelling there for a dismal meeting with her mother and sister at which Christabel told her that 'a working women's movement was of no value' and that '"You have your own ideas. We do not want that; we want all our women to take their instructions and walk in step like an army."' Christabel suggested that they should occasionally meet 'not as Suffragettes, but as sisters', but the time for that had passed. 'To me the words seemed meaningless,' recorded Sylvia, 'we had no life apart from the movement.'[26] It was many years before they were reconciled.

Back in Britain the EFF provided both funds and workers for Labour candidates in several by-elections up until the outbreak of war in 1914. Ironically, the NUWSS's long history of election work meant that its organisers were far more experienced than local Labour Party and ILP members, and after one campaign in the Potteries town of Hanley the NUWSS's paper, *Common Cause*, observed that:

> The plain moral which we have always tried to drive home is 'organise and organise now'. The spirit and fire of the Labour Party is wonderful, but you can't mobilise forces without the machine of mobilisation.[27]

The relationship between the Party and the NUWSS was not without its points of friction. Sometimes there was not complete agreement over which candidates to support, and there were occasional difficulties over funds. In addition, Ramsay MacDonald was prone to outbursts which suggested that he was against women's suffrage, and he was constantly having to be nudged back into line by Henderson. In fact, his objections were largely class-based: despite having married a middle-class woman and despite there being a general commitment to adult as well as female suffrage, he clearly felt that the suffrage movement was irredeemably bourgeois. At one point the NUWSS's parliamentary secretary, Catherine Marshall, wrote to him to inquire: 'Why do you hate us so? ... Your accusation of class-feeling on our side, against the working women, wounds – and shows that you have missed the significance of the Women's Movement.'[28]

Had Margaret MacDonald still been alive she might have been able to influence his attitude, but she might also have been equally exasperated by the antics of George Lansbury, the MP for Bow and Bromley. Lansbury was a committed supporter of female suffrage and, particularly, of the WSPU, and over the two years he had been in Parliament had been a problem for the Labour whip. This was not merely a matter of voting against the Party line; in June 1912 he was suspended from the House of Commons for crossing the floor, shaking his fist in Asquith's face and shouting at him that 'you're beneath contempt. You call yourself a gentleman, and you forcibly feed and murder women in this fashion. You ought to be driven out of office.' In October he resigned his seat in order to fight a by-election on the issue of the franchise and the treatment of suffrage prisoners. Predictably, and much to MacDonald's irritation, he lost, and did not return to Parliament again until 1922.[29]

The forcible feeding of women suffrage prisoners had begun in 1909 after they started to go on hunger strike because they maintained that they were political, not criminal, prisoners and should be treated accordingly.

The government, on the other hand, thought that if it conceded political status to the women it would legitimate not only their demands, but also their methods. Reluctant to allow women to starve to death in its gaols, it allowed them to be force fed by means of a tube inserted into the throat through the nose. This procedure was brutal, particularly where the woman struggled or refused to co-operate. Between 1909 and 1913 hundreds of women, including the Pankhursts, had been force fed, often with calamitous results for their health and all with a degree of violence which, in the opinion of many people, amounted to torture. Some women were subjected to this repeatedly, yet still persisted with a courage which even people who opposed the WSPU's tactics admired. But the government saw a real danger of women starting to die, and therefore devised an ingenious if callous way of averting it. The Prisoners (Temporary Discharge for Ill-Health) Act passed in April 1913 allowed women who were weak or ill to be released on licence part way through their sentences and rearrested again once they had recovered. Women said that the net effect was that of a cat playing with a mouse, and thus the Act acquired the name by which it is now universally known. Women were now continually arrested, force-fed, released and rearrested to go through the whole cycle again. Many people thought that there was something particularly wrong and horrible about this, and public opinion, which had been keen to see something done to curb the militants' activities, was generally opposed to that something being the Cat and Mouse Act. Labour women who remained committed to universal adult suffrage now began to appear more supportive of the militants' plight. Mary Macarthur took part in a delegation of protest to the Home Secretary, and in June, after Emily Wilding Davison's death at Epsom, she wrote a generous obituary of her in Labour Woman.[30] This drawing together of women who had hitherto been opposed to one another ironically had the effect of isolating the WSPU, which now suffered a fall in membership and organi-sational capacity, even as its activities became increasingly extreme, moving from window-breaking to arson and deeds such as the destruction of paintings and the uprooting of plants at Kew Gardens.

The atmosphere of instability which permeated the years before the outbreak of war in 1914 was not by any means solely attributable to the activities of the WSPU. In fact, Emmeline and Christabel Pankhurst looked with some envy – and no small alarm – at the domestic unrest which surrounded their own movement and attracted attention and press coverage away from it. Not the least of these was the situation in Ireland.

The Home Rule Bill introduced in April 1912 promised limited self-government with many caveats and reservations of powers to Westminster, but nevertheless it was a step forwards and the Irish Parliamentary Party leader, John Redmond, was prepared to support it. Meanwhile in Ulster the unionists under Sir Edward Carson were beginning to drill volunteers and buy guns to resist Home Rule, to which they were adamantly opposed. Nationalists were doing the same to support it, or at the very least to be able to resist Carson. As the situation became increasingly intense, incidents escalated and the government became more emollient towards Carson's demands. Christabel Pankhurst interpreted this as meaning that governments listened only when threatened by militant action, though the prospect of insurrection and civil war in Ireland was perhaps of a rather different order from even the very dramatic campaigns now being waged by the WSPU.

There were also still hundreds of strikes going on in scores of industries. By 1912 there was a fevered atmosphere of militancy in many quarters, and since industrial action periodically erupted into violence the situation was very tense. Strikers were killed by troops in the South Wales coalfield and in Liverpool, and Winston Churchill's assertion that the soldiers had been sent in at the request of the employers fooled almost no one. In some cities citizens' militias were formed, prefiguring the strike-breaking organisations of the General Strike more than a decade later. At one point gunboats sailed into the mouths of the Mersey and the Humber.

Events at home were compounded by those abroad, particularly in Russia, which had long been a cause célèbre for the left and a source of anxiety for the right-wing press. In April 1912, nearly 300 people in Lena were killed by tsarist troops sent in to quell a strike in the Siberian goldfields, and this had led to a substantial increase in industrial action and revolutionary feeling among Russian workers. Across Europe there was unrest and unease and a sense that the rule of law was breaking down. Conference agendas were full of angry resolutions, and the streets full of angry striking workers.

Not for the last time, the Labour leadership in Parliament found itself caught between the militancy of its members and trade union supporters and the need to present an electable face to the public at large. Despite the supposed unpopularity of the two old parties they both continued to win by-elections, and despite the efforts of the EFF Labour regularly came towards the bottom of the poll. Any sense of momentum that had been created by the general elections of 1906 and 1910 had now stalled, with

Labour looking increasingly unlikely to become the third party at the next election, due to take place in 1915.

As 1914 opened the scale of industrial action looked unlikely to decrease, whilst suffrage militancy continued and Carson still drilled his troops in Ulster. In Yorkshire alone over 100,000 miners were on strike, and in Leeds 5,000 local government employees had struck for higher wages, supported by hundreds of gasworkers. In South Wales, young miners began to talk about forming quasi-military brigades. In London dock workers, coal transporters and building workers were all on strike, and the military had to be brought in to shift supplies.

On 10 March the suffragette Mary Richardson entered the National Gallery and slashed the Velázquez painting known as the 'Rokeby Venus' with a meat axe. She said at the time that it was because of the way in which Emmeline Pankhurst was being treated, but later said also that she hated 'the way men visitors to the gallery gaped at it all day'.[31] Gallery owners now became alarmed, and unaccompanied women were banned from many exhibitions. Public sympathy for the militants was by now in decline following several arson attempts, including the planting of a bomb (which failed to explode) in St Paul's Cathedral and one at Lloyd George's half-built house in Surrey.

The Great Unrest might have gone on for much longer, but for the assassination of an archduke in Sarajevo in June 1914 and a network of treaty obligations which left the British government 'honour-bound' to go to war if Belgium was attacked. On 4 August, German troops crossed the border. The worst fears of many socialists were about to be realised as the tragedy of World War I shattered the precarious peace of Europe.

10

War and Peace

In 1912 the Women's Labour League (WLL) sent several resolutions to the Labour Party conference in Birmingham. One dealt with industrial unrest and was moved jointly with the Independent Labour Party (ILP) delegates. Another became the resolution on suffrage which Arthur Henderson moved and which was the spur for the agreement with the National Union of Women's Suffrage Societies (NUWSS). Others related to industrial dirt, school clinics and education. But there was also one on secret diplomacy, which was moved by Katharine Bruce Glasier and Marion Phillips and passed unanimously. Writing afterwards in the *League Leaflet*, Katharine recorded that the press:

> had sneered at the Women's Labour League for bringing a resolution against the secret diplomacy that rules our foreign policy today ... But the women showed that they were as alive as men to the evils of a system that ... has led us 'to risk war with Germany in the interests of French financiers over Morocco, to condone the Italian outrage in Tripoli, the Russian theft in Mongolia, and above all to join hands with Russia in making an assault upon the national independence and freedom of Persia'.[1]

The outbreak of World War I in August 1914, which is often presented as having come as a total shock to almost everyone, had in fact been both feared and foreseen by many socialists, feminists and peace campaigners. 'We stand,' Marion Phillips had written in the *League Leaflet* in early 1913, 'the Labour and socialist forces of the world, the champions of human life, proclaiming a sacred right to freedom from the hideous nightmare of slumdom and the rule of force and the murderous threat of the world's great armies.'[2] Many Labour women considered themselves as anti-war at the very least; some, such as Margaret Bondfield and the Quaker Isabella Ford, were actively pacifist. Nor were they alone. Keir Hardie and Ramsay

MacDonald, though disagreeing on so much else, came together on their opposition to militarism and rearmament, and consistently sounded alarm bells as the international situation became increasingly dangerous.

The labour movement had always had an internationalist flavour, and foreign policy had always been one of its concerns. The Second International, which brought together socialist parties from various countries, offered opportunities for both women and men to make international connections, and many people had a wide circle of correspondents in Europe. Margaret and Ramsay MacDonald had welcomed people from around the world to their Sunday afternoon 'at homes', and Margaret had been secretary of the British Section of the Women's International Council of Socialist and Labour Organisations which Margaret Bondfield chaired. There were many ties between the socialist movements in Britain and Germany, and many people had German friends who opposed the development of German militarism just as they themselves opposed rearmament at home. Unfortunately, however, the focus on points of agreement obscured the fact that in both countries the population as a whole was much more enthusiastic about the prospect of war than socialist MPs and leaders were. As Ramsay MacDonald remarked to the government chief whip a few days before war broke out, 'no war was at first unpopular'.[3]

For many socialists, the great enemy was not Germany, but Russia. For decades the tsarist government had been seen as the most reactionary and repressive of regimes and opposed by leftists across Europe. When the Fabian Edith Nesbit published *The Railway Children* in 1905 she included a Russian political prisoner as one of the characters, and after the Russian Revolution of that year much socialist time and effort was put into fundraising to help refugees. In 1909 there were mass demonstrations against the visit of the Tsar, and many people had met exiled Russian socialist leaders such as Lenin at international conferences or in London, and supported them in their opposition to a despotic and undemocratic system. Germany, on the other hand, though also to some extent deficient in democracy, seemed to have progressive social and economic policies and to be closer to Britain in both culture and development than many other European countries.

This did not mean, however, that Labour leaders were blind to the threats of increasing militarism and the developing arms race with Germany. On the contrary, there were lengthy discussions about what the response should be if war came. In 1911, a special Party conference was held to debate the international situation. The ILP wanted a general strike while the trade unions largely opposed it. Hardie and MacDonald both supported the ILP line: a general strike, MacDonald argued, might not make much difference to whether or not war was declared, but it would be an act of solidarity with workers across international borders.

As international relations deteriorated, Labour leaders became increasingly distrustful of the ability – or even the will – of the Liberal government to avoid war. Lloyd George and Churchill, in particular, seemed hell-bent on conflict. Churchill was already detested by the left because of his action in sending in troops to break up strikes. If his attitude was transferred to foreign policy, MacDonald wrote in 1912:

> millions upon millions of our national wealth will be squandered, and whilst there is no public opinion demanding that Ministers must have some policy other than merely building more ships than their neighbours, there will be no end to the folly except war.[4]

The situation was complicated by the fact that much diplomacy was conducted in private and treaties were not brought to Parliament for debate or agreement. As a result, nobody was sure what obligations had been entered into and what the implications of any pacts with foreign powers might be. Secret diplomacy caused both anger and alarm, and opposition to it remained a major plank of Labour's foreign policy platform for many years to come.

In June 1914 the heir to the Austro-Hungarian empire was assassinated in Sarajevo, setting in train a series of events which resulted in the threat of a German invasion of Belgium. Britain's obligations under the 1839 Treaty of London meant that, once this had happened, war became almost inescapable. On 31 July the British section of the International Socialist Bureau issued an 'Appeal to the British Working Class' signed by Keir Hardie and Arthur Henderson. It called upon workers to:

> Hold vast demonstrations against war, in London and in every industrial centre. Compel those of the governing class, and their Press, who are eager to commit you to co-operate with Russian despotism, to keep silence ... There is no time to lose; already, by secret agreements and understandings of which the democracies of the civilised world know only by rumour, steps are being taken which may fling us into the fray. Workers! – stand together, therefore, for peace.[5]

On the same day a petition signed by organisations representing 12 million women from 26 countries was delivered to the Foreign Office and a number of embassies. Signed by Millicent Fawcett, among others, it said that:

> Powerless though we are politically, we call upon the governments and powers of our several countries to avert the threatened unparalleled disaster ... [we] appeal to you to leave untried no method of concili-ation or arbitration ... which may help to avert deluging half the civilised world in blood.[6]

On 2 August a huge demonstration was held in Trafalgar Square addressed by Keir Hardie, Arthur Henderson, Marion Phillips, George Lansbury and many others. On 3 August the foreign secretary, Sir Edward Grey, announced to the House of Commons that war was now only a matter of time and that Britain was honour-bound to join it. Ramsay MacDonald put the Labour Party's position, which was that Britain should remain neutral. He was particularly scathing about the concept of 'honour':

> There has been no crime committed by statesmen of this character without those statesmen appealing to their nation's honour. We fought the Crimean War because of our honour: we rushed to South Africa because of our honour. ... What is the use of talking about coming to the aid of Belgium, when as a matter of fact you are engaged in an old European war, which is not going to leave the map of Europe in the position it is now?[7]

The following day a women's protest meeting was held at Kingsway Hall. With the exception of the Women's Social and Political Union (WSPU), which was pro-war, almost every element of the women's movement was represented both in the audience and on the platform. Millicent Fawcett took the chair, and speakers included Mary Macarthur and Marion Phillips as well as Emmeline Pethick-Lawrence and the indomitable Charlotte Despard. But it was in vain: as Margaret Bondfield said, 'when we came out the Guards were on their way to Dover. The die was cast. We were at war. Events had got beyond control.'[8]

The trade unions immediately suspended all industrial action, the NUWSS and the WSPU suspended the suffrage campaign, and the

Pankhursts came home from Paris. In Ireland the situation remained complex, though men on both sides of the Home Rule question joined up to fight abroad. For socialists, and for socialist women in particular, the issue of what their role in the war should be became crucial. In the September edition of *Labour Woman*, Marion Phillips filled the front page with a heartfelt denunciation of the conflict. Under the heading 'Will the light come?', her opening paragraph laid the blame squarely onto the secret diplomacy where she thought it belonged. But she also looked more hopefully to the future:

> There is one other freedom to achieve – the freedom of women. On them falls with terrible weight the burden of war. From them must come the inspiration in the power of which the new world of Peace shall be built. ... The dead bodies of men will lie upon the battlefields and deep in the sea ... But the women will remain to lead the world in the rebuilding of the new time. We believe that women will be ready to take up the task.[9]

In the meantime, the position outlined by Ramsay MacDonald in the House was beginning to unravel. The Parliamentary Labour Party (PLP), which had initially agreed with the neutrality stance he had outlined, now wanted to support the government's request for funding for the war. On 5 August MacDonald resigned as chairman of the PLP, effectively resigning also as leader of the Party as a whole. Although not a pacifist, he believed that the war was morally wrong and should be opposed as the Boer War had been. He, Snowden and Hardie, to whom hostilities, though not unexpected, had come as a dreadful shock, stood firm on their opposition to the conflict, and while this earned them the applause of the ILP, pacifists and people in favour of a negotiated peace, it also brought down public hatred and opprobrium from most other quarters. There were calls for them to be arrested and tried for treason, some from former friends and comrades. Hardie was already frail when the war broke out, and died a year later, robbing the Labour Party of its father figure as well as an iconic advocate for peace.

Emmeline and Christabel Pankhurst turned the WSPU into a pro-war organisation and its paper, the *Suffragette*, into *Britannia*. Suffrage prisoners were released and the militant campaign ended, though the Women's Freedom League (WFL) continued to lobby. Some socialists, such as Robert Blatchford, were pro-war, as was British public opinion, if only because people believed that it would be over very quickly. ILP members, on the other hand, were very much opposed, even though their leaders in Parliament were mainly in favour, as were many trade unionists, particularly at grass-roots level. Thus both the Labour and the women's movements found themselves split over the issue, with real heartache on both sides and the loss of long-standing friendships.

These divisions came as something of a shock to women who had worked together through international organisations for years. The Hungarian feminist and pacifist Rosika Schwimmer, who was based in London when the war broke out, noted that 'All the chirping peace voices were drowned by the deafening thunder clap of the first shot. ... It ... opened the gate for the deluge of fire and blood.'[10] Isabella Ford tried hard to keep good relationships with old suffrage friends, but the strain became very great. At the NUWSS conference held to discuss what part suffragists should play in the war, she 'declaimed against co-operation with the government for war purposes with a pugnacity of word and gesture which took everyone's breath away, and then, having had her say, stamped off the platform and down the hall in almost ferocious style'.[11] Writing to Millicent Fawcett she said that 'I hate Prussianism as heartily as you do – & I long for it to go – But I do not think that war ever destroyed war – & real salvation can only come to people and nations from within.'[12]

Many suffrage campaigners supported the war because they believed that it offered women the chance to show that they could contribute as much as men and should therefore be granted the vote once the war was over. On the other hand, many Labour and trade union women who opposed it believed that if they did not protect working-class women's interests nobody else would. Thus women such as Margaret Bondfield and Mary Macarthur found themselves in the rather curious position of both campaigning for peace and working as part of the war effort. The different groups and opinions in the labour movement could have found themselves drifting irrevocably apart under the stresses the war brought; that they did not was due at least in part to Arthur Henderson's determination to keep lines of communication open.

Having again become Labour leader, Henderson was acutely aware of the dangers the Party faced, and set up the War Emergency: Workers' National Committee (WNC) to draw people together. Protagonists from both pro- and anti-war camps were able to maintain contact with one another as well as to defend workers' interests at a time when they were threatened by the development of state intervention and capitalist profiteering. The Committee was chaired by Henderson himself and included both MacDonald and the pro-war Henry Hyndman, whose Social Democratic Federation (SDF) had now become the British Socialist Party. Mary Macarthur and Marion Phillips were also members, as were Margaret Bondfield, Susan Lawrence, Sidney Webb, Robert Smillie, president of the Miners' Federation, and Jim Middleton, the Labour Party's assistant secretary. Any Labour organisation was eligible to affiliate, and the Fabian Women's Group (FWG) was represented, as well as the Women's Industrial Council (WIC) and a number of suffrage societies.

The other route through which contacts were maintained was the Union of Democratic Control (UDC), set up in November 1914 by Ramsay MacDonald and a number of other opponents of the war. The UDC was not a specifically pacifist body, although pacifists such as Isabella Ford were members, and it worked for a non-violent solution to the conflict. Like the WNC it enabled people who differed profoundly on principle to work together on the points about which they agreed, and it kept conversations open which might otherwise have been closed by enabling the agreement of a common set of aims for the anti-war cause.

Broadly speaking, the UDC had two basic lines of policy. The first was to try to secure a negotiated peace by constitutional means, but the second, which many people found very attractive, was about what should happen after the war, and what should be done to prevent wars from happening in future. This included rooting foreign policy in democratic structures rather than secret networks, reducing armaments, ensuring self-determination for nations and populations, and establishing international courts and other structures at which disputes between governments could be resolved. Taken as a whole, these aspirations in one form or another informed most subsequent twentieth-century attempts to avert war, and to this day continue to underpin many internationalist and democratic ideas.

On 9 February 1915 the UDC's executive agreed that 'democracy must be based on the equal citizenship of men and women' and specifically invited women to join. Many did, but even so the UDC remained a tiny and highly unpopular organisation. Pro-war feeling was very high for the first couple of years of conflict and again at the end, and those opposed to it were regarded as public enemies. Ramsay MacDonald, who was treated as a hero by many in the various peace movements, was singled out for particular hatred by the pro-war press, who even printed his birth certificate, calling it their 'very painful and unsavoury duty' to reveal the 'libeller and slanderer of his country' as 'the illegitimate son of a Scotch servant girl' who had been registered at birth as 'James McDonald

Ramsay' and therefore, having lied about his name, should be ineligible to sit in Parliament.[13] MacDonald had never hidden his antecedents, but he found the sheer malice of the article much more depressing than the insults and death threats he received daily. His expulsion from the golf club at Lossiemouth, of which he had been one of the first members, was also a blow. 'I am in receipt,' he wrote bitterly to them, 'of your letter informing me that the Moray Golf Club has decided to become a political association with the Golf Course attached ...'[14]

In the months after MacDonald's resignation as leader Henderson had some hopes of tempting him back, but to no avail. The Party's National Executive Committee (NEC) and PLP found themselves caught between the anti-war feeling among the socialists in the ILP and the pro-war feeling among the majority of trade unionists. This caused some embarrassment as decisions about how to act were made and then reversed, sometimes in a matter of days. In 1915 Asquith decided to form a coalition government, and invited Labour to join it. The PLP declined, but the NEC wanted to accept. It took a joint meeting of both bodies to get agreement, after which Henderson became Labour's first cabinet minister as President of the Board of Education. The debate the following year over whether or not to support conscription produced even more confusion. The Special Conference held in 1916 voted against. The NEC then decided that this would mean withdrawing from the coalition. Within days a joint meeting of the NEC and the PLP decided to remain.

At the Party's annual conference a few days later the WLL moved that 'this Conference declares its opposition to the Military Service (No. 2) Bill and in the event of it becoming law, decides to agitate for its repeal'.[15] After some discussion the conference voted on the resolution in parts, accepting the first by a large margin but narrowly defeating the second. Thus the Labour Party position was to oppose conscription in principle, but not to mandate MPs to campaign for its repeal. By April, in the face of huge losses, the government was extending conscription; this time the unions backed them and within 24 hours the NEC had decided to call, and then not to call, another special conference. Unused to government and torn by widely conflicting views, the Party seemed unable to come to firm conclusions about even the most fundamental issues.

Once conscription was brought in, many young men had to decide whether or not to accept it or try to claim exemption. Margaret and Ramsay MacDonald's oldest son, Alister, was 18 in 1916 and as a pacifist volunteered as a non-combatant orderly in the Friends' Ambulance Unit. For three years he worked on an ambulance train carrying wounded soldiers through northern France, experiencing, like many others, horrors which stayed with him for life. The process for gaining exemption was difficult, and those who applied often became the object of active hatred, particularly if they succeeded. In Lancashire the feminist and socialist Hannah Mitchell described her anguish at the thought that her 19-year-old son might be called up. She said:

> I waited in such agony of mind, that I look back on that time as a reprieved man might look back on the time spent in the condemned cell. As the time drew near for his call-up I felt I couldn't bear to live if I knew he had killed another woman's son, but it was for him to decide ...[16]

In the event Hannah's son also applied for exemption, and was set to tree-felling in Ireland. After he sustained a serious injury there he was held in a camp near Dublin, and at the end of the war he was in hospital with influenza during the epidemic. When he finally returned home Hannah saw that 'he was not the happy, care-free lad of the pre-war years ... he had suffered in spirit, and felt the tragedy of war very keenly'.[17]

The WLL was one of the first organisations to affiliate to the UDC, which it did in January 1915, sending Jennie Baker to the UDC's council. However, while Labour women campaigned against conscription and on some of the moral and ethical issues thrown up by the war, particularly in relation to motherhood, it was the exponential increase in employment which the war eventually brought which transformed life for many women workers.

In employment terms, the war brought immediate challenges. One of its initial consequences was a sudden and dramatic upturn in unemployment, particularly among the lowest-paid women. It was estimated that within a month of the outbreak of hostilities over 100,000 women had lost their jobs,[18] particularly in industries such as domestic service where employers could easily make patriotic economies by shedding staff. An additional problem was caused by middle-class women enrolling for war work, which initially consisted primarily of making clothing for soldiers. This led to the development of a distinctly odd acquaintanceship: Queen Mary, who was co-ordinating the work, sent for Mary Macarthur in order to make sure that the activities of volunteers could 'supplement and not supplant paid labour'.[19] The two women got on surprisingly well, and Mary Macarthur was invited onto the committee of the Queen's Work for

Women Fund, which functioned as part of the National Relief Fund, on whose committee Mary also sat.

The plethora of committees set up to manage various aspects of war work included the Central Committee on Women's Employment, of which Mary was the secretary and to which four other Labour women – Margaret Bondfield, Marion Phillips, Mrs Gasson (a member of the Women's Co-operative Guild) and Susan Lawrence – were appointed by the WNC. Susan Lawrence, who would go on to become one of Labour's first female MPs in 1923, had begun life as a Conservative, but converted to socialism in 1912 after meeting Mary Macarthur during a strike of charwomen employed by the London County Council, of which she was a member. She was a tall, rather intimidating woman of formidable intellect who wore a monocle and chain-smoked, but she was capable of inspiring great loyalty and even affection, becoming known throughout the labour movement in London as 'Our Susan'. Like many other people from Margaret Bondfield onwards, Susan Lawrence found Mary Macarthur inspirational, and during the war years Mary became the linchpin around which the organisation of women in industry revolved.

Long before conscription was introduced men had begun to join up in large numbers, and by early 1915 it was clear that the war was going to be both longer and bloodier than most people had thought. In March, the government issued an invitation to women to register for industrial work. No guarantees were given about either rates of pay or conditions, and Sylvia Pankhurst, who was opposed to the war and was still organising East End women, suggested a conference to agree some common demands. This was held on 16 April at Caxton Hall in London and chaired by Mary Macarthur. Margaret Bondfield moved a set of conditions which women should demand as part of their participation in war work. These included trade union membership, equal pay, a living wage, adequate training, and postwar arrangements. Male trade unions, such as the engineers, were urged to accept women members, and there was a demand for adult suffrage. By the end of the day there was a clear platform of demands upon which women in industry could agree, and these formed the basis of negotiations both during the war and after it.

Margaret Bondfield was now working as the assistant secretary of the National Federation of Women Workers (NFWW), and she launched a nationwide recruitment campaign which lasted for the whole of the war. In 1914 there were 358,000 women in trade unions, most of them in the textile unions of Lancashire and Yorkshire. By 1918 there were over a million women trade unionists, nearly 20 per cent of the female workforce, and some unions which had not admitted women as members before the war had now changed their minds. But even the increase in organisation could not cater for the huge numbers of women now employed, many of whom had no experience of either industry or trade unions, and although Mary, Margaret, Gertrude Tuckwell and many others worked tirelessly to try to protect them from exploitation it was impossible to organise everyone.

The challenges trade union women faced were considerable. The Factory Acts had been suspended, which meant that women now had to work long shifts on very low pay, and despite all denials the government was effectively allowing the extension of sweated labour. The factories into which women were being invited were not equipped to receive them. There were very few facilities at all, and none for women. Conditions were unpleasant and insanitary, and, particularly in munitions, often downright dangerous. 'Munitionettes' were much mythologised in the media, but in reality they faced very high risks for very poor remuneration. Male trade unionists were often resistant to women workers in principle, particularly where they were 'diluting' male skills, rates and conditions of work. Equal pay was next to impossible to get, though women transport workers struck successfully for an equal bonus in 1918. For most of the war, strikes were illegal, many employers refused to recognise women's unions, and workers in munitions factories were not allowed to leave their jobs, even if they were underpaid and exploited. There was even a rise in the use of child labour in some industries.

In February 1916 Marion Phillips and others set up the Standing Joint Committee of Industrial Women's Organisations (SJC), the core members of which were the women's trade unions, the WLL, the Women's Co-operative Guild and the Railway Women's Guild. This body initially worked on pensions, but soon came to function as the main point of contact for working women's organisations. It modelled itself to some extent on the WIC, researching and publishing authoritative reports on various aspects of women's employment. Government ministries actively consulted it, and when the Ministry of Food set up its Consumers' Council three SJC members were appointed to it. It also had an international remit: Marion was both secretary of the SJC and chair of the British Section of the Women's International Council of Socialist and Labour Organisations. When, in 1917, Lloyd George set up the Reconstruction Committee to draw up plans for what should happen after the war, Marion Phillips and Beatrice Webb were its only female members.

Perhaps not surprisingly, they found it difficult to work together. Beatrice had never been part of either the WLL or any of the other women's organisations, but regarded herself as the ultimate authority on industrial matters. She did indeed have an imposing record in this field, but so in a different way did Marion, and Beatrice clearly felt threatened, remarking in her diary that 'Marion Phillips is shrewd and capable, but she is contentious and she tries to oppose anything I propose out of some vague desire not to be considered as a Webb disciple.'[20]

Thus Labour women were heavily involved in the fight for workers' rights, but many of them were also deeply engaged in the peace movement. Through the UDC they campaigned to change the public's mind about the war and persuade the government to work for a negotiated peace. They spoke on public platforms and at street corners, earning derision and abuse just as they had done when speaking for women's suffrage or trade unionism. They wrote articles and letters and came to be regarded with deep suspicion by the authorities. When they attempted to travel to international conferences they were prevented and the media treated them as pro-German traitors to both their country and their sex. In 1915 the International Women's Suffrage Alliance planned to hold a meeting in The Hague, which was in a neutral country. This became the International Congress of Women held on 28 April. The UDC helped to convene a national women's conference in London to 'discuss the basis of a permanent peace settlement'. The organising committee included Mary Macarthur, Margaret Bondfield, Ethel Snowden and Marion Phillips, as well as Isabella Ford, Charlotte Despard and the co-operator Margaret Llewelyn Davies. At least 180 women had applied to go to The Hague, but the government was alarmed at the prospect of so many women travelling and refused to grant them passports. They would, however, allow a smaller delegation of 24 to go, including Margaret Bondfield, Isabella Ford, Ada Salter and Esther Roper. Winston Churchill called them 'dangerous women' and when the delegation arrived at Tilbury they found that, by coincidence, the shipping lanes had all been closed. They waited ten days for them to reopen again, 'marooned', as Margaret Bondfield observed, 'by the Government's decision to suspend all passenger service boats from Tilbury as long as we besieged Tilbury dock'.[21] The pro-war press reported the situation with glee: under the headline 'Hopeless dawn at Tilbury', the *Daily Express* said that 'A dismal group of Peacettes are waiting at Tilbury for a boat to take them to Holland for the International chirrup with the German fraus.'[22]

The only British women who got to The Hague were those, including Emmeline Pethick-Lawrence, who were already abroad, but from it was born in the autumn the Women's International League for Peace and Freedom (WIL), upon the committee of which many Labour women served. Throughout the war, and despite continuous attack, women continued to campaign for a negotiated peace, which, as Margaret Bondfield said, would be 'no flabby, emasculated thing – no drooping angel on a damp cloud – but something strong, real and robust'.[23] After the war, those who had worked so hard for peace tried to prevent an unjust and punitive settlement being visited on Germany. 'I would rather,' said Mary Macarthur prophetically during the 1918 general election campaign, 'lose a thousand seats than be party to a settlement containing the seeds of a future war.'[24]

◆ ◆ ◆ ◆ ◆

The last general election had been held in 1910, and by the terms of the 1911 Parliament Act the next one should have been held by 1916 at the latest. It was clear, however, that this would be untenable while the war was still being fought, if only because many men would be disenfranchised by the simple fact of being away fighting. There was also an acceptance that it would be unreasonable to allow one man struggling in the mud of northern France to vote and not the man standing next to him simply on the grounds of a property qualification, and so there were already moves to bring in a franchise bill to allow all men to vote. The campaign for female suffrage had been suspended at the start of the war, but the NUWSS knew that if they did not take advantage of the opportunity they would be unlikely to get another chance in the near future.

When Asquith indicated in 1915 that it was doubtful whether women would be included in any future franchise bill they again began to hold demonstrations and meetings. However, he was soon replaced as prime minister by Lloyd George, and early in 1916 the NUWSS wrote to the government to remind it that before the war it had promised that women would be included in any new suffrage legislation. At the Labour Party conference in January 1916, even the miners supported the inclusion of women. Prominent Labour women now worked alongside the NUWSS, and for the first time there was general alignment between universal adult and female suffragists. A petition beginning 'We, the undersigned workers, believing that if a woman can cast a shell she can cast a vote ...'[25] was circulated to factories and trade union branches with a good response.

Throughout the summer the pressure was maintained, and in August a Speaker's Conference was set up in Parliament to look at the whole issue of electoral registration and the franchise.[26]

Women's organisations had anticipated that some women might be included in the conference's membership, but the fact that this turned out not to be the case sounded the first note of alarm. Issues around male suffrage were resolved fairly quickly, but there was not the same kind of consensus on what to do about women. In the end the report, issued in January 1917, recommended that women should be included, but that there should be both a property threshold and an age qualification of either 30 or 35.

Inevitably, this would exclude a large number of working-class women, and many Labour and trade union women were therefore reluctant to accept what was being offered. Throughout the first few months of 1917 there were meetings, demonstrations and petitions to try to persuade Parliament to legislate for an equal – or at least a more equal – suffrage, but to no avail. There were still people opposed to enfranchising women at all, and even some reservations about enfranchising all men. In May the Representation of the People Bill was introduced into the House of Commons and had a fraught passage through the legislative process. Despite last-ditch attempts in the House of Lords to block it, it finally became law in early 1918. All men, and all women over the age of 30 who met the property requirement, or who were university graduates, were to be allowed to vote at the next general election. The sex bar had finally been breached.

For women such as Mary Macarthur and Margaret Bondfield, however, it was hard to celebrate when so many of the women they represented had been left out. Margaret Bondfield said that they 'felt that it was a mean and inadequate little Bill, creating fresh anomalies which had to be overcome'.[27] It would be another ten years before women were able to vote on an equal basis with men.

In the meantime, as the franchise bill was being debated, the Russian Revolution changed the whole configuration of politics across Europe. One immediate fear was that the new government under Kerensky would take Russia out of the war, and there was a rush of visitors, including Emmeline Pankhurst, to try to persuade them to stay. There were proposals to hold an international conference of socialists in Stockholm to discuss war aims. At first Arthur Henderson did not think this would be helpful and proposed instead a gathering of allied socialist parties in London. When the Petrograd Soviet announced that it supported the

Stockholm plan, Lloyd George allowed Henderson to visit Russia to try to generate support for the London meeting. He arrived in Russia in June 1917, and what he found there persuaded him not only that the Stockholm conference could not be prevented, but that the Labour Party should participate. Lloyd George was furious. Delegates were denied passports, and Henderson resigned from the government. His visit to Russia had also convinced him that the political landscape was shifting, that democracy would have to be fought for and defended, and that the Labour Party had definitively to disconnect itself from the Liberals and become a genuine alternative party of government. He believed – not entirely accurately – that the public no longer trusted the old parties which had taken the country into the war, and he thought that a restructured, unified and re-energised Labour Party with a clear electoral purpose and capability could reap the rewards. Working with Beatrice and Sidney Webb he set about a major reconstruction of the Party which included the absorption of the WLL.

Throughout the Labour Party's short history it had been possible for it to speak with several voices, but this could not continue if Henderson's objectives were to be achieved. The greatest challenge was to persuade the trade unions to agree to a structure which included individual membership, thus on the face of it increasing the influence of local members whilst actually making it possible for the NEC to have much more control over what local parties did. It would no longer be possible, for instance, for local parties to run by-election candidates in defiance of the leadership's decision, and it would be much easier to achieve some unity in policy terms, too.

The approach of the enfranchisement of even some women also added urgency to the particular question of what the WLL's future relationship with the Labour Party should be. At the time it was by no means either clear or certain that women generally would follow the same patterns of political affiliation as men; in April 1917 a WLL subcommittee looking at the prospect of Labour women having the vote observed that they 'should not be caught by any of the separate women's organisations which are bound to be set on foot. It is most important that, as workers, they should join with men and not form a special women's party.'[28] Throughout the war the WLL continued to campaign on the issues that mattered to women, especially housing and the feeding of children, adding new, war-related questions such as conscription, prostitution and support for unmarried mothers. But the organisation itself continued to become increasingly centralised as Marion Phillips tightened her grip on it, and in any case local activity became harder to maintain as branches weakened or failed and women found themselves having to concentrate on war work.

From the Labour Party's point of view the extension of the franchise presented threats as well as opportunities. The WLL had been accustomed to ploughing its own furrow when it came to policy. Its conference had not always agreed with the Labour Party over issues such as suffrage, and many of its leading women had connections with women in the wider women's movement which did not accord with the Party's ideology or opinion. Under Marion Phillips's guidance there had been some drawing together, but the WLL still retained the capacity to take its own line where it thought that would benefit women. But millions of women were about to be enfranchised, and the Party needed to be able to reach them directly. The WLL with its network of connections and its organising experience offered the possibility of being able to do this quickly and efficiently. Thus it is easy to see why Henderson and the Webbs would want the Party to clip the women's wings in one way while supporting them in another. What is less explicable is how the WLL executive allowed a situation to arise in which women were admitted to individual membership of the Party only as second-class members, with little access to either public office or power within the new structures, and no autonomy.

The events of the war had changed perceptions on all sides and, in particular, led to a readjustment in the perceived relationship, among women as well as men, between class and gender. The WLL had viewed themselves as part of both struggles, and believed that, in the plight of working-class women, those struggles intersected. But one effect of the war was to increase the importance of class issues, particularly after the Russian Revolution of 1917. Both the war and the revolution heightened the view of the left that class was the overriding factor in terms of oppression; just as Emmeline Pankhurst had believed that the vote would solve the evils of unemployment, so women on the left now thought that removing class and economic oppression would also do away with the oppression of women.

In addition, for many women the ultimate goal had always been integration with what Marion Curran had called 'the men's party', just as Mary Macarthur always saw the NFWW as ultimately becoming part of the wider trade union movement. Some women were prepared to argue for women-only spaces, and others did not necessarily believe that women were yet ready to be part of larger, older political and trade union structures, but by the middle of the war the WLL was largely run by women for whom integration was an immediate and achievable goal, and Marion Phillips was very definitely of this view.

The negotiations by which the Labour Party 'acquired' the WLL, therefore, were largely conducted on this basis by Marion, Mary Longman (with whom she lived) and Arthur Henderson. He and the Webbs had developed a plan to introduce individual membership and local branches. The Party's NEC was to be restructured so as to allow the representation of grass-roots members and to recognise changes in the size and role of the trade unions. There was also to be a new constitution with a much greater emphasis on socialism and, in particular, nationalisation (in the form of the famous Clause IV), which had been found to work well under pressure during the war and now came to be seen as the ideal form of economic regulation. In these much larger negotiations the question of what to do about women was a small, if important, part, and Henderson himself dealt with the arrangements. These were presented to a WLL executive meeting on 12 October 1917, which Henderson attended to explain what was proposed.

It is clear from the minutes that members did not give Marion or Henderson an easy time of it. Whilst they agreed with most of the proposals, they were not happy about women's representation on the NEC, and there was 'a good deal of discussion on details of organisation'. There was also a very strong feeling that 'special provision should be made for women to have opportunities of discussing special women's questions or problems from the women's standpoint'.[29] Discussion continued for some months afterwards, and the issues were debated at the WLL's last conference in January 1918. But by then it was much too late to change anything; the Party's new constitution was to be agreed at its annual conference the following day. Women were to be allowed to be individual members of the Labour Party, but at a subscription half that of men's. Henderson had earlier talked about women helping 'not only with their votes, and with work at election times, but in helping to form the policy of the party and in the way of political education'.[30] There were to be separate sections for men and women, but women-only spaces would be restricted to the local level, and there would be no national women's conference. Holding one would be 'impossible without giving a similar weight to men's sections, and thereby instituting a sectionalism of a national kind throughout the party'.[31]

The WLL was effectively being presented with a fait accompli and had no option but to accept it, though both then and for years afterwards there were protests, and the question of the status of a women's conference and the degree of independent action open to socialist feminists is still a point of debate within Labour to this day. In 1918 many women found their relegation to second-class members unappetising, and acted accordingly. 'I believe,' said Hannah Mitchell, 'in complete equality, and was not prepared to be a camp follower, or a member of what seemed to me a permanent Social Committee, or official Cake-maker to the Labour Party.'[32] She concentrated her activity on the ILP, and she was probably not alone. The WLL was formally dissolved into the Labour Party in June 1918 and the SJC became the Women's Advisory Committee. Marion Phillips became the Party's first national women's officer.

The first woman to be selected to fight as a Labour candidate in a general election was Mary Macarthur, who was invited to contest the Stourbridge seat in the Black Country. Stourbridge included Cradley Heath, where less than a decade previously she had led the chain-makers' strike and was still known as 'Our Mary'. So quick was the Party to install her as the candidate that at the point at which she was adopted, in August 1918, the legislation allowing women to stand had still not been passed. Her huge popularity meant that there was fierce competition to secure her as a candidate: she was offered a choice of seven seats, and even the male trade unions were unanimous in their support of her. Nevertheless, unlike most other women candidates she had time in which to get organised, and it was widely expected that she would be elected as Britain's first female member of parliament.

The Armistice on 11 November was followed very quickly by the calling of a general election. This was to be held on 14 December 1918, and for the first time in history was to be held on a single day rather than over a period of weeks. The Labour Party had already withdrawn from the coalition government and was therefore standing, as Henderson had wanted, entirely clear of any Liberal connection. Apart from anything else, the Liberals' electoral deal was now with the Conservatives. Candidates from either party who had supported the coalition received a letter of support signed by both Lloyd George (as prime minister) and Andrew Bonar Law, the Conservative leader. This letter became known as a 'coupon', and Liberals and Conservatives did not stand against each other where one or other candidate had been thus approved. Herbert Asquith, whom Lloyd George had displaced as prime minister, led the rump of the Liberal Party. But despite Henderson's efforts the Labour Party also had its problems: George Barnes, who had replaced Henderson as leader in 1917, refused to resign from the coalition in 1918 and thus had to be expelled from the Party and replaced by Scots mining MP William Adamson. Despite this, however, the Party fielded a record number of candidates in the 1918 election, standing in over 350 constituencies.

In addition to Mary, Labour fielded just three other women candidates. Charlotte Despard, at 74 the grande dame of suffrage, socialism and pacifism, stood in Battersea. In Rusholme, Emmeline Pethick-Lawrence stood on a firmly feminist and socialist platform. Millicent Mackenzie, who stood for a university seat in Wales, was the first woman to become a professor at a major university and had campaigned for female suffrage. Across the country only 13 other women got themselves onto ballot papers: four Liberals, one Conservative, five independents, two Sinn Feiners (including Constance Markievicz) and one Women's Party candidate. There was considerable press interest in the women candidates, *The Times* noting that 'When a woman enters the lists the novelty of the situation and the freshness of her point of view contrive to banish indifference and apathy.'[33] There was also much speculation about how well prepared women electors might or might not be and how they might vote. Many constituencies ran women's meetings so that women could question the candidates, and these were well attended and often very lively.

Mary Macarthur's own campaign had got off the ground early, but ran into trouble when she went to hand in her nomination papers. To her astonishment the returning officer refused to accept them. He maintained that she had not correctly entered her name, and that he would not allow her to be a candidate unless she did. He believed her legal name to be, not Mary Macarthur, as everyone knew her, but her married one of Mary Reid Anderson, and this was the only name that he was prepared to countenance. Given that the Liberal candidate in Mansfield, Violet Markham, was standing in a seat her brother had held for many years and was allowed to do so under her maiden name rather than her married one of Carruthers, this seemed particularly arbitrary, but the returning officer was immovable.

Ballot papers at that time carried no reference to candidates' party affiliations, and electors were expected to recognise the name of the person they wanted to vote for. But most of the people who wanted to vote for Mary Macarthur were voting for the first time, and some were barely able to read. Despite her popularity and fame, and despite a strong campaign, it was hard to dispel the confusion understandably felt by many new male and female voters. Her election address was uncompromising in its commitment to equality, socialism, peace and economic justice, and she also appealed particularly to women. 'If I am returned to the House of Commons,' she said, 'I shall try to voice in a special sense the aspirations of the women workers of this land, to whose cause I have been privileged to devote my life ....'[34] The three-page document was signed 'Mary R. Macarthur (Mrs W. C. Anderson)'.

Mary Macarthur came closer to winning in the 1918 election than any other of the Labour women, but still lost by 1,333 votes. She claimed not to be too disappointed, and to be much more upset by her husband's loss of his seat in Sheffield Attercliffe, but the result was undoubtedly a blow. She never forgave the returning officer, accusing him of robbing her of her good name and maintaining that despite the figures she regarded the result as 'a remarkable victory'.[35]

In neighbouring Smethwick, Christabel Pankhurst stood for the Women's Party. This had been set up primarily as a vehicle to get her into Parliament, and she was its only candidate. It had a programme rooted as much in the war as in feminism, with 'Victory, National Security and Social Reform' as its watchwords, and explaining that 'it is felt that women can best serve the nation by keeping clear of men's party political machines and traditions'.[36] Sylvia Pankhurst was scathing. 'Here is obviously a Tariff Reform, Tory, Imperial jingo organisation,' she said, 'and we who are Socialist and internationalist have other ideas.'[37] During the campaign Christabel, who was the only female candidate to receive Lloyd George's coupon, was in a straight fight with a Labour man, whom she accused of both pacifism and Bolshevism. She advocated equality between the sexes, but also punitive reparations against Germany, more stringent rationing and the abolition of trade unions. Her pro-war views meant that she was, despite her feminism, popular among many working-class voters, and the Labour Party was seriously worried that she might win. Resources were diverted from neighbouring constituencies, including Stourbridge, and Mary Macarthur took time out from her own difficult campaign to go and speak for the Labour candidate. Christabel Pankhurst lost by 600 votes. In all, every female candidate except one was defeated. Constance Markievicz, then imprisoned in Holloway Gaol for her part in the 1916 Easter Rising in Dublin, became the first woman ever to be elected to the British Parliament.

In general, a triumphant electorate took its revenge on the Labour pro-peace MPs, including Ramsay MacDonald, Philip Snowden and Will Anderson, who all lost their seats. Despite his time in the Cabinet, Arthur Henderson also lost. But overall Labour representation in Parliament rose to 57, leaving the Party still in fourth place, but with more influence than Sinn Fein who, though numerically the third party, did not take their seats. The Irish Parliamentary Party was no longer represented. Labour was effectively now a substantial force in the House of Commons. The Conservative Party won most seats, but David Lloyd George remained as prime minister. Asquith, who had led the non-coupon Liberals, lost the seat he had represented for over 30 years.

As the men began to return from the front lines, so women started to retreat from employment. Women who had left their homes in their thousands to work in factories, transport and farming now found themselves forced out of their jobs and back into their kitchens. Men had been promised that they would get their jobs back at the end of the war, and keeping that promise meant that the women had to be ejected. Many of these were the same women who had been denied the vote, and there was much dissatisfaction. The ambivalence about the desirability of women working continued for decades, with professions such as the civil service and teaching continuing to ban the employment of married women until after World War II.

For the Labour Party, and for the women in it, a new era was opening. The 1920s would bring the first Labour governments, a general strike and a catastrophic financial crash. Women would slowly find their feet in electoral politics, and although there would still be controversy and debate about their role in the Labour Party they would settle in as an established part of the political landscape. But the memory of their contribution to the building of that landscape would almost entirely disappear; Millicent Fawcett could have been writing about all Labour and trade union women when she wrote of Isabella Ford that no-one would 'ever fully know all that she did in framing the mental attitude and outlook of the founders of the Independent Labour Party'.[38] The new era would bring new challenges, and the next two decades would set the scene for both another world war and the landmark Labour government that followed it. In the twenty-first century women's position in politics is very different, and the world in which the first Labour women asserted their place in the movement seems very distant. Despite this, however, their legacy lives on, and continues to inform, encourage and inspire the women who are in the room today.

Epilogue

In the end, the vote did not turn out to be the magical answer to all problems that the long fight for it had allowed it to appear. Eight and a half million women could vote, and all women could stand for Parliament, but no woman took her seat in the House of Commons until 1919,[1] and the number of women MPs did not reach double figures for another decade. As a consequence their influence on legislation and events was limited; they did score some successes, but the expectation that once women could vote both politics and society would change radically was not fulfilled.

During the 1920s the Labour Party became a party of government. In 1923 Margaret Bondfield, Susan Lawrence and Dorothy Jewson became Labour's first women MPs. In January 1924 Ramsay MacDonald, who had returned to Parliament in a by-election in 1922, became the first Labour prime minister and the first from a working-class background. Despite probable dalliances with various women he had never remarried, and the memory of Margaret remained with him; their daughter Sheila later recalled: 'After crossing the threshold of No. 10 Downing Street for the first time as prime minister he wrote in his diary "Ah, were she here to help me. Why are they both dead, my mother and she?"'[2]

The new government was a coalition with the Liberals, but it included Margaret Bondfield as parliamentary secretary at the Ministry of Labour, the first woman to hold ministerial office. She had been elected to the Trades Union Congress (TUC) General Council in 1918 and in 1923 had become the first woman to chair it. Of her elevation to government she later wrote: 'I was both sad and glad; I was leaving the greatly prized Chair of the industrial world, of which I knew something from the inside, and I was going on a strange adventure.'[3] In the election held in October 1924 she lost her highly marginal seat; George Bernard Shaw, still a stalwart Fabian and supporter of women, wrote to her:

You are the best man of the lot, and they shove you off on a place where the water is too cold for their dainty feet just as they shoved Mary [Macarthur] off on Stourbridge and keep the safe seats for their now quite numerous imbeciles.⁴

Margaret's later career became a vivid illustration of the old adage that all political careers end in failure. In 1926 she was elected for the Tyneside seat of Wallsend, and in 1929 she became the first woman cabinet minister when Ramsay MacDonald appointed her as Minister of Labour. Again, her account of the appointment records a mix of emotions:

I pointed out to him [MacDonald] that a brilliant group of women had been returned in our Party, and asked him if he was quite sure he had made the best choice in myself. He said very decidedly that he was quite sure, upon which I said that I would do my best to merit his confidence. … Once more I am torn up by the roots from official Trade Union work which has been such a large part of my life.⁵

This moment proved to be the high point; the Wall Street crash soon after Labour took power ultimately broke the Labour Party as well as the economy, and took many reputations into the wilderness with it, including Margaret's. As part of measures to address the crisis she proposed cuts in unemployment benefits, and for many people, particularly in the trade unions she loved, this was unforgivable. When MacDonald formed a coalition National Government with the Conservatives in 1931, Margaret refused to join it and remained with the Labour Party but, like 200 other Labour MPs, including all the women, she lost her seat in the ensuing general election. Overall, Labour lost 200 seats, returning almost to a pre-1918 level of representation. MacDonald himself was expelled from the Party and died in 1937. His ashes were buried with Margaret's at Lossiemouth.

Long after Margaret Bondfield's death in 1953, Barbara Castle was asked by the Fabian Society to write something about her for a publication to mark the centenary of her birth. Barbara was said to have declined, on the grounds that Margaret's action in 1931 had brought her close to betrayal of the movement; as Harold Wilson's Minister of Labour, Barbara was even said to have changed her department's name to avoid any taint of association. Margaret's name was almost entirely omitted from the Party's centenary celebrations in 2000.

Following MacDonald's defection to the National Government George Lansbury became leader, taking the Party into the 1935 election in which it regained a hundred of its lost seats. He was then replaced as leader by Clement Attlee who remained in post for the next 20 years. Meanwhile the Independent Labour Party (ILP), whose drift away from the Labour Party had begun even before the Great War, finally disaffiliated from it in 1932 and was never again the formidable force in the politics of the left that it had once been.

Women did not achieve an equal franchise with men until 1928, and even then only after a steady, almost weary campaign. The Women's Social and Political Union (WSPU) had been wound up in 1917 and Christabel Pankhurst, who lived abroad between 1921 and 1926, did not take much part in the campaign, but Emmeline returned to Britain in the mid-1920s and was active to some degree, dying in London a few weeks before the 1928 Act was passed. The youngest daughter, Adela, had emigrated to Australia in 1914 and took no further part in British politics. Sylvia remained in London, becoming an early member of the Communist Party and later campaigning against racism and fascism. She developed a career as a writer, and lived with her partner, Silvio Erasmus Corio. In 1927 she gave birth to a son, Richard Keir Pethick Pankhurst, and later became famous for her work in defence of Ethiopia following its invasion by Italy in 1935. Christabel died in 1958, Sylvia in 1960 and Adela in 1961.

After the war ended Millicent Fawcett retired from active political life, although she continued to participate in some charities and causes. In 1928, however, she was in the gallery of the House of Commons to see the Equal Franchise Bill passed which finally granted universal adult suffrage. In her diary she wrote: 'It is almost exactly 61 years ago since I heard John Stuart Mill introduce his suffrage amendment to the Reform Bill on May 20th, 1867. So I have had extraordinary good luck in having seen the struggle from the beginning.'[6] She died a year later at the age of 81.

Marion Phillips remained as the Labour Party's National Woman Officer until her death in 1932. In 1929 she was elected to Parliament for the constituency of Sunderland, one of nine women – including Ethel Bentham and Mary Agnes Hamilton – returned in the first election held on the basis of universal adult suffrage. When she died of cancer in 1932 she was working on the Party's national campaign to recruit a million new individual members. Arthur Henderson wrote of her that she:

was a woman of striking intellectual force, powerful personality and great industry. The keen sense of personal love I had for her is shared by every member of the National Labour Party Executive. The women's section of the Labour Party is a monument to her great organising ability.[7]

Mary Macarthur never stood for Parliament again. Will Anderson died suddenly in the influenza epidemic in February 1919, leaving Mary a widow with a small daughter, Nancy. In 1920 she was diagnosed with breast cancer. Neither she nor Margaret Bondfield had envisaged the National Federation of Women Workers (NFWW) as a permanent fixture, believing that it would eventually merge with one of the 'mainstream' unions. Now Mary negotiated its absorption into the National Union of General and Municipal Workers, with Margaret taking the National Women's Officer role that had originally been intended for Mary. On the day that the merger took effect, 1 January 1921, Mary Macarthur died at the age of 40.

The Labour Party's postwar structure ensured that women became and remained active members, but it deprived them of much independence of action and made little space for them either in public office or at senior levels of organisation or policy making. There were women candidates in every election, but most found themselves in marginal seats or, like their early male counterparts, in one of the few remaining two-member seats. Between the crash of 1931 and Ellen Wilkinson's election in Jarrow in 1935 there were no Labour women in Parliament at all. In 1945, 21 were elected, a level not achieved again until 1987, and only the introduction of positive action measures for the 1997 election took the number of Labour women MPs above a hundred. Similarly, women were slow to break into government; in 1964 Barbara Castle became only the fourth woman (and third Labour woman) cabinet minister, and not until after 1997 did it become common for more than a couple of women to sit in Cabinet together.[8]

The absorption of the Women's Labour League (WLL) into the Labour Party in 1918 had several consequences, not all of them either foreseen or intended. It gave Labour women a formal place in the Party's structures, with a guaranteed presence on the National Executive Committee (NEC) and a voice on the floor of Conference. But the reduced membership rate led to a widespread perception that women were second-class members, and in many local parties this was how they were seen. Hannah Mitchell's apprehension that women would be treated as 'official Cake-makers' was all too frequently justified, and it took women decades to achieve the measure of equality that Marion Phillips had probably thought would come more quickly. Women continued to work on the issues that concerned them, and scored a number of successes through campaigning and lobbying. They were also prominent in advancing developments in public health and housing in local government, particularly between the wars. As a whole, however, they were never valued as highly as they might have been. Labour was not unique in this, but its rigid structures and rules contributed to the difficulties and women found it hard to break out of the roles they seemed to have been assigned in 1918.

There were other side-effects, too. Labour women now found themselves bound (as WLL women had not been) by a narrowly inter-preted party loyalty which had been much less marked in the pre-war years. Then there had been a certain fluidity when it came to women's activism, and much of the suffrage movement as well as the Women's Industrial Council (WIC), the women's trade unions, the peace movement and many other organisations had enabled women to work together across ideological lines. Women of all parties became more partisan during the 1920s, but this was particularly true of Labour women for whom socialism and class politics had been much invigorated by both the war and the Russian Revolution. The wedge driven between them and the wider women's movement at this time proved hard to dislodge even as successive waves of feminism washed over society in subsequent decades. To some extent the breach remains to this day.

The loss of the WLL also contributed to the loss of Labour women's history. Even before 1918 the records of Labour women's activism had begun to disappear: after Margaret MacDonald's death the Executive Committee itself destroyed many records and there does not seem to have been any intention of creating a permanent record or archive after the merger. What remains is currently held in the People's History Museum in Manchester and is a combination of the Labour Party's official corre-spondence and minutes and Mary Middleton's papers, which were kept by her widower, J. S. Middleton, and ultimately preserved by his fourth wife, Lucy, who was elected to Parliament in 1945. As women's sense of themselves as a distinct political entity faded – and was actively discouraged in some quarters – so their foremothers became harder to find, and their personalities less distinct. Both the Labour Party and the trade unions retained their traditional masculine tone and appearance, and women began to look outside the labour movement for their political roots. They found them in the suffrage movement, but in doing so they lost the richness and vigour of their own history and largely forgot women's role in laying Labour's foundations.

The WLL remained the only independent organisation of Labour women until 1988, when the Labour Women's Network was formed in the wake of the 1987 general election. More than a century after Margaret MacDonald's death, Margaret Bondfield's challenge to Labour women on her behalf is still being answered: 'She was sure we would become an effective force in Labour politics. Are we strong enough to justify her faith?'

The Women in the Room

The following list gives brief details for many of the women mentioned in this book. For most of them, more exhaustive biographies can be found in the excellent *Oxford Dictionary of National Biography* (www.oxforddnb. com) or in volumes such as Cheryl Law's *Women: A Modern Political Dictionary* (London, 2000). A small number of them wrote autobiographies or memoirs; an even smaller number have had biographies written about them.

Addis, Maria: delegate to the TUC from the Dressmakers' Society eight times between 1881 and 1895. Moved a suffrage resolution at the TUC in 1884.

Baker, Jennie (d.1939): socialist, universal adult suffragist and peace campaigner, member of the Women's Labour League Executive and later Secretary of the National Council for Unmarried Mothers.

Becker, Lydia (1827–90): feminist, suffragist, botanist, radical Liberal reformer, campaigner for women's property rights and education, Secretary of the National Society for Women's Suffrage, the first national suffrage organisation (based in Manchester), in 1867.

Bentham, Ethel (1861–1931): physician, feminist and socialist, member of the Women's Labour League, President 1913 onwards, ran the League's Memorial Baby Clinic, MP 1929–31.

Besant, Annie (1847–1933): campaigner, politician, socialist, Fabian, feminist, free-thinker, theosophist and journalist.

Billington-Greig, Teresa (1876–1964): teacher, feminist, suffragette and journalist, founder member of the Women's Freedom League.

Black, Clementina (1853–1922): trade unionist, researcher, socialist, suffragist, author and campaigner, especially on consumer issues, sweated labour and a legal minimum wage. Co-founded the Women's Industrial Council in 1894.

Bondfield, Margaret (1873–1953): trade unionist, socialist, feminist, adult suffragist, pacifist, first woman to occupy many political posts, including female Labour MP, government minister, cabinet minister and Chair of the TUC.

Bruce Glasier, Katharine (née Conway) (1867–1950): socialist, journalist, and campaigner, public speaker for the Fabians, the Independent Labour Party and the Socialist Church, campaigner for pithead baths for miners.

Chew, Ada Nield (1870–1945): working-class socialist, suffragist, organiser, campaigner, trade unionist and author.

Cooper, Selina (1864–1946): trade unionist, feminist, suffragist, socialist, National Union of Women's Suffrage Societies organiser and peace campaigner.

Craigen, Jessie (1835–99): working-class feminist, trade unionist, suffrage and Irish Home Rule campaigner

Despard, Charlotte (1844–1939): feminist, socialist and suffrage campaigner, co-founder of the Women's Freedom League and one of Labour's first female parliamentary candidates in 1918.

Dilke, Emilia (Lady Dilke) (1840–1904): trade unionist, campaigner for women's rights and art historian. Founding member of the Women's Protective and Provident League, the Women's Trade Union League and the Women's Industrial Council.

Fawcett, Millicent (1847–1929): women's rights campaigner and suffrage leader, first woman to speak on a public platform for votes for women, President of the National Union of Women's Suffrage Societies.

Ford, Isabella (1855–1924): Leeds-based feminist, trade unionist, suffragist, pacifist, member of the Independent Labour Party executive, first woman to speak at a Labour Party conference.

Gore-Booth, Eva (1870–1926): feminist, trade unionist, suffragist and pacifist, partner of Esther Roper.

Hanson, Marion Coates (1870–1947): feminist, socialist and suffragette, co-founder of the Women's Freedom League.

Hicks, Amie (Annie) (1839–1917): trade unionist, socialist and Marxist, member of the Social Democratic Federation.

Irwin, Margaret (1858–1940): Scottish trade unionist, suffragist and women's rights campaigner, Parliamentary Secretary of the Scottish TUC.

Lawrence, Susan (1871–1947): trade unionist and socialist, Fabian, one of Labour's first three women MPs elected in 1923.

Lee, Annie: trade unionist, feminist and socialist, first woman delegate to Labour Party conference in 1901, later one of Manchester's first women councillors and aldermen.

Macarthur, Mary (1880–1921): trade unionist, feminist, socialist and peace campaigner, founded the National Federation of Women Workers in 1906, led the chain-makers' strike in 1910.

MacDonald, Margaret (née Gladstone) (1870–1911): socialist, feminist, trade unionist, social reformer, co-founder of the Women's Labour League in 1906.

Macpherson, Mary Fenton (1859–1933): linguist and journalist, activist in Railway Women's Guild, co-founder of the Women's Labour League.

Marland-Brodie, Annie (1861–1947): trade unionist, socialist, first woman to be appointed as a national trade union organiser.

Martyn, Caroline (1867–96): itinerant speaker and lecturer for the Independent Labour Party.

Marx, Eleanor (1855–98): socialist, feminist and trade unionist, founding member of the Social Democratic Federation.

McMillan, Margaret (1860–1931): Christian socialist, Fabian, Independent Labour Party speaker, campaigner for children's health and education.

Middleton, Mary (1870–1911): socialist co-founder of the Women's Labour League in 1906, Secretary 1907–11.

Mitchell, Hannah (1872–1956): Manchester-based socialist, feminist, suffragette and pacifist, later councillor.

Nesbit, Edith (1858–1924): socialist, feminist, Fabian, journalist, advocate of the 'new life', celebrated children's author.

Pankhurst, Adela (1885–1961): feminist and suffragette, third daughter of Emmeline and Richard Pankhurst, emigrated to Australia.

Pankhurst, Christabel (1880–1958): feminist and suffragette leader, eldest daughter of Emmeline and Richard Pankhurst, candidate in the 1918 general election, emigrated to the United States.

Pankhurst, Emmeline (1858–1928): feminist and suffragette leader, founder member of the Independent Labour Party in 1893, co-founded the Women's Social and Political Union in 1903.

Pankhurst, Sylvia (1882–1960): feminist, socialist, trade unionist, pacifist and suffragette, second daughter of Emmeline and Richard Pankhurst.

Paterson, Emma (1848–86): trade unionist and women's rights campaigner, co-founded the Women's Protective and Provident League in 1874, jointly with Edith Simcox the first woman delegate to the TUC in 1875.

Pethick-Lawrence, Emmeline (1867–1954): feminist, socialist and suffragette, one of Labour's first women parliamentary candidates in 1918.

Phillips, Marion (1881–1932): socialist and feminist, Secretary of the Women's Labour League 1911–18, Labour Party's first National Women's Officer 1918 onwards, MP 1929–31.

Roper, Esther (1868–1938): Manchester-based trade unionist, feminist, suffragist and pacifist, partner of Eva Gore-Booth.

Simcox, Edith (1844–1901): feminist, trade unionist, shirtmaker and anthropologist, jointly with Emma Paterson the first woman delegate to the TUC in 1875, and the first woman to speak at it.

Snowden, Ethel (née Annakin) (1881–1951): socialist, feminist, suffragist, journalist, public speaker and peace campaigner.

Stacy, Enid (1868–1903): socialist, trade unionist and women's rights campaigner, itinerant speaker and lecturer for the Independent Labour Party.

Tuckwell, Gertrude (1861–1951): trade unionist, social reformer, adult suffrage campaigner, niece of Emilia Dilke and President of the Women's Protective and Provident League after 1904.

Varley, Julia (1871–1952): trade unionist and campaigner, worked with Mary Macarthur in the chain-makers' strike, later became Chief Woman Organiser for the Transport and General Workers' Union.

Webb, Beatrice (1858–1943): social reformer, later socialist, expert on industrial conditions and trade unions, coined the term 'collective bargaining', co-author of the Labour Party's 1918 constitution.

Whyte, Eleanor (d.1913): trade unionist, bookbinder and women's rights campaigner, attended every TUC meeting for over 20 years, sometimes as the only female delegate.

Wilson, Charlotte (1854–1944): anarchist, Fabian, suffragist, feminist, first woman to write a Fabian Tract (1884), founder in 1908 of the Fabian Women's Group.

Notes

Preface

1. Quoted in Margaret Bondfield. A Life's Work, p 245.

Introduction

1. Mary Agnes Hamilton, *Mary Macarthur: A Biographical Sketch* (London, 1925), p. 124.
2. E. Sylvia Pankhurst, *The Suffragette Movement: An Intimate Account of Persons and Ideals* (London, 1931), p. 334.
3. Mary Middleton to Lisbeth Simm, 30 January 1911, quoted in Mary Middleton Memorial Booklet (Correspondence of Margaret Ethel MacDonald, The National Archives, PRO 30/69/902).
4. Beatrice Webb, *Diary*, vol. 1: *1873–1892: Glitter Around and Darkness Within* (London, 1986), 27 November 1887, p. 223.
5. Clementina Black, 'On Marriage: A Criticism', *Fortnightly Review*, April 1890.
6. Margaret Bondfield, *A Life's Work* (London, 1948), p. 37.
7. Ibid., p. 76.
8. Gifford Lewis, *Eva Gore-Booth and Esther Roper: A Biography* (London, 1988), pp. 6–8.
9. Martin Pugh, *The Pankhursts: The History of One Radical Family* (London, 2001), p. 94.
10. Quoted in Jill Liddington, *The Road to Greenham Common: Feminism and Anti-Militarism in Britain Since 1820* (Syracuse, NY, 2005), p. 73.

1. Trade Unionists

1. Sidney Webb and Beatrice Webb, *The History of Trade Unionism* (London, 1898), pp. 227–8.
2. Quoted in Henry Pelling, *A History of British Trade Unionism* (London, 1992), p. 64.
3. Chartism was a campaign for political rights for working people in the 1830s and 1840s. It was the first mass working-class movement and, although it enjoyed huge support, was ultimately unsuccessful in its own campaigns. It disappeared after 1848, but all of its demands except annual parliamentary elections have since been realised. They did not include votes for women.

4. Address to the trade unionists of the United Kingdom and working men generally, Labour Representation League minute book, 17 March 1873 (LSE Archives and Special Collections, GB 97 SR 0061).
5. TUC Report, October 1875, p. 24.
6. *Women's Trade Union Review*, July 1897, p. 19.
7. TUC Report, 1877, p. 18.
8. Harold Goldman, *Emma Paterson: She Led Women Into a Man's World* (Essex, 1974), p. 28.
9. Quoted in ibid., p. 28.
10. *Labour News* was not a Labour newspaper, but a place where jobs were advertised which also took articles on subjects of interest to both employers and the employed.
11. WPPL Annual Report, 1875 (TUC Library Collections, London Metropolitan University).
12. TUC Report, 1874, p. 80.
13. Ibid., p. 28.
14. Emma Paterson, *Labour News*, April 1874.
15. *Sheffield Daily Telegraph*, 14 October 1875.
16. WPPL Annual Report, 1879 (TUC Library Collections, London Metropolitan University).
17. Quotations in this paragraph are all taken from TUC Report, 1878, pp. 31–2.
18. TUC Report, 1880, p. 30.
19. TUC Report, 1889, p. 42.
20. TUC Report, 1891, p. 73.
21. This was Mrs Woodcock, of Nottingham; 1894 was the only year in which she attended, and nothing more seems to be known about her.
22. *Women's Union Journal*, January 1887 (TUC Library Collections, London Metropolitan University).
23. Annie Marland-Brodie was a textile worker from Lancashire who first met Emilia Dilke at a Women's Liberal Federation meeting in London in 1891. Though Annie soon became a socialist, their friendship and working relationship lasted until Emilia's death in 1904.
24. Quoted in Barbara Drake, *Women in Trade Unions* (London, 1920; repr. 1987), pp. 23–4.
25. TUC Report, 1887, pp. 42–3.
26. TUC Report, 1888, p. 43.
27. Quoted in Drake, *Women in Trade Unions*, p. 20.
28. TUC Report, 1888, p. 43.
29. TUC Report, 1889, p. 31.
30. TUC Report, 1891, pp. 86–7.
31. Quoted in Drake, *Women in Trade Unions*, p. 11.
32. Bondfield, *A Life's Work*, p. 28.
33. Ibid., p. 51.
34. TUC Report, 1899, p. 64.
35. Ibid., pp. 65–6.
36. Bondfield, *A Life's Work*, p. 52.

2. Socialists

1. Margaret Bondfield, *A Life's Work* (London, 1948), p. 48.
2. Quoted in James H. Billington, *Fire in the Minds of Men: Origins of the Revolutionary Faith* (Piscataway, NJ, 1998), p. 245.
3. Quoted in ibid.
4. Quoted in Henry Pelling, *The Origins of the Labour Party*, 2nd edn (Oxford, 1965), p. 14n.
5. Henry Mayers Hyndman, *The Record of an Adventurous Life* (London, 1911), p. 181.
6. Ibid., p. 272.
7. *Morning Post*, 26 September 1889. The woman, Mary Griffith, drowned her illegitimate son in the Serpentine in Hyde Park. She was found guilty, but the sentence was remitted to three months' hard labour because of her mental state at the time of the baby's death.
8. *Daily Herald*, 30 June 1913.
9. Quoted in Rachel Holmes, *Eleanor Marx* (London, 2014), p. 233.
10. Quoted in Billington, *Fire in the Minds of Men*, p. 417.
11. Conservative Central Office had been set up in 1870 to provide professionalism for Conservative campaigns.
12. Edward R. Pease, *History of the Fabian Society* (London, 1916), p. 32.
13. Ibid., p. 33.
14. Fabian Society, *Tract 1, Why Are the Many Poor?*, 1884 (LSE Digital Library, Fabian Society Tracts).
15. Wells retaliated by caricaturing the Blands in his books and suggesting in the final part of his autobiography (not published until long after both men were dead) that Bland's relationship with his daughter was 'unfatherly' to the point of incest: H. G. Wells, *Postscript to an Experiment in Autobiography* (London, 1984).
16. Quoted in Margaret Cole (ed.), *The Webbs and their Work* (London, 1949).
17. George Bernard Shaw, *The Fabian Society: What it Has Done and How it Has Done It* (London, 1892), p. 1.
18. Fabian Society Minutes, 5 June 1885 (LSE Digital Library, Fabian Society Minute Books).
19. Charlotte Wilson *et al.*, *What Socialism Is* (London, 1886), p. 6.
20. Fabian Society Minutes, 17 September 1886 (LSE Digital Library, Fabian Society Minute Books).
21. Ibid.
22. Ibid. A note observes that 'This was because one Graham, a tinsmith and an anarchist follower of Morris came drunk and conducted himself with unseemly heat.'
23. Quoted in Laurence Thompson, *The Enthusiasts* (London, 1971), p. 72.
24. Ibid., p. 75.
25. 'Some Eminent Trade Unionists, No. 8, Miss Isabella Ford', *Leeds Weekly Citizen*, 12 June 1914.
26. Samuel Cunliffe Lister also owned the Ackton Hall pit in Featherstone, where in 1893 troops fired on striking miners, killing two, in the Featherstone Massacre.

27. Pete Curran, *Bradford Observer*, 25 June 1892, quoted in David Howell, *British Workers and the Independent Labour Party 1888–1906* (Manchester, 1983), p. 434n.
28. Quoted in Pelling, *Origins of the Labour Party*, p. 97.
29. *The Fabian Election Manifesto*, 1892 (LSE Digital Library, Fabian Society Tracts (Tract 40)), p. 10.
30. H. H. Champion, who in 1885 had been Hyndman's co-conspirator in the 'Tory gold' scandal, had by this time reappeared and arranged for donations of £100 each to the campaign funds of four independent candidates, including Hardie and John Burns, who was also elected. The source of the money was never disclosed, leaving Hardie open to later charges of being a closet Tory.
31. Parnell had been having an affair for many years with Kitty O'Shea, the wife of a former army captain and MP. When O'Shea failed to gain control of an inheritance she had been expecting, he filed for divorce. The case was sensational and destroyed Parnell's career. He married Kitty and died a year later.
32. ILP Conference Report, 1893 (ILP Archive, People's History Museum), p. 3.
33. Ibid.
34. Ibid.
35. Ibid.
36. Ibid., p. 16.
37. In October 1889, 700 tailoresses in Leeds struck in an attempt to prevent their employers charging them for the power used to run the sewing machines. Their six-week strike was unsuccessful, but led to the setting up of a number of trade unions in the West Yorkshire clothing trades.
38. Quoted in June Hannam, *Isabella Ford* (Oxford, 1989), p. 34.

3. Foundations

1. Beatrice Webb, *Our Partnership*, ed. Barbara Drake and Margaret Cole (London, 1948), pp. 126–7, quoting from her diary.
2. Of these, ten were the result of an MP's resignation, seven to an election being declared void, six to the death of the incumbent, three to the incumbent's promotion to the peerage, two to the incumbent being appointed to another post, and one because the MP concerned stood and was elected in two seats, thus causing a by-election in the seat he chose not to take.
3. ILP Conference Report, 1894 (ILP Archive, People's History Museum).
4. Ibid., p. 10.
5. The 1894 Local Government Act enfranchised women who were ratepayers, plus married women owning property in their own right.
6. ILP conference reports listed all members, male and female, elected during this period.
7. Women were not able to stand for metropolitan or county councils until 1907.
8. ILP Conference Report, 1895 (ILP Archive, People's History Museum).
9. Ibid.
10. Ibid.

11. Quoted in Henry Pelling, *The Origins of the Labour Party*, 2nd edn (Oxford, 1965), pp. 165–6.

12. *Daily Chronicle*, 19 July 1895.

13. Beatrice Webb, *Diary*, vol. 2: *1892–1905: All the Good Things of Life* (London, 1986), 16 July 1895.

14. Ramsay MacDonald to Margaret Gladstone, 16 June 1895 (James Ramsay MacDonald Papers, The National Archives, PRO 30/69).

15. Quoted in David Marquand, *Ramsay MacDonald* (London, 1977), p. 49.

16. Margaret Bondfield, *A Life's Work* (London, 1948), p. 48.

17. Reported in the *Yorkshire Evening Post*, 15 July 1924.

18. Quoted in Laurence Thompson, *The Enthusiasts*, pp. 94–5.

19. Quoted in Isabella Fyvie Mayo, *Recollections of Fifty Years*, 1910, Chapter VI, www.gerald-massey.org.uk/fyvie-mayo/c_recollections_04.htm, accessed 11 June 2018.

20. Quoted in Lena Wallis, *The Life and Letters of Caroline Martyn* (Glasgow, 1898), p. 73.

21. *Labour Leader*, 1 August 1896.

22. A. Besant, *Annie Besant: An Autobiography* (London, 1910), Chapter XIII, www.gutenberg.org/files/12085/12085-h/12085-h.htm, accessed 11 June 2018.

23. Quoted in Paula Bartley, *Emmeline Pankhurst* (London, 2002), p. 58.

24. ILP Conference Report, 1896 (ILP Archive, People's History Museum).

25. Ibid.

26. ILP Conference Report, 1900 (ILP Archive, People's History Museum).

27. The Second Boer War began in October 1899 and lasted until the middle of 1902. Triggers for it included the British objective of absorbing the independent Boer states into the Empire and control of the gold-mining industry.

28. J. Ramsay MacDonald, *Margaret Ethel MacDonald: A Memoir* (London, 1912), pp. 248–9.

29. TUC Report, 1898, p. 70.

30. *Labour Leader*, 1 October 1898.

31. Margaret Irwin to Ramsay MacDonald, 4 May 1899, quoted in Kenneth O. Morgan, *Keir Hardie: Radical and Socialist* (London, 1975), p. 99.

32. *Railway Review*, 3 March 1899, quoted in Frank Bealey and Henry Pelling, *Labour and Politics, 1900–1906* (London, 1958), p. 23.

33. The Good Woman Hotel's site is now occupied by a café and a restaurant. The plaque to commemorate the meeting held there is nearby in Doncaster railway station.

34. TUC Report 1899, pp. 64–5.

4. 'The Men's Party'

1. The Memorial Hall was demolished in 1968 and replaced by an office building which was used by British Telecom. This was in turn demolished in 2004, and the site is now occupied by 5 Fleet Place.

2. *Clarion*, 3 March 1900.

3. Quoted in Christine Collette, *For Labour and for Women: The Women's Labour League, 1906–1918* (Manchester, 1989), p. 10.
4. Steadman remained a Liberal all his life, resigning from the LRC because he could not hold dual membership.
5. Report of the Labour Representation Conference, 1900, *The Labour Party Foundation Conference and Annual Conference Reports 1900–1905*, Hammersmith Reprints of Scarce Documents No. 3 (London, 1967), p. 14.
6. Ibid., p. 18.
7. Ibid.
8. Ibid., p. 20.
9. Fabian Society Executive Minutes, 9 March 1900 (LSE Digital Library, Fabian Society Minute Books).
10. Equivalent to about £42,750 a year in 2018, with proportionately greater buying power since prices and rents were relatively low. As a comparator, a Board of Trade report of 1899 found that the average annual wage for a young female domestic servant was just over £16 (Clara Collett, 'Money Wages of Domestic Servants', Board of Trade Labour Department Report (Eyre and Spottiswoode, HMSO, 1899)).
11. Margaret Gladstone to Ramsay MacDonald, 2 July 1896 (James Ramsay MacDonald Papers, The National Archives, PRO 30/69).
12. Margaret Gladstone to Ramsay MacDonald, 15 June 1896 (James Ramsay MacDonald Papers, The National Archives, PRO 30/69).
13. Ramsay MacDonald to Margaret Gladstone, 21 June 1896 (James Ramsay MacDonald Papers, The National Archives, PRO 30/69).
14. Margaret Bondfield, *A Life's Work*, p. 307.
15. Frank Bealey and Henry Pelling, *Labour and Politics, 1900–1906* (London, 1958), pp. 36–7.
16. Report of the First Annual Conference of the Labour Representation Committee, 1901, *Labour Party Foundation Conference Reports*, p. 32.
17. Report of the Labour Representation Conference, 1900, *Labour Party Foundation Conference Reports*, p. 17.
18. Ibid., pp. 18–19.
19. Iain Dale (ed.), *Labour Party General Election Manifestos 1900–1997* (London, 2000), p. 9.
20. Report of the First Annual Conference of the Labour Representation Committee, 1901, *Labour Party Foundation Conference Reports*, p. 33.
21. Circular letter from Ramsay MacDonald to candidates, October 1900 (Labour Party Archive, People's History Museum).
22. Quoted in David Marquand, *Ramsay MacDonald* (London, 1977), p. 73.
23. Quoted in Jill Liddington, *The Road to Greenham Common: Feminism and Anti-Militarism in Britain Since 1820* (Syracuse, NY, 2005), p. 53.
24. This account of the Taff Vale dispute is based on that given in Bealey and Pelling, *Labour and Politics, 1900–1906*, pp. 57–72.
25. Ibid., p. 67.
26. TUC Report, 1901, p. 37.
27. Quoted in Marquand, *Ramsay MacDonald*, p. 75.
28. *Lancashire Evening Post*, 31 July 1902.

29. In 1910 Shackleton joined the Civil Service. In 1916 he became permanent secretary at the Ministry of Labour, the first working-class person to hold such a post. He was knighted in 1917 and died in 1938.
30. *Burnley Express*, 16 July 1902.
31. Quoted in Sonja Tiernan, *Eva Gore-Booth: An Image of Such Politics* (Manchester, 2012), p. 73.
32. Eva Gore-Booth to John McNeill, 9 October 1902, LRD/5/402 (Labour Party Archive, People's History Museum).
33. Esther Roper, *Poems of Eva Gore-Booth, Complete Edition* (London, 1929), p. 9.
34. Quoted in Tiernan, *Eva Gore-Booth*, p. 75.

5. Women's Work

1. *Daily News*, 28 November 1867.
2. Eleanor Marx and Edward Aveling, 'The Woman Question: From a Socialist Point of View', *Westminster Review*, January–April 1886, www.marxists.org/archive/eleanor-marx/works/womanq.htm, accessed 12 June 2018.
3. Clara Zetkin, speech to the Gotha Congress, October 1896, reported by Eleanor Marx in *Justice*, 7 November 1896.
4. Isabella Ford, 'Women and the Franchise', *Labour Leader*, 1 March 1902.
5. TUC Report, 1880, p. 38.
6. TUC Report, 1881, p. 34.
7. TUC Report, 1884, p. 44.
8. Ibid.
9. TUC Report, 1901, p. 28.
10. Ibid., p. 80.
11. Ibid.
12. E. Sylvia Pankhurst, *The Suffragette Movement: An Intimate Account of Persons and Ideals* (London, 1931), pp. 177–8.
13. Margaret Bondfield, *A Life's Work* (London, 1948), p. 37.
14. Quoted in Matthew Worley, *Labour's Grassroots: Essays of the Activities of Local Labour Parties and Members, 1918–1945* (London, 2005), p. 83.
15. Bondfield, *A Life's Work*, p. 43.
16. Report of the LRC Conference, 1904, *The Labour Party Foundation Conference and Annual Conference Reports 1900–1905*, Hammersmith Reprints of Scarce Documents No. 3 (London, 1967), p. 174.
17. Ibid. In fact there were no women on Labour's NEC until 1918.
18. *Labour Leader*, 3 February 1905.
19. The text of the resolution and the account of the debate which followed it are taken from the Report of the LRC Conference, 1904, *Labour Party Foundation Conference Reports*, pp. 235–7.
20. This was the house in Nelson Street which is now the Pankhurst Centre. Though smaller than the family was used to, it was still large enough to be described as a 'villa'.
21. Harry Pankhurst died in 1910 at the age of 20.

22. John Nodal to Emmeline Pankhurst, 29 November 1902, quoted in June Purvis, *Emmeline Pankhurst: A Biography* (London, 2002), p. 61.
23. Emmeline Pankhurst to John Nodal, 29 November 1902, quoted in ibid., p. 62.
24. Christabel Pankhurst, *Unshackled: The Story of How We Won the Vote* (London, 1959), p. 43.
25. Enid Stacy had been one of the ILP's most popular speakers. In 1897 she married the Revd Percy Widdrington but died of an embolism in September 1903 at the age of 35.
26. *Labour Leader*, 31 October 1903.
27. Pankhurst, *Suffragette Movement*, p. 184.
28. Bondfield, *A Life's Work*, p. 69.
29. Quoted in Mary Agnes Hamilton, *Mary Macarthur: A Biographical Sketch* (London, 1925), p. 6.
30. Mary Agnes Hamilton, *Margaret Bondfield* (London, 1924), p. 95.
31. Mary Agnes Hamilton, *Women at Work: A Brief Introduction to Trade Unionism for Women* (London, 1941), p. 59.
32. Bondfield, *A Life's Work*, p. 55.
33. Pankhurst, *Suffragette Movement*, p. 180.
34. Quoted in June Hannam, *Isabella Ford* (Oxford, 1989), p. 5.
35. Bedford College is now part of Royal Holloway, University of London. The Mary Macpherson Essay Prize is still awarded each year.
36. Fabian Tract No. 96, the author of which is given as Mrs Fenton Macpherson.
37. *Clarion*, 16 December 1904.
38. *Clarion*, 13 January 1905.
39. *Labour Leader*, 7 October 1904.
40. *Labour Leader*, 28 April 1905.
41. Mary Macpherson to Ramsay MacDonald, 2 November 1904 (WLL Papers, Labour Party Archive, People's History Museum, LRC/17).
42. WLL Papers, Labour Party Archive, People's History Museum, LRC/24/284.
43. Quoted in Christine Collette, *For Labour and for Women: The Women's Labour League, 1906–1918* (Manchester, 1989), p. 32.

6. Breakthrough

1. Ramsay MacDonald and Keir Hardie, 'The ILP's Programme', *Nineteenth Century* xlv (January 1899), quoted in David Marquand, *Ramsay MacDonald* (London, 1977), p. 75.
2. *Daily News*, 25 March 1902. The Wakefield by-election, in which Philip Snowden was the Labour candidate, had been held earlier that year.
3. *Daily News*, 9 July 1902.
4. Iain Dale (ed.), *Labour Party General Election Manifestos 1900–1997* (London, 2000), p. 10.
5. Elizabeth Pollock to the LRC, 10 January 1906 (Labour Party Archive, People's History Museum).
6. Jim Middleton to Elizabeth Pollock, 11 January 1906 (Labour Party Archive, People's History Museum).

7. Together with the Conservative victories of 1931 and 1983 and the Labour successes of 1945 and 1997, the Liberal win of 1906 ranks as one of the biggest of the twentieth century.
8. *The Times*, 31 January 1906.
9. Ramsay MacDonald to Margaret MacDonald, 28 January 1906 (James Ramsay MacDonald Papers, The National Archives, PRO 30/69).
10. Pete Curran was elected for Sunderland but was an alcoholic and died in 1909. Victor Grayson was famously elected in 1907 in Colne Valley as the standard-bearer for the left, youth and women's vote. He lost his seat in 1910, became an outspoken supporter of World War I, and disappeared in 1920.
11. WLL *League Leaflet* No. 12, December 1911 (WLL Papers, Labour Party Archive, People's History Museum).
12. Ray Strachey, *The Cause* (London, 1928), pp. 244–5.
13. E. Sylvia Pankhurst, *The Suffragette Movement: An Intimate Account of Persons and Ideals* (London, 1931), p. 178.
14. Malcolm MacDonald, 'Constant Surprise' (Durham University Library, Special Collections, GB-0033-MAC), p. 22.
15. Margaret MacDonald to Jim Middleton, 4 September 1905 (Labour Party Archive, People's History Museum).
16. Quoted Marquand, *Ramsay MacDonald*, p. 52.
17. Quoted in ibid.
18. Margaret Bondfield to Margaret MacDonald (James Ramsay MacDonald Papers, The National Archives, PRO 30/69).
19. Note of WLL inaugural meeting (Labour Party Archive, People's History Museum, GC/1/344).
20. Pankhurst, *Suffragette Movement*, pp. 244–5.
21. Report of the First Conference of the Women's Labour League, p. 1 (WLL Papers, Labour Party Archive, People's History Museum).
22. Ibid., p. 4.
23. Report of the Second Annual Conference, 18 May 1907, p. 19 (WLL Papers, Labour Party Archive, People's History Museum).
24. Mary Macpherson to Margaret MacDonald, 20 March 1907 (WLL Papers, Labour Party Archive, People's History Museum).
25. Margaret MacDonald to Mary Middleton, 21 March 1907 (WLL Papers, Labour Party Archive, People's History Museum).
26. Margaret MacDonald in Mary Middleton Memorial booklet, April 1911 (James Ramsay MacDonald Papers, The National Archives, PRO 30/69).
27. Lisbeth Simm to Mary Middleton, 1908 (WLL Papers, Labour Party Archive, People's History Museum).
28. General Correspondence, Labour Party Archive, People's History Museum, GC/14/385.
29. Ibid., GC/14/342.
30. Twenty-nine Labour members were elected at the 1906 general election, but there was also one miners' MP who joined them when Parliament met.
31. Six were caused by death, two MPs resigned to take up posts as judges, and two resigned in order to move to the colonies. One resigned to allow Arthur Balfour to get back into Parliament, and the seat of another was taken by future

Conservative leader Arthur Bonar Law, who had also lost his seat in the general election. Two Irish MPs resigned because they had, perfectly legally, been elected in two constituencies and had to choose which one to represent, thus triggering by-elections in the ones they rejected. One was unseated after an electoral petition, and another after being expelled from the Irish Nationalist Party. The remainder were the result of resignations mainly for business or health reasons.

32. Ramsay MacDonald to Margaret MacDonald, 9 September 1908 (James Ramsay MacDonald Papers, The National Archives, PRO 30/69).
33. Letter to *Labour Leader*, 17 May 1907.
34. Adela Pankhurst emigrated to Australia in 1914 where she became a prominent and highly controversial political figure. She married, had four children, and died in 1961.
35. Marion Coates Hanson, letter to *Labour Leader*, 24 September 1907.
36. Isabella Ford, 'Why Women Should be Socialists', *Labour Leader*, 1 May 1913, p. 10.
37. Details of both speeches are from Margaret Bondfield, *A Life's Work*, pp. 83–5.

7. Suffrage and Sweating

1. Quoted in Kenneth O. Morgan, *Keir Hardie: Radical and Socialist* (London, 1975), p. 160.
2. *Report of the Seventh Annual Conference of the Labour Party*, 1907, pp. 49–50.
3. Ibid., pp. 61–3.
4. John Bruce Glasier to Ramsay MacDonald, 5 November 1908 (James Ramsay MacDonald Papers, The National Archives, PRO 5/18).
5. Campbell-Bannerman died three weeks after resigning. Unusually, he had remained in Downing Street after his successor had taken office, and was the last prime minister to die there.
6. Quoted in Sonja Tiernan, *Eva Gore-Booth: An Image of Such Politics* (Manchester, 2012), p. 125.
7. Quoted in Laurence Thompson, *The Enthusiasts* (London, 1971), p. 136.
8. Quoted in Christine Collette, *For Labour and for Women: The Women's Labour League, 1906–1918* (Manchester, 1989), pp. 97–8.
9. Helen Bosanquet to Professor Alfred Marshall, 30 September 1902, in *The Correspondence of Alfred Marshall, Economist: Volume 2*, ed. John K. Whittaker (Cambridge, 1996).
10. Quoted in Ellen Mappin, *Helping Women at Work: the Women's Industrial Council 1889–1914* (London, 1915; repr. 1983), p. 88.
11. Mary Agnes Hamilton, *Mary Macarthur: A Biographical Sketch* (London, 1925), p. 65.
12. *Daily News*, 2 May 1906.
13. TUC Report, 1906, pp. 149–50.
14. Margaret MacDonald, *Labour Leader*, 17 May 1907.
15. Mary Macarthur, *Labour Leader*, 14 June 1907.
16. Margaret MacDonald, *Labour Leader*, 31 May 1907.
17. Mary Macarthur, *Labour Leader*, 21 June 1907.

18. Mary Macarthur, *Labour Leader*, 28 June 1907.
19. Wages boards were expanded after World War I and remained in existence until abolished in 1993. A national minimum wage was introduced in 1999. Disagreement over the merits of wages legislation continues to this day.
20. Report of the Second Annual Conference of the Women's Labour League (WLL Papers, Labour Party Archive, People's History Museum), pp. 14–16.
21. Ramsay MacDonald to Margaret MacDonald, 24 September 1908 (James Ramsay MacDonald Papers, The National Archives, PRO 30/69).
22. The research for this report was being carried out at this point; the report itself was not published until 1915.
23. *Labour Leader*, 10 May 1907.
24. Ben Tillett, *Is the Parliamentary Labour Party a Failure?* (London, 1908), p. 3.
25. Quoted in Thompson, *The Enthusiasts*, p. 156.
26. Ibid., p. 157.
27. ILP Conference Report, 1909 (ILP Archive, People's History Museum).
28. Hansard, 29 April 1909.
29. Hansard, 30 May 1911.

8. Changes

1. Diary entry for 4 July 1910, quoted in David Marquand, *Ramsay MacDonald* (London, 1977), p. 131.
2. Quoted in Christine Collette, *For Labour and for Women: The Women's Labour League, 1906–1918* (Manchester, 1989), p. 110.
3. This involved women standing outside polling stations and accosting men as they went in or out; in some places police threatened to arrest women as prostitutes if they continued to do this.
4. Millicent Fawcett to Lady Frances Balfour, 28 November 1910, quoted in June Purvis, *Christabel Pankhurst: A Biography* (Oxford, 2018), p. 94.
5. *Votes for Women*, 23 February 1912 (British Library Newspaper Archive, MFM. M39669).
6. Quoted in Mary Agnes Hamilton, *Mary Macarthur: A Biographical Sketch* (London, 1925), p. 100.
7. Quoted in Hamilton, *Mary Macarthur*, p. 71.
8. Quoted in Hamilton, *Mary Macarthur*, p. 57.
9. TUC Report, 1909, p. 168.
10. Beatrice Webb, *My Apprenticeship* (London, 1926), p. 336. Beatrice believed that industrial production should all be concentrated in large factories, which would eliminate sweated homeworking, married women in the workforce and middlemen all in one swoop.
11. Quoted in Hamilton, *Mary Macarthur*, p. 84.
12. *County Express for Worcestershire & Staffordshire*, 1 September 1910, quoted in Sheila Blackburn, *A Fair Day's Wage for A Fair Day's Work? Sweated Labour and the Origins of Minimum Wage Legislation in Britain* (Aldershot, 2007), pp. 132–3 (note).
13. Hamilton, *Mary Macarthur*, p. 89.

14. TUC Report, 1910, pp. 121–2.
15. *Labour Leader*, 17 May 1907.
16. Diary entry for 11 June 1910, quoted in Marquand, *Ramsay MacDonald*, p. 127.
17. Ramsay MacDonald to Margaret MacDonald, October 1910 (James Ramsay MacDonald Papers, The National Archives, PRO 30/69).
18. Iain Dale (ed.), *Labour Party General Election Manifestos 1900–1997* (London, 2000), p. 14.
19. Ibid., p. 15.
20. Arthur Henderson to Ramsay MacDonald, 2 January 1911 (James Ramsay MacDonald Papers, The National Archives, PRO 5/21).
21. Quoted in Ramsay MacDonald and Margaret MacDonald, *A Singular Marriage: A Labour Love Story in Letters and Diaries*, ed. Jane Cox (London, 1988), p. 367.
22. Mary Middleton to Lisbeth Simm, 30 January 1911, quoted in Mary Middleton Memorial Booklet (Correspondence of Margaret Ethel MacDonald, The National Archives, PRO 30/69/902).
23. Quoted in ibid.
24. Margaret Bondfield, *A Life's Work* (London, 1948), p. 80.
25. This account is taken from Ramsay MacDonald, *Margaret Ethel MacDonald: A Memoir* (London, 1912), pp. 260–1.
26. Amie Hicks to Margaret MacDonald, 1 May 1908 (James Ramsay MacDonald Papers, The National Archives, PRO 30/69).
27. *Daily News*, 28 November 1911.
28. The clinic moved to Tavistock Road in 1924, was taken over by the local authority in 1936 and absorbed into the National Health Service in 1948. It was closed soon afterwards.
29. Quoted in MacDonald and MacDonald, *A Singular Marriage*, p. 372.
30. Quoted in ibid.
31. This seat was unveiled in 1914 and still stands on the north side of Lincoln's Inn Fields.
32. Quoted in Margaret Ethel MacDonald Memorial Booklet (James Ramsay MacDonald Papers, The National Archives, PRO 30/69), p. 22.
33. Ibid., p. 23.
34. Dora Montefiore was involved in a relationship with George Belt, a married ILP organiser in Hull. Correspondence between them came into Margaret MacDonald's hands and she showed it to other people. Dora sued for libel, and Ramsay MacDonald had to settle the case out of court.
35. Quoted in Margaret Ethel MacDonald Memorial Booklet (James Ramsay MacDonald Papers, The National Archives, PRO 30/69), p. 22.

9. The Great Unrest

1. *The Times* ran a 'Deaths from Heat' column throughout the summer of 1911. A total of 17,400 people died in London in July, August and September, many from heat-related causes.
2. *Daily News*, 14 September 1911.

3. *Women's Trade Union Review,* October 1911, quoted in Mary Agnes Hamilton, *Mary Macarthur: A Biographical Sketch* (London, 1925), p. 106.
4. Beatrice Webb, *Our Partnership,* ed. Barbara Drake and Margaret Cole (London, 1948), p. 474.
5. Ibid.
6. Outdoor poor relief was help given in the form of food, clothing or money to people who stayed outside the workhouse; indoor relief was the provision made in the workhouse.
7. Hamilton, *Mary Macarthur,* p. 111.
8. This was changed in 1913 following a strong campaign led by the Women's Co-operative Guild.
9. *Fabian News,* February 1912 (Fabian Society Archive, LSE Library Archives & Special Collections), p. 21.
10. E. Sylvia Pankhurst, *The Suffragette Movement: An Intimate Account of Persons and Ideals* (London, 1931), p. 354.
11. Quoted in Hamilton, *Mary Macarthur,* p. 110.
12. Quoted in Christine Collette, *For Labour and for Women: The Women's Labour League, 1906–1918* (Manchester, 1989), p. 102.
13. Quoted in Caroline Benn, *Keir Hardie* (London, 1992), p. 272.
14. Margaret Bondfield, *A Life's Work* (London, 1948), p. 125.
15. Ibid., p. 126.
16. Quoted in Christine Collette, *The Newer Eve: Women, Feminists and the Labour Party* (London, 2009), p. 37.
17. Quoted in Collette, *The Newer Eve,* p. 37.
18. Quoted in Collette, *For Labour and for Women,* p. 144.
19. *Common Cause,* 12 July 1912, quoted in Sandra Holton, *Feminism and Democracy* (Cambridge, 1986), p. 74.
20. Bondfield, *A Life's Work,* p. 86.
21. Ibid., p. 85.
22. *Labour Leader,* 2 February 1912.
23. Millicent Fawcett to Ramsay MacDonald, 28 January 1912 (James Ramsay MacDonald Papers, The National Archives, PRO 30/69).
24. H. N. Brailsford to Arthur Henderson, 4 May 1912, quoted in Holton, *Feminism and Democracy,* p. 74.
25. Isabella Ford to Edward Carpenter, 25 August 1913, quoted in June Hannam, *Isabella Ford* (Oxford, 1989), p. 156.
26. Pankhurst, *Suffragette Movement,* pp. 517–18.
27. *Common Cause,* 18 July 1912, quoted in Holton, *Feminism and Democracy,* p. 83.
28. Catherine Marshall to Ramsay MacDonald, 19 October 1912 (James Ramsay MacDonald Papers, The National Archives, PRO 30/69).
29. George Lansbury later became leader of the Labour Party in the aftermath of the 1931 election crash, resigning in 1935. He died in 1940. His grandchildren include the actor Angela Lansbury and the children's animator Oliver Postgate (*Bagpuss* and *Noggin the Nog*).
30. *Labour Woman* replaced the *League Leaflet* in 1913 and was published regularly until 1970, covering a wide variety of issues and campaigns.
31. Quoted in Lucinda Hawksley, *March, Women, March* (London, 2015), p. 210.

10. War and Peace

1. Katharine Bruce Glasier, *League Leaflet*, February 1912 (British Library Newspaper Archive, MFM.M39928).
2. Marion Phillips, *League Leaflet*, February 1913 (British Library Newspaper Archive, MFM.M39928).
3. Diary entry for 23 September 1914, quoted in David Marquand, *Ramsay MacDonald* (London, 1977), p. 164.
4. *The Pioneer*, 27 July 1912 (British Library Newspaper Archive, 013898431).
5. Quoted in Margaret Bondfield, *A Life's Work* (London, 1948), p. 140.
6. Quoted in Jill Liddington, *The Road to Greenham Common: Feminism and Anti-Militarism in Britain Since 1820* (Syracuse, NY, 2005), p. 78.
7. Hansard, 3 August 1914.
8. Bondfield, *A Life's Work*, p. 142.
9. *Labour Woman*, September 1914 (British Library Newspaper Archive, MFM. M39928).
10. Quoted in Liddington, *Road to Greenham Common*, p. 77.
11. I. O. Ford, *New Leader*, 25 July 1924, quoted in Liddington, *Road to Greenham Common*, pp. 163–4.
12. Quoted in June Hannam, *Isabella Ford* (Oxford, 1989), p. 166.
13. *John Bull*, 4 September 1915, quoted in Marquand, *Ramsay MacDonald*, p. 190.
14. Quoted in Marquand, *Ramsay MacDonald*, p. 192.
15. *Report of the Fifteenth Annual Conference of the Labour Party*, 1916.
16. Hannah Mitchell, *The Hard Way Up* (London, 1968), p. 186.
17. Ibid., p. 187.
18. Quoted in Mary Agnes Hamilton, *Mary Macarthur: A Biographical Sketch* (London, 1925), p. 136.
19. Ibid., p. 137.
20. Beatrice Webb, Diary (LSE Digital Library, Beatrice Webb Typescript 9 December 1916–10 October 1924), 3 June 1917, p. 30.
21. Bondfield, *A Life's Work*, p. 156.
22. Quoted in Julie V. Gottlieb, *'Guilty Women': Foreign Policy, and Appeasement in Inter-War Britain* (London, 2015), p. 272.
23. *Labour Leader*, 4 March 1915.
24. Quoted in Hamilton, *Mary Macarthur*, p. 177.
25. Quoted in Cheryl Law, *Suffrage and Power: The Women's Movement, 1918–1928* (London, 1997), p. 33.
26. A Speaker's Conference is a rare mechanism used to consider such issues, and action is usually (though not always) taken as a result of its deliberations.
27. Bondfield, *A Life's Work*, p. 87.
28. Quoted in Christine Collette, *For Labour and for Women: The Women's Labour League, 1906–1918* (Manchester, 1989), p. 158.
29. WLL Executive Minutes, 12 October 1917 (WLL Papers, Labour Party Archive, People's History Museum).
30. WLL Annual Conference Report 1918 (WLL Papers, Labour Party Archive, People's History Museum), p. 46.

31. WLL Executive Committee report on the Draft Constitution of the Labour Party (WLL Papers, Labour Party Archive, People's History Museum), p. 3.
32. Mitchell, *Hard Way Up*, p. 189.
33. *The Times*, 12 December 1918.
34. Mary Macarthur's election address, Stourbridge, 1918 (TUC Library Collections, London Metropolitan University), p. 1.
35. Quoted in Law, *Suffrage and Power*, p. 121.
36. Quoted in Pamela Brookes, *Women at Westminster* (London, 1967), p. 9.
37. *Aberdeen Evening Post*, 18 October 1918 (British Newspaper Archive).
38. Millicent Fawcett, 'Isabella Ormston Ford', *Woman's Leader*, 25 July 1924, quoted in Hannam, *Isabella Ford*, p. 111.

Epilogue

1. Nancy Astor was elected in Plymouth Sutton in a by-election caused by her husband's elevation to the peerage in 1919.
2. Quoted in Ramsay MacDonald and Margaret MacDonald, *A Singular Marriage: A Labour Love Story in Letters and Diaries*, ed. Jane Cox (London, 1988), p. 379.
3. Margaret Bondfield, *A Life's Work*, p. 255.
4. Ibid., p. 245.
5. Ibid., p. 277.
6. Diary entry for 2 July 1928, quoted in Jane W. Grant, *In the Steps of Exceptional Women: The Story of the Fawcett Society, 1866–2016* (London, 2016), p. 62.
7. *Daily Herald*, 25 January 1932.
8. In 1970 Margaret Thatcher became only the sixth woman cabinet minister from any party. By the centenary of women's suffrage in 2018 only 45 women had ever held cabinet office (of whom 23 were Labour).

Bibliography

Archival Sources

British Library Newspaper Archive.
Durham University Library, Special Collections
    GB-0033-MAC: Malcolm MacDonald, 'Constant Surprise'.
London Metropolitan University, TUC Library Collections.
London School of Economics, Archives and Special Collections
    GB 97 SR 0061: Labour Representation League minute book.
London School of Economics, Digital Library
    Beatrice Webb Diary, 9 December 1916–10 October 1924.
    Fabian Society Minute Books.
    Fabian Society Tracts.
London School of Economics, Women's Library, Papers of Ross Davies.
The National Archives
    PRO 5/18, 5/21 and 30/69: James Ramsay MacDonald Papers.
    PRO 30/69/902: Correspondence of Margaret Ethel MacDonald.
People's History Museum, Manchester
    Independent Labour Party Archive.
    Labour Party Archive.

Printed Primary Sources

The Labour Party Foundation Conference and Annual Conference Reports 1900–1905,
    Hammersmith Reprints of Scarce Documents No. 3 (London, 1967).
TUC Reports, Reports of TUC Annual Congresses, 1868–1918, www.unionhistory.
    info/reports/index.php, accessed June 2017–February 2018.

Newspapers and Periodicals

Aberdeen Evening Post
Burnley Express
Clarion
Common Cause
Daily Chronicle

Daily Herald
Daily News
Fortnightly Review
Justice
Labour Leader
Labour News
Lancashire Evening Post
Leeds Weekly Citizen
Morning Post
The Pioneer
Sheffield Daily Telegraph
The Times
Women's Trade Union Review
Yorkshire Evening Post

Biographies, Autobiographies and Diaries

Bartley, Paula, *Emmeline Pankhurst* (London, 2002).
Benn, Caroline, *Keir Hardie* (London, 1992).
Besant, A., *Annie Besant: An Autobiography* (London, 1910), www.gutenberg.org/files/12085/12085-h/12085-h.htm, accessed 11 June 2018.
Bondfield, Margaret, *A Life's Work* (London, 1948).
Cole, Margaret (ed.), *The Webbs and their Work* (London, 1949).
Fyvie Mayo, Isabella, *Recollections of Fifty Years*, 1910, www.gerald-massey.org.uk/fyvie-mayo/b_recollections.htm, accessed 12 June 2018.
Goldman, Harold, *Emma Paterson: She Led Women Into a Man's World* (Essex, 1974).
Goronwy-Roberts, Marian, *A Woman of Vision: A Life of Marion Phillips MP* (Wrexham, 2000).
Gottlieb, Julie V., *'Guilty Women': Foreign Policy, and Appeasement in Inter-War Britain* (London, 2015).
Hamilton, Mary Agnes, *Margaret Bondfield* (London, 1924).
———, *Mary Macarthur: A Biographical Sketch* (London, 1925).
Hannam, June, *Isabella Ford* (Oxford, 1989).
Herbert, Lucy, *Mrs Ramsay MacDonald* (London, 1924).
Holman, Bob, *Keir Hardie: Labour's Greatest Hero?* (London, 2010).
Holmes, Rachel, *Eleanor Marx* (London, 2014).
Hyndman, Henry Mayers, *The Record of an Adventurous Life* (London, 1911).
Leventhal, F. M., *Arthur Henderson* (Manchester, 1989).
Lewis, Gifford, *Eva Gore-Booth and Esther Roper: A Biography* (London, 1988).
MacDonald, J. Ramsay, *Margaret Ethel MacDonald: A Memoir* (London, 1912).
MacDonald, Ramsay and Margaret MacDonald, *A Singular Marriage: A Labour Love Story in Letters and Diaries*, ed. Jane Cox (London, 1988).
Marquand, David, *Ramsay MacDonald* (London, 1977).
Marshall, Alfred, *The Correspondence of Alfred Marshall, Economist: Volume 2*, ed. John K. Whittaker (Cambridge, 1996).
Mitchell, Hannah, *The Hard Way Up* (London, 1968).

Morgan, Kenneth O., *Keir Hardie: Radical and Socialist* (London, 1975).
Morgan, Kevin, *Ramsay MacDonald* (London, 2006).
Pankhurst, Christabel, *Unshackled: The Story of How We Won the Vote* (London, 1959).
Pankhurst, E. Sylvia, *The Suffragette Movement: An Intimate Account of Persons and Ideals* (London, 1931).
Pugh, Martin, *The Pankhursts: The History of One Radical Family* (London, 2001).
Purvis, June, *Christabel Pankhurst: A Biography* (Oxford, 2018).
———, *Emmeline Pankhurst: A Biography* (London, 2002).
Roper, Esther, *Poems of Eva Gore-Booth, Complete Edition* (London, 1929).
Thompson, E. P., *William Morris: Romantic to Revolutionary* (London, 1976).
Thompson, Laurence, *The Enthusiasts* (London, 1971).
Tiernan, Sonja, *Eva Gore-Booth: An Image of Such Politics* (Manchester, 2012).
Wallis, Lena, *The Life and Letters of Caroline Martyn* (Glasgow, 1898).
Webb, Beatrice, *Diary*, vol. 1: *1873–1892: Glitter Around and Darkness Within* (London, 1986).
———, *Diary*, vol. 2: *1892–1905: All the Good Things of Life* (London, 1986).
———, *My Apprenticeship* (London, 1926).
———, *Our Partnership*, ed. Barbara Drake and Margaret Cole (London, 1948).
Wells, H. G., *Postscript to an Experiment in Autobiography* (London, 1984).

Secondary Works

Barnsley, Tony, *Breaking Their Chains: Mary Macarthur and the Chainmakers' Strike of 1910* (London, 2010).
Barrow, Logie and Ian Bullock, *Democratic Ideas and the British Labour Movement* (Cambridge, 1996).
Bealey, Frank and Henry Pelling, *Labour and Politics, 1900–1906* (London, 1958).
Billington, James H., *Fire in the Minds of Men: Origins of the Revolutionary Faith* (Piscataway, NJ, 1998).
Black, Clementina (ed.), *Married Women's Work* (London, 1915; repr. 1983).
Blackburn, Sheila, *A Fair Day's Wage for A Fair Day's Work? Sweated Labour and the Origins of Minimum Wage Legislation in Britain* (Aldershot, 2007).
Boston, Sarah, *Women Workers and the Trade Unions*, 3rd edn (London, 2015).
Brookes, Pamela, *Women at Westminster* (London, 1967).
Clayton, J. (ed.), *Why I Joined the Labour Party: Some Plain Statements* (Leeds, 1897).
Collette, Christine, *For Labour and for Women: The Women's Labour League, 1906–1918* (Manchester, 1989).
———, *The Newer Eve: Women, Feminists and the Labour Party* (London, 2009).
Collins, Clare, 'Women and Labour Politics in Britain, 1893–1932' (Ph.D. thesis, London School of Economics, 1991).
Crick, Martin, *The History of the Social-Democratic Federation* (Keele, 1994).
Dale, Iain (ed.), *Labour Party General Election Manifestos 1900–1997* (London, 2000).
Davis, Mary, *Comrade or Brother? The History of the British Labour Movement 1789–1951* (London, 1993).
Drake, Barbara, *Women in Trade Unions* (London, 1920; repr. 1987).
Fawcett, Millicent Garrett, *Women's Suffrage* (London, 1912).

Grant, Jane W., *In the Steps of Exceptional Women: The Story of the Fawcett Society, 1866–2016* (London, 2016).

Hamilton, Mary Agnes, *Women at Work: A Brief Introduction to Trade Unionism for Women* (London, 1941).

Hannam, June and Karen Hunt, *Socialist Women: Britain, 1880s to 1920s* (London, 2002).

Hawksley, Lucinda, *March, Women, March* (London, 2015).

Hollis, Patricia, *Ladies Elect: Women in English Local Government, 1865–1914* (Oxford, 1987).

Holloway, Gerry, *Women and Work in Britain Since 1840* (Abingdon, 2005).

Holton, Sandra, *Feminism and Democracy* (Cambridge, 1986).

Howell, David, *British Workers and the Independent Labour Party 1888–1906* (Manchester, 1983).

Hunt, Karen, *Equivocal Feminists: The Social Democratic Federation and the Woman Question, 1894–1911* (Cambridge, 1996).

Law, Cheryl, *Suffrage and Power: The Women's Movement, 1918–1928* (London, 1997).

———, *Women: A Modern Political Dictionary* (London, 2000).

Liddington, Jill, *The Road to Greenham Common: Feminism and Anti-Militarism in Britain Since 1820* (Syracuse, NY, 2005).

Liddington, Jill and Jill Norris, *One Hand Tied Behind Us: The Rise of the Women's Suffrage Movement* (London, 2000).

Mappin, Ellen, *Helping Women at Work: the Women's Industrial Council 1889–1914* (London, 1915; repr. 1983).

Marx, Eleanor and Edward Aveling, 'The Woman Question: From a Socialist Point of View', *Westminster Review*, January–April 1886, www.marxists.org/archive/eleanor-marx/works/womanq.htm, accessed 12 June 2018.

Owen, James, *Labour and the Caucus: Working Class Radicalism and Organised Liberalism in England, 1868–1888* (Liverpool, 2014).

Pease, Edward R., *The History of the Fabian Society* (London, 1916).

Pelling, Henry, *A History of British Trade Unionism* (London, 1992).

———, *The Origins of the Labour Party*, 2nd edn (Oxford, 1965).

Pugh, Martin, *The Making of Modern British Politics, 1867–1945* (London, 2002).

———, *Speak for Britain: A New History of the Labour Party* (London, 2011).

Renwick, Chris, *Bread for All: The Origins of the Welfare State* (London, 2017).

Rowbotham, Sheila, *Hidden from History: 300 Years of Women's Oppression and the Fight Against It*, 3rd edn (London, 1977).

Shaw, George Bernard, *The Fabian Society: What it Has Done and How it Has Done It* (London, 1892).

Smith, Harold L., *The British Women's Suffrage Campaign, 1866–1928* (Harlow, 2010).

Strachey, Ray, *The Cause* (London, 1928).

Tanner, Duncan, *Political Change and the Labour Party, 1900–1918* (Cambridge, 1990).

Thorpe, Andrew, *A History of the British Labour Party*, 4th edn (London, 2015).

Tillett, Ben, *Is the Parliamentary Labour Party a Failure?* (London, 1908).

Webb, Sidney and Beatrice Webb, *The History of Trade Unionism* (London, 1898).

Wilson, Charlotte *et al.*, *What Socialism Is* (London, 1886).

Worley, Matthew, *Labour's Grassroots: Essays of the Activities of Local Labour Parties and Members, 1918–1945* (London, 2005).

Index